STUDIES OF THE AMERICAS

edited by

James Dunkerley

Institute for the Study of the Americas
University of London
School of Advanced Study

Titles in this series are multi-disciplinary studies of aspects of the societies of the hemisphere, particularly in the areas of politics, economics, history, anthropology, sociology, and the environment. The series covers a comparative perspective across the Americas, including Canada and the Caribbean as well as the United States and Latin America.

Titles in this series published by Palgrave Macmillan:

Cuba's Military 1990–2005: Revolutionary Soldiers during Counter-Revolutionary Times
By Hal Klepak

The Judicialization of Politics in Latin America
Edited by Rachel Sieder, Line Schjolden, and Alan Angell

Latin America: A New Interpretation
By Laurence Whitehead

Appropriation as Practice: Art and Identity in Argentina
By Arnd Schneider

America and Enlightenment Constitutionalism
Edited by Gary L. McDowell and Johnathan O'Neill

Vargas and Brazil: New Perspectives
Edited by Jens R. Hentschke

When Was Latin America Modern?
Edited by Nicola Miller and Stephen Hart

Debating Cuban Exceptionalism
Edited by Bert Hoffman and Laurence Whitehead

Caribbean Land and Development Revisited
Edited by Jean Besson and Janet Momsen

Cultures of the Lusophone Black Atlantic
Edited by Nancy Priscilla Naro, Roger Sansi-Roca and David H. Treece

Democratization, Development, and Legality: Chile, 1831–1973
By Julio Faundez

The Hispanic World and American Intellectual Life, 1820–1880
By Iván Jaksic'

The Role of Mexico's Plural in Latin American Literary and Political Culture: From Tlatelolco to the "Philanthropic Ogre"
By John King

Faith and Impiety in Revolutionary Mexico
    Edited by Matthew Butler

Reinventing Modernity in Latin America: Intellectuals Imagine the Future, 1900–1930
    By Nicola Miller

The Republican Party and Immigration Politics: From Proposition 187 to George W. Bush
    By Andrew Wroe

The Political Economy of Hemispheric Integration: Responding to Globalization in the Americas
    Edited by Diego Sánchez-Ancochea and Kenneth C. Shadlen

Ronald Reagan and the 1980s: Perceptions, Policies, Legacies
    Edited by Cheryl Hudson and Gareth Davies

Wellbeing and Development in Peru: Local and Universal Views Confronted
    Edited by James Copestake

The Federal Nation: Perspectives on American Federalism
    Edited by Iwan W. Morgan and Philip J. Davies

Base Colonies in the Western Hemisphere, 1940–1967
    By Steven High

Beyond Neoliberalism in Latin America? Societies and Politics at the Crossroads
    Edited by John Burdick, Philip Oxhorn, and Kenneth M. Roberts

Visual Synergies in Fiction and Documentary Film from Latin America
    Edited by Miriam Haddu and Joanna Page

Cuban Medical Internationalism: Origins, Evolution, and Goals
    By John M. Kirk and H. Michael Erisman

Governance after Neoliberalism in Latin America
    Edited by Jean Grugel and Pia Riggirozzi

Modern Poetics and Hemispheric American Cultural Studies
    By Justin Read

Modern Poetics and Hemispheric American Cultural Studies

Justin Read

MODERN POETICS AND HEMISPHERIC AMERICAN CULTURAL STUDIES
Copyright © Justin Read, 2009.
Softcover reprint of the hardcover 1st edition 2009 978-0-230-61596-0

All rights reserved.

First published in 2009 by
PALGRAVE MACMILLAN®
in the United States—a division of St. Martin's Press LLC,
175 Fifth Avenue, New York, NY 10010.

Where this book is distributed in the UK, Europe and the rest of the
world, this is by Palgrave Macmillan, a division of Macmillan Publishers
Limited, registered in England, company number 785998, of Houndmills,
Basingstoke, Hampshire RG21 6XS.

Palgrave Macmillan is the global academic imprint of the above companies
and has companies and representatives throughout the world.

Palgrave® and Macmillan® are registered trademarks in the United States,
the United Kingdom, Europe and other countries.

ISBN 978-1-349-37957-6   ISBN 978-0-230-62334-7 (eBook)
DOI 10.1057/9780230623347

Library of Congress Cataloging-in-Publication Data
Read, Justin.
   Modern poetics and hemispheric American cultural studies /
Justin Read.
      p. cm.—(Studies of the Americas)
     Includes bibliographical references and index.
      1. American poetry—20th century—History and criticism.
   2. Latin American poetry—20th century—History and criticism.
   3. Modernism (Literature)—America. 4. Culture and globalization—
America. 5. Culture conflict in literature. I. Title.
PS310.M57R43 2009
809.1′9112—dc22   2008055737

A catalogue record of the book is available from the British Library.

Design by Newgen Imaging Systems (P) Ltd., Chennai, India.

First edition: August 2009

10 9 8 7 6 5 4 3 2 1

For Ania:
A Work of Love

Contents

List of Figures	ix
Preface	xi
Acknowledgments	xxxi
Credits	xxxiii
Abbreviations	xxxv
1 Enter the Cannibal: Dependency, Migration, and Textuality in William Carlos Williams's *Spring and All*	1
2 The Reversible World: America as Dissonance in Mário de Andrade's *Pauicéia desvairada*	59
3 Verse Reverse Verse: Fake Autobiographies, Lost Translations, and New Originals of Vicente Huidobro's *Altazor*	103
4 Alien Sedition: Anti-Semitism and Censorship in *The Cantos of Ezra Pound*	157
Notes	197
Bibliography	215
Index	223

Figures

2.1 Front-cover of the first edition of *Paulicéia desvairada* (© The Family of Mário de Andrade, used by permission). 100

2.2 A drawing of Anhangabaú park that appears between the "Prefácio interessantíssimo" and lyrical poems in the first edition of *Paulicéia desvairada* (© The Family of Mário de Andrade, used by permission). 101

2.3 "The conclusion, therefore, is that there are two capital forces: love, which multiplies the species; and the nose, which subordinates it to the individual. Procreation, equilibrium." 102

3.1 The "Molinos" of the first edition of *Altazor* (reprinted under the authorization of the Fundación Vicente Huidobro). 134

3.2 The "Molinos" of the manuscript of *Altazor*; pages appear in reverse order from the printed version, indicated by "12" coming before "11" (reprinted under the authorization of the Fundación Vicente Huidobro). 142

3.3 The first manuscript page of the "Prefacio" in French (reprinted under the authorization of the Fundación Vicente Huidobro). 146

3.4 A title page of Huidobro's manuscript (reprinted under the authorization of the Fundación Vicente Huidobro). 147

3.5 An associational vector. 151

3.6 An associational mapping (reprinted under the authorization of the Fundación Vicente Huidobro). 152

3.7 The *first* title page of Huidobro's manuscript (reprinted under the authorization of the Fundación Vicente Huidobro). 153

3.8 "Todo el resto fué escrito ~~en Chile~~ en 1919 y corregido en 1920" (reprinted under the authorization of the Fundación Vicente Huidobro). 154
4.1 "The sun rises in the east." 172
4.2 *The Cantos of Ezra Pound* (Fifth paperbound printing, 2007?), pp. 256–257 (reprinted with the permission of New Directions Publishing Corporation). 181
4.3 *The Cantos of Ezra Pound* (First clothbound printing of *Cantos 1–117* in one volume, 1970), pp. 256–257 (reprinted with the permission of New Directions Publishing Corporation). 181
4.4 Table of Contents for *Cantos LII–LXXI* (reprinted with the permission of New Directions Publishing Corporation) 184

Preface

The poem is process. A production process. But not a process toward some final product. The poem has no final answer—you cannot say what it means in the end—because the poem always moves along before you can say it. In a sense, the poem is an act of refusal. Before producing sense, the poem refuses sense. Not entirely (or sometimes entirely), but refuses sense *for the moment*. The poem puts sense in its place, semantics in equal measure to the nonsemantic aspects of words, the abstract grammar of language and the concrete presence of the words themselves (typescript, handwriting, voice, digital image). The poetry of the poem resides not in its meaning, but in its musicality: the aural resonance created by the sound of one word next to another word, words on top of words. The spatial resonance of marks and symbols set against the page, the screen, the sidewalk. The physical resonance, the way one's head rings, the way the poet holds on to the time and space of the audience, the way words come through your stereo speakers and knock on your chest. And yes, the erotic, emotional resonance, the feeling the poem leaves on your skin or in your head or on your heart. Only at this point does the semantic sense of the *text* reenter into *context*: amidst the multiplied resonances of the poem one finds sense, creates new sense, starts making sense where no sense was before. All of this may take a flash of a moment to occur, or it may take years or decades of concerted study. In any event, the poem is the process by which all of this comes to pass.

And once it passes, the poem must be read again. The process continues. The poem always changes *in relation* to the time and space in which it is produced, reproduced, and received. *Text* is always a function of *context*. You cannot say what the poem means in the end. But you can work through its process, and *within* its process.

However, because the poem is process, the poem is not the thing to which most contemporary scholars will turn in order to fix the meaning of culture, identity, or history. Despite the importance of context, the poetic process can appear to be self-organizing and self-contained. The poem can rapidly become an exercise in its own formality, whereby certain structural properties of language, certain sound-effects, certain sense-effects are all elicited without having much relation to the world around the poem. The American New Critics called this the "well-wrought urn," a perfect creation, left by some unknowable master, replete with its own internal tensions and manners. The Structuralists likewise viewed the poem as the ultimate expression of the abstract language system, as a self-operating machine of language. In short, for these schools of the twentieth century, the poem held a *privileged* place in literary and cultural scholarship. The refusal of sense inherent to the poetic process came to maximize the impression of poetry as the highest, purest form of linguistic expression. Yet the refusal of sense also came to be seen as a lack of engagement with the real world, as if the poem/urn/machine were "above all that."

This sense of privilege has also necessarily been interpreted as *socioeconomic* privilege. Post-structuralism and deconstruction accomplished necessary work with respect to the institutions of cultural scholarship and cultural power, and their relations to class antagonisms. After deconstruction, language could not be accepted de facto as natural, but rather always socially constructed. Any use of language, particularly written language, published in historical, cultural, or otherwise social discourses could likewise never be taken out-of-hand as fully naturalized. It was finally recognized, for instance, that poetry had no *natural* place of privilege over prose, journalism, film scripts, or even comic books and advertisements. Rather, its privilege was by and large the product of the power invested in it historically by educational, academic, and cultural institutions. There can be no mistake, therefore, of the shift over the past half-century to narrative—*prose* narrative—as the predominant focus of cultural studies. If one understands how certain socially constructed narratives of history and nation come to accumulate power, then it stands to reason that you can understand how these narratives might be altered, and how narratives of *other* histories and nations might be validated. The formalism and formality of poetry appeared to be ill-suited to such tasks.

Yet we should notice here that the problem is not with poetry or the poetic itself, but with how poems and poetics *have been read*. The process of poetry always stands in relation to time and space. Thus, the process of poetry always relates to its historical, material, and spatial contexts. Indeed as I would like to show in this book, the poem can even *devour* its time and space.

Why Read?

This book poses difficult questions: How does the process of poetry relate to larger historical processes of culture, politics, and economics in the American Hemisphere? Why is poetry necessary to understanding the Americas as temporal, spatial, and historico-cultural contexts?

The growth of Hemispheric, Inter-American cultural studies has been nothing short of impressive over the past decade. When I began the present project almost a decade ago, such a thing as Inter-American studies scarcely existed in literary-cultural studies. True a few trailblazing figures such as Earl Fitz, Djelal Kadir, and Vera Kutzinski had published substantive works, but these did not in themselves manage to coalesce into a distinct discipline or subdiscipline of "Hemispheric American Studies."[1] Instead, "American Studies" in the U.S. academy was understood to mean "U.S. Studies" only, and even its decidedly "Anglo" bent often did not include English-speaking Canada or the Caribbean. The use of "American" to mean "U.S." was even institutionalized in the very name of the American Studies Association (ASA). (For the remainder of this study, "American" means "of the Americas"; "U.S.-American" means, well, "U.S.-American.") Latin American studies has a separate trade organization, the Latin American Studies Association (LASA), the membership of which—if I may be so bold to generalize—has tended to regard the ASA with suspicion, if LASA regards it at all. Even within Latin American cultural studies, Spanish America and Brazil were usually studied in isolation—with minimal crossover. With American literary-cultural studies split into several distinct spheres (North America, Spanish America, Brazil, also Francophone Caribbean and Quebec), truly inter-American comparative work in the last half of the twentieth century was spearheaded by social scientists and diplomats who tended to have a specific geopolitical agenda. Until only recently, that is, Hemispheric studies have largely served the Organization of American States, the Inter-American Development Bank, International Monetary Fund, World Bank—organizations promoting either the hegemony of the United States or that of global capitalism.

Since the turn of the twenty-first century, however, something remarkable has occurred. The ASA speaks openly of "internationalizing" American studies, so as to correct the biases of American Exceptionalism. This veritable sea change in Anglo-American studies (at least at the institutional level) has been accompanied by, if not led directly to, extended anthologies and monographs in the field, notably written or edited by Donald Pease, Werner Sollors, and Anna Brickhouse.[2] Whether such scholars have successfully shed any and all hints of Exceptionalism remains a point of heated debate, of course, as witnessed by a special issue of *PMLA* on "Globalizing American Studies" edited by Djelal Kadir, especially in Djelal's pointed critique of Pease.[3] Nevertheless, "hemispheric" and "international" have become the keywords of the day.

Concurrent to these developments in Anglo-American studies, Latin American cultural studies have undergone their own remarkable transformations. A generation ago, Latin Americanists appeared committed to a certain form of regional insularity, perhaps justifiably so. The region was perceived (not incorrectly, by the way) to be afflicted by its dependence on the "First World," so that developing a distinctly Latin American cultural theory—to read and understand Latin America on its own terms—became an urgent task. This effort was led by Roberto Fernández Retamar, who in addition to his official role in Cuba's Casa de las Américas also penned the seminal works *Para una teoría de la literatura hispanoamericana* and the beautiful *Calibán*.[4] By the 1980s and early 1990s, a few exceptional figures did begin to call for more "openness," notably the Argentinean/Brazilian critic Jorge Schwartz in his essay "¡Abajo Tordesillas!"[5] U.S. scholars such as Earl Fitz and Richard Morse began sketching out—although not theorizing—means of a comparative Anglo-Latin American field.[6] Yet such exceptions were just that...exceptional.

The previous "insularity" in Latin Americanism has all but faded away over the past 15 years. Nowadays, cultural scholars routinely move between different linguistic traditions within Latin America, especially by incorporating both Brazilian and Spanish-American cultures. Recent notable examples of this are Luíz Madureira's *Cannibal Modernities* and Fernando Rosenberg's *The Avant-Garde and Geopolitics in Latin America*.[7] Moreover, Latin Americanists such as Deborah Cohn and Debra Castillo have begun to read both Latin- and Anglo Americas in terms of inherent bilingual and bicultural connections between them.[8] At the same time, a rich body of hemispheric work from Anglo-Americanists has emerged, albeit work from a distinct theoretical and methodological perspective than that of Latin Americanism: Anna Brickhouse's *Transamerican Literary Relations*, Gretchen Murphy's *Hemispheric Imaginings*, and the collection *Hemispheric American Studies* edited by Caroline Levander and Robert Levine.[9] More impressively, border studies has emerged as a *central* field of cultural studies internationally, in its analysis and theorization, not only U.S.-Mexican and U.S.-Caribbean border cultures, but also the central presence of Latinos and Latin American culture in the north. The significance of this emergence cannot be underestimated. Key concepts of contemporary cultural studies—"hybridity," "border," "deterritorialization"—cannot be utilized in contemporary scholarship without mentioning the work of Gloria Anzaldúa, José David Saldívar, Nestor García Canclini, or Walter Mignolo, to name but a few.[10] In short, there is no question that, far from remaining "derivative" of trends in France and the United States, Latino and Latin American studies and theory have moved to the forefront of cultural studies worldwide.

In light of these developments, we can say with a good measure of confidence that both Anglo-American Studies and Latin American Studies have "embraced" the outside world since 1990. The transformation in both fields has been one from a state of relative closure, in which geo-cultural regions were thought to be unique, exceptional, and/or special to one of relative openness, in which connections, migrations, and exchanges between Anglo and Latin, North and South, assume primary critical importance.

But what has really brought about these "tectonic" shifts in both Anglo and Latin American studies? As I just mentioned, Hemispheric American studies *have* existed for some time now, just not in the realm of cultural studies in the humanities. Hemispheric American studies have a much more extensive history in the "quantitative" social sciences, and in correlative professional spheres of international relations, politics, and commerce. And in an "obverse" way, politics, economics, and social science have driven cultural scholars to think "hemispherically." Economic crises across Latin America and the Caribbean in the 1970s and 1980s—combined with political oppression supported directly and indirectly by the United States and Canada—drove large populations of Latin Americans to relocate northward. The United States and Canada have long been "Latin" countries in their way, of course: Québec, the U.S. Southwest, Louisiana, South Florida, and so on. Yet by 1990 it became readily apparent that a wholesale demographic shift had occurred in nominally "North" or "Anglo" American nations. Furthermore, after 1990 the Latin American economy began to expand again—spurred by accelerated globalization of the region's national economies.[11] Large, intercontinental economic spheres such as Mercosur, the Central American Free Trade Agreement, and North American Free Trade Agreement have been ratified since the early 1990s, with greater and lesser degrees of success. In short order, American governments and multinational corporations began to imagine an all-encompassing Free

Trade Agreement of the Americas encompassing half of the planet. To a certain extent economic interdependence with the North has fostered an "Anglicization" of Latin American cultural practices, primarily in the adoption of consumer-cultural practices among more affluent classes.

Thus, it is no accident that interest in Hemispheric American cultural studies corresponds to the "Latinization" of Anglo America, the "Anglicization" of Latin America, and the political-economic integration of the Americas through globalized free trade. Even in the face of stiff opposition to neoliberalism (both in the form of popular movements and populist demagoguery), American nations have become mutually dependent. Cultural scholars generally remain opposed to globalization and integration, largely out of a sincere ethical obligation to oppose increasingly advanced forms of economic exploitation and political oppression. Nevertheless, we would be amiss to think that inter-American cultural studies have nothing to do with inter-American free trade: opposition to free trade has been born from the very practice of free trade.

This is a dangerous position in which to find oneself. Power dynamics and spheres-of-influence in the Americas are in a state of flux these days, yet there can be no doubt that Anglo-Latin American relations have been marked by disequilibrium, with greater political and economic power exerted from the North than from the South. On one hand, the imbalance has created the impression—particularly amongst Anglo-Americans (or academics working in Anglo America)—that Latin American and Caribbean *cultures* are underdeveloped, even though political-economic "underdevelopment" has nothing to do with cultural value. At the same time, Latin American scholars have, to repeat, viewed Anglo America (and Anglo-Americans) with suspicion as to their true intentions. The fear among Latin Americanists is that hemispheric Americanism would dilute the significance, the specificity, and ultimately the viability of Latin American cultures, even though cultural insularity is no longer acceptable. Their fear would be a real one, however, if Anglo-Americanists were to persist—tacitly or explicitly—in reading Latin America merely as an addendum to Anglo America, and in so doing disregard the impressive body of Latin American cultural scholarship (not to mention cultural production) that has developed over the past 150 years.

This is perhaps the primary question posed by this book: In raising culture as integrally related, and perhaps forcefully resistant, to an integrated Free Trade Agreement of the Americas, how do we avoid creating a homogenized Free Trade Agreement of Hemispheric American Cultural Studies?

The Negative Space of Hemispheric American Studies

By raising this question I mean that Hemispheric American studies cannot be practiced without recognizing the institutional effects of that practice. Hemispheric studies are in the process of emerging as a defined discipline, but they are doing so "in translation" between the extant cultural-scholarly institutions of Anglo-American and Latin American Studies, each of which have already derived their own particular predilections, methods, and theories. At some point the institutional differences between the two fields will have to be negotiated, and I hope this present work will move Hemispheric studies in this direction. However, any inter-Americanist will immediately have to confront the questions of how and where to begin the work of translation and negotiation. Even Earl Fitz, whose knowledge of American cultures from Québec and Nunavut down through Patagonia is perhaps unparalleled, begins his *Rediscovering the New World* with the following apology:

> My methodology in this undertaking has been to identify several key issues that seem endemic to literature in the New World, to select certain representative texts from each of the five largest New World cultures...and to read these texts against one another....One of the daunting problems encountered in an undertaking such as this was precisely the issue of text selection, for not all the works that relate to any given topic could possibly be discussed. Given the multitude of issues and texts that are available for consideration, on what rationale does one pick certain ones over others?[12]

Fitz admirably elaborates a *methodology* for his comparative study, and seems to suggest that this methodology will provide a basis for the *theorization* of the vexing multiplicities at play in different parts of the hemisphere. Yet he also stands down from moving beyond the methodology of thematic cohesion, and thus also stands down from an overarching theory of Americanism valid across the hemisphere.

The unmistakable goal of my own work, here and elsewhere, is to provide such an overarching theorization. To begin such work we need to assess the institutions of Americanism that have come *before* inter-Americanism, to "begin before the begin" as it were. But if we are thinking of institutional comparisons between different fields of American literary-cultural studies, we will find something quite stunning. Over the past century, Anglo and Latin American studies have been united only to the extent that they have afforded relatively *little* intrinsic value to American cultures. Traditionally, literary historians and critics have considered American cultures too "new" to have a defined culture, properly speaking; or they have viewed them as mere replicas of their foreign progenitors. In either case, Americanist scholarship—whether Anglo-Americanist or Latin Americanist—has viewed the "American" through a profound *lack* of its own culture.

In one of the earliest U.S.-American literary histories, for instance, Walter C. Bronson begins his 1919 *A Short History of American Literature* by stating:

> For the first two centuries, indeed, our literature is chiefly valuable, not as art, but as history, as an expression of the spirit of the people and the times. Nor can its full significance be seen until we widen our view still more and recognize that American literature is one branch of the greater English literature, a part of the life of a great race as well as of a great nation.[13]

All "American" literature (Bronson, of course, ignores the fact that "American" would be anything other than "U.S.-American") essentially exists as a mere extension of English literature—and an inferior version of the English at that, not yet "art" but mere historical documentation. Similar sentiments are expressed among Bronson's contemporaries. John Macy would write in 1913 that "American literature is a branch of English literature, as truly as are English books written in Scotland or South Africa."[14] We can make no mistake about it: both Bronson and Macy reduce American culture to the service of a single "great" (and very white) *race*. In doing so they tacitly suggest the "American" as a diluted offshoot of that race.

Generally speaking U.S.-American literary history has tended not only to deny value to the literature it studies, but to deny value to the "American," in general. In 1980, Robert E. Spiller would complain:

> ...[A]s recently as a half century ago, it was generally assumed that there was no such thing as an *American* literature. At that time there were no departments and few courses in American literature as such in our colleges and universities; there were no scholarly societies or journals devoted to its study; the specialists in American literary research could be counted on one hand, and to so announce oneself was virtually to commit professional suicide; and histories of the subject were generally deprecatory and apologetic.[15]

Such institutional myopia seems to have been "corrected" in the aftermath of World War II, when the valorization of U.S. culture was perceived as a matter of vital national security, as a counterweight to Soviet aggression and propaganda.[16] Nevertheless, lest we view the depreciation of "American" value to be a thing of the past, Hortense J. Spillers writes in 1991:

> The construction and invention of "America," then—a dizzying concoction of writing and reportage, lying and "signifying," jokes, "tall tales," and transgenerational nightmares, all conflated under the banner of Our Lord—exemplify, for all intents and purposes, the oldest game of *trompe de l'oeil*, the perhaps-mistaken-glance-of-the-eye, that certain European "powers" carried out regarding indigenous Americans. *Misprision*, therefore, constitutes law and rule of "Our America" in its "beginnings" for Europe. "Made up" in the gaze of Europe, "America" was as much a "discovery" on the retinal surface as it was the appropriation of land and historical subjects.[17]

"America" in Spillers' view amounts to little more than a dream (or nightmare) "made up" for the advancement of European hegemony, which is a perfectly valid way of addressing the issue. All the same, according to Spillers "America" can *only* be defined under the limits imposed on it by Europe. Although she attacks the lack of agency afforded to Americans to define themselves in the harshest of terms, she nonetheless perpetuates this very lack of agency in her own argument.

This notion of *lack* as a constitutive aspect of American literatures and cultures is by no means limited to U.S. intellectuals either. César Vallejo, arguably the greatest poet from any America of any generation, writes in 1927 that "Today, as yesterday, the writers of America practice a borrowed literature, which goes tragically bad for them. The aesthetic—if one may so call that grotesque simian nightmare of American writers—lacks therefore, today perhaps more than ever, its own proper physiognomy."[18] Here, Vallejo may have been echoing the thoughts of the *modernista* poet, Rubén Darío, who prefaced one of his masterworks, *Prosas profanas* (1895/1901), by bluntly stating that his work was "neither useful nor timely." Why?:

> a) Because of the absolute lack of mental elevation in the thinking majority of our continent, over which rules that universal personality classified by Remy de Gourmont with the name *Celui-qui-ne-comprend-pas*. *Celui-qui-ne-comprend-pas* is among us professor, correspondent academic with the Real Academia Española, journalist, lawyer, poet, *rastaquouére*.

b) Because the collective work of the new [poets] of America is still vain, with so many of the best talents remaining in the limbo of complete ignorance of the very Art to which they devote themselves.[19]

Such views are not limited to writers, but have historically been the province of Latin American literary critics as well. In arguably the greatest work of Brazilian literary history, the two-volume *Formação da literatura brasileira*, Antonio Candido states just as bluntly: "Our literature is a secondary branch of the Portuguese, in its turn a shrub of secondary order in the garden of the Muses.... Compared to the greats, our literature is poor and weak."[20] As late as 1992, in the introduction to the *Borzoi Anthology of Latin American Literature*, Emir Rodríguez Monegal takes a somewhat different stance: "It cannot yet be said that there is a cohesive Latin American literature, at least in the continental sense.... Latin American literature is more an intention than a fact simply because Latin America itself has never achieved cultural integration."[21] Although Rodríguez in fact names Latin America as a collective entity in a text that anthologizes literary work from the region, he nevertheless defines "Latin America" as a sort of intentional fallacy. Rodríguez's concern is not that Latin American literature exhibits gross aesthetic shortcomings, for in fact he introduces an anthology of Latin American literary genius. Rather, Latin American literature lacks an extant, integrative cultural space in the first place. Without such a space, "Latin America" can only be held as an immaterial prospect or intention of some future unification. Indeed, the view of "Latin America" as a promise geared toward the future emerges from a long history in Latin American criticism, dating in the twentieth century back to the work of Pedro Henríquez Ureña, and indeed as far back as Andrés Bello in the postindependence period of the nineteenth century.[22]

Taken hemispherically, Americanist literary criticism has been caught—until relatively recently—in a peculiar sort of conundrum similar to the old Brazilian joke: "O Brasil é o país do futuro...e sempre será!" ("Brazil is the country of the future...and always will be.") Evidently, American culture (or at least literature) is not yet fully formed. It may not be inferior to Europe, but it nevertheless has a long way to go before it can move from belief and intention to reality. American culture is something that may be glimpsed, but nothing that has definition or form. Or rather, its form and definition always emanate from somewhere else external to it: its indigenous (Amerindian), Asian, or African roots to be sure; but more likely as a cultural extension of its

European colonizers. Such views have dissipated substantially over the past 20 years, and yet they continue to linger still.

In terms of literary-cultural studies as an institution, the American has been, shall we say, *spectral*... but only if one believes in ghosts. My own view is that the material condition of the American histories is just that: material and historical. Yet matter and history are always *in migration*, movement that has made American cultures rather hard to nail down. The question of American cultural studies in the global or hemispheric sense, therefore, is not *if* something can be known, but *how* and *why* it should be known. The question is not *if* the American exists, but *the process by which* the American has been announced, *how* it has been materialized.

Or perhaps we should begin to frame the problem of inter-American studies around how the Americas *continue* to materialize, rather than merely accepting the region as already concretized. Perhaps the Americanists just mentioned have tended to confuse "process" with "lack." They have been looking for a culture that has been fully embodied or incorporated. Yet American cultures may *only* be defined as a *process of integration*, as an ongoing process of cultural migration and cultural translation. The problem of Hemispheric American cultural studies in such a context is not whether one can compare a text from one America to a text from another America. The problem is that to do so would tend to assume that a "Latin America" has *already* been differentiated, realized, and stabilized as a region and as a field of study, even if one finds a lack of cultural value there. Such assumed self-realization may then distinguish Latin America from an already differentiated, realized, and stabilized Anglo America that likewise lacks intrinsic value. And vice versa. In order to make comparisons, it seems, one must assume that one America has *already* been reconciled unto itself, and that another America *already* reconciled unto itself, in order to overcome the *irreconcilable* differences between them.

The Plan of the Present Work

Modern Poetics and Hemispheric American Cultural Studies therefore addresses several problems that will prove fundamental to the formation of the discipline:

What Is the "American"?

There is no such thing as "America" until the sixteenth century, at which point the hemisphere was named by foreign (European) cartographers. Furthermore, indigenous peoples of the hemisphere are in fact pre-American (not necessarily "native" American) since their cultures and societies far predate any existence of America per se. Indigenous peoples, rather, have been *forced to become American*, usually by means of violence and coercion, just as have many other subsequent cultural groups (Africans especially prior to the 1890s, many Asian groups until the 1960s as key examples). However, the mere naming of America after Amerigo Vespucci is not the sole determining factor of what America is, or what an American is. The "American" comes into being as a result of migration and encounter. In other words, there is no such thing as "American" until two extant cultures meet and are thereby compelled to communicate, even if this results in *mis*communication. As secondary (and very strange) consequences of this fact, the "American" simultaneously exists *only* in modern historical time (post-1492), and is therefore *cut off* from any historical origin. That is, the real historical "origin" of the Americas is in fact a present, continuing historical process of cultural migration, encounter, and translation between populations. Yet these populations will always locate their "true" historical and cultural origins in another time and place (Europe, Africa, Asia, preconquest, even if these are myths). The American is in fact the ~~American~~.

What Is American Culture?

To say that American cultures are "multicultural" is not forceful enough. As a process of migration and encounter, American culture is always a matter of *cultural translation*. The process of cultural translation is best theorized and analyzed through the Latin American concept of "transculturation," a concept first coined by Fernando Ortiz and developed by Angel Rama, Antonio Cornejo Polar, Walter Mignolo, among others.[23] These thinkers see clearly that the process of cultural translation is not (just) one of *acculturation* or assimilation to a "dominant" culture; instead, certain elements acculturate, others "deculturate" and are lost, but in any case both "dominant" and "dominated" exchange culture, merge into one another, even if they remain overtly hostile to one another. This is how Latin American *mestizaje* has come to be understood since 1940, and I see no reason why the transcultural model would not apply to Anglo America as well. However, we should not be mistaken that transculturation results in *telos*, with the emergence of a fully formed *mestizo* national subject. The process of transculturation continues, and continues to result in more conflicts between cultures and ethnicities than it resolves. Any American culture is therefore best defined as "pluriform transculture" marked by continual historical tension and cultural conflict, even violently so. In this sense it is best to hold onto radicalized interpretations of transculturation, such as that of Alberto Moreiras's "savage hybridity" or "cannibalism" as developed by Haroldo de Campos *via* Oswald de Andrade.[24]

What Is American Language?

Notably, there is no such thing—or more precisely, not *yet* such a thing—as a language called "American." Languages in the hemisphere are either indigenous/*pre*-American (Aymara, Tupi-Guarani, Quechua, Quiche, Hopi, Lakota, Inuit, etc.), or they are imported/*non*-American (English, French, Portuguese, Spanish, Chinese, Vietnamese, Yoruba, etc.). If the Americas are, as Silviano Santiago has suggested, the "space in-between" (in-between different cultures and societies), then the true language of the Americas would likewise have to occupy a space in-between.[25] Since American cultures are always already "transculturated," that is, formed through cultural translation, then it stands to reason that the language of the Americas is *translation* itself. The problem, of course, is that translation is not a language in its own right, only a relation between two or more *other* languages. Moreover, as I and others have noted previously, the "good" translation is the one that remains transparent, whereas the "bad" translation is typically one in which the reader, listener, or receiver recognizes that something is being translated—it is not the original but a secondary copy.[26] To make translation *deliberately* visible or material is, shall we say, rather uncivilized and uncouth. As I state a bit later on in this Preface, and prove in the rest of this book, the problem of translation is particularly *poetic*.

What Is an American Subject?

This final question is by far the most difficult one, and the most incendiary insofar as it will lead directly to ideological conflict both within academic disciplines and between academia and the rest of the world. Perhaps the greatest historical question facing any and all American societies is the determination of who *is* American and who *is not* American, un-American. American political systems rest on the foundational question of who may receive full citizenship, and hence receive representation in the official realm of state power. In response to this predicament, the predominant mode of cultural studies in the Americas (particularly in the United States) has been the valorization of subaltern subject-positions. The goal of working through subaltern subjectivity is political in nature: either to dismantle existing political structures so as to create new systems in which subaltern subjects are given their just place or to integrate subaltern subjects into existing state structures in ways that do not infringe on justice and human rights. The problems as I see it with such lines of inquiry stem from *how* any American subject would be incorporated into any form of state, whether into the modern nation-state or some entirely new form. The matter of state incorporation requires the subject to be translated into an *objective* fact—for subjectivity to be objectified in some way, shape, or form. Furthermore, the dominant forces of political and economic power *only* care about objective facts: they only care about how objects (commodities, goods, products, people) can be pushed around, and how efficiently they can be pushed. Any focus on subjectivity alone will therefore tend to be disregarded by such forces. This is not to say that we must disregard subjectivity or subalterity altogether—not at all. Rather, we must find ways to understand the *relation in-between* subjects and objects. As involved in an ongoing process of transculturation and translation, the American subject is never *reconciled* to history or to itself, but is always migrating between cultures and histories, even as a matter of "internal" psychological formation. Consequently, the American subject (subject-position) will never be reconciled or fixed to any objective location (object-position) within a state system. Rather than the *re-conciliation* of the subject, we must look to the continual and continuing *non-conciliation* of subject-object relations as the hallmark of "American." This may sound confusing now, but it will become clear by the end of the book.

Outlines of the Modern

I have thus far outlined two different sorts of process: The poem as a contextual process, and the American as a modern, historical process. But how do these two processes intersect or overlap? The concept of the *modern* is the key link between the two. Before I go any further, I should say that I reject the concept of "modernity" as formulated in the "modern-traditional" binary of Weberian social science. Civilization and culture are always coeval. One is never *more* "modern" than the other, especially not because one is less "traditional." Rather, some cultures are more wealthy than others, some cultures have more things and machines than others. By contrast my understanding of "modern" is probably closer to the concept of the "modern/colonial" as formulated by Mignolo *via* Aníbal Quijano and Immanuel Wallerstein.[27] "Modernity" is at its base a worldwide political-economic system that begins with the "discovery" and the colonization of Americas, Africa, Asia, and Oceania.

This conceptual distinction is important in that aesthetic and cultural *modernisms* (ca. 1910–1960) gave voice to modernity—not in the sense of destroying "tradition," as is commonly held, because "modernity" and "tradition" are not binary opposites. Rather, modern poets in particular concretized the modern political-economic order as a matter of culture.[28] But the difficulty in making such an assertion, albeit a true one, is that modernists and *vanguardistas* were not mere handmaidens of capitalism or the status quo. After Whitman, Machado de Assis, Darío, *samba*, jazz, and *tango* it had become readily apparent by the 1920s that American cultures were now distinct from their colonial forebears. Modern poets sought to materialize this distinction, to *inscribe* the American voice and American identity, through a poetics based in *migration, translation,* and *transculturation*. However, the poetic process is not just about specifying the meaning of language. The poem is a process that generates critical insight for its participants as to how meaning is created in a particular context—so that one can derive ways to *mutate* contexts. Modern poets tended to be, in the words of Haroldo de Campos, the "*Oi barbaroi*." They were not merely interested in giving meaning to modernity, but often in attacking modernity and creating new possibilities for it. This is therefore not a matter of the superstructure (culture, literature, poetry) giving symbolic meaning to the base (capitalism). Modern poetry is more likely a matter of the superstructure trying to *devour* the base, grind it down, make it into something different.

I outline how this is the case in the four chapters to follow, each focused primarily on a single poetic work, but with each work placed into far-ranging contexts. The chapters are organized more or less in chronological order, although I must caution that I am not trying to construct a chronology of Hemispheric Americanism. In the first chapter, I analyze William Carlos Williams's 1923 volume of prose and poetry, *Spring and All*. Although Williams's parents were British/West Indian and Puerto Rican, I reject any revision of Williams as a "hemispheric" subject. Instead, I focus on hemispheric possibilities that emerge from the text itself in an objective sense, in its migrations between prose and poetry. Although modernism (and Williams's brand of objectivism in particular) is often read as an evasion of politics and society, I work through links between Williams's poetics and those of the Brazilian poet Oswald de Andrade, in order to demonstrate how *Spring and All* may require Latin American dependency theory in order to be properly understood. The meaning of "So much depends on a red wheel barrow" may itself depend on dependency.

Chapters 2 and 3 concentrate squarely on Latin American texts and cultures. In chapter 2, I examine Mário de Andrade's invention of "harmonic verse" in his 1922 volume, *Paulicéia desvairada*, not only as a poetic-linguistic structure but also as a means to structure transcultural relations in modern Brazil. In poeticizing the modern (economic and cultural) capital of São Paulo, Mário works to "harmonize" and "modernize" Brazil in a highly duplicitous fashion. Brazil is structured as at once a modern nation and a schizophrenic spectacle that sets the reader's head ringing. A similar pattern emerges (in chapter 3) through Vicente Huidobro's 1931 epic, *Altazor*, although in a much stranger way (as if things could get much stranger than *Paulicéia desvairada*). *Altazor* must be read as a search for origins, although it is not clear whether the work seeks a "pre-Babelian" origin of language or a "postmodern" origin of a new utopia. What is clear is that the recent "discovery" of Huidobro's manuscripts for the work has provided us a "new origin" for *Altazor*. And this new origin locates the work in a particularly American problematic of transcultural translation. Through an admittedly strange act of historical recuperation, I "discover" how *Altazor* reasserts the Chilean nation despite itself—a Chile falling down on itself in ironic and comedic fashion. Taken in tandem, *Paulicéia desvairada* and *Altazor* do not provide firm locations for their respective nations; rather, the nation, and the national subjects incorporated into it, are always already caught in movement, caught in translation.

These works, in other words, allow us to recognize the (re-)assertion of the American nation as "non-grounded" and non-conciliated: as grounded in both subject-subject and subject-object oscillation. This provides me a means to assess the highly problematic Americanism of *The Cantos of Ezra Pound* in chapter 4. The author of the *Cantos*, of course, was virulently anti-Semitic, racist, and likely insane. He was also found to be officially un-American by the U.S. government, due to his vocal support of Mussolini during (and after) World War II. However, at the height of Pound's anti-American support of Italian fascism, the *Cantos* veer sharply into U.S.-American history—in the section (first published in 1940) that has come to be known as the "China/Adams" cantos. In that section, Pound constructs a history of *ethical* political-economic thought rooted in the writings of Confucius and John Adams. Pound's ethics—such as they are—would only emerge from a transcultural and translational encounter between China and the United States, always framed in relation to modern European culture. By reading *The Cantos of Ezra Pound* through the prism of Latin American thought—notably theories of "cannibalistic" translation of Haroldo de Campos—we will find efficacious ways to judge the untenable contradictions the work produces. The Americanism of the *Cantos* occurs in its *refutation* of authorship, authority, and authoritarianism, even as the work *asserts* all these things in its focalization of U.S.-American history. This only becomes available in the context of textual transmission and translation, which are the ultimate bases for any determination of authorship and subjectivity in the work.

The ends of this book are therefore a beginning: *The foundation of American culture is migration. The original language of the Americas is only ever translation.* The poem is the process by which the language of migration—*translation*—materializes in its own right.

Limitations

If the aim of this book is to make Hemispheric American studies comprehensible, it makes no claims whatsoever to being *comprehensive*. I do not in any way, shape, or form include *all* literary and cultural histories of the Americas, for that would be as foolish as it is impossible. Rather, this book sketches the general theoretical and methodological track I take in subsequent books and articles—a track I hope others will follow, expand, and revise after reading this book.

I do first want to recognize, however, several gaps in my presentation of the argument. Within the realm of poetry of the Americas, even the casual reader will notice the absence of Argentinean, Andean, Canadian, and Caribbean authors. And in particular to the field of modernist/modernizing poetry of the Americas, I have not included key figures such as Jorge Luis Borges, César Vallejo, Octavio Paz, Pablo Neruda, Lezama Lima, T. S. Eliot, Langston Hughes, Marianne Moore, HD...the list could continue. The reasons for these apparent "elisions" are both personal and practical. My interests and strengths as a reader lie in the analysis of texts in microscopic detail, and in the relation of "microscopic" readings to the "macroscopic" scale of world order. Beyond the fact that this style does not permit a vast number of works to be analyzed, however, I am not particularly interested in *cataloguing* the wide variety of possible texts and areas that could be covered. If my readers are interested in such broad-based work, they are best advised to consult excellent works such as *Latin American Vanguards* by Vicky Unruh, *The Pound Era* by Hugh Kenner, or *The Futurist Moment* by Marjorie Perloff, all of which are now widely considered classics in their respective fields. Yet, given my interests and my style of literary criticism, the addition of another mass of microscopic details would make the book as a whole untenable, or rather, impractical to read.

Second, my readers might be surprised to encounter a theoretical work of cultural studies that does not include a theory of race, gender, sexuality—at least not explicitly so. I would caution against such a judgment on the reader's part, however. My goal—to reiterate—is not to create a common sphere of Americanism. This means that I reject any attempt to create a common sphere of indigenous culture, of blackness, of queerness, of woman. The disparities in American nations, I believe, are too vast to posit absolute subject-positions of "black", "gay," "lesbian," "macho," or even "woman," with absolute certainty. Yet I do not at all reject theories of the same per se, especially because they are in fact of central importance to this book. One should notice how questions of race, sexuality, and gender are in fact folded into each argument made in the pages to follow. Above and beyond this fact, though, I seek to provide a productive platform for hemispheric American studies into which all questions of race, gender, and sexuality may be addressed without erasing the patent cultural, political, and economic differences between various Americas. With this book I am not attempting to pinpoint *specific* kinds of social difference; instead I am trying to show how multiple forms of difference function (or malfunction) *differentially* in general.

I myself do not view this book as self-contained or complete, however. I should note that I will likely follow the present work with a more general *Theory of Hemispheric American Cultural Studies* that will address theories of race, gender, and sexuality directly. And I have already begun another book project, *Alternative Functions*, which examines the nexus between urbanization, modernization, modernist architecture, and modernist poetry in the Americas. The latter book focuses primarily on the Latin American city, specifically readings of Buenos Aires, Lima, São Paulo, Brasília, and Mexico City; but it will end in Los Angeles. More importantly in terms of the plan and scope of *Modern Poetics, Alternative Functions* begins with readings of Jorge Luis Borges, Oliverio Girondo, and César Vallejo, and will include other notable figures such as Octavio Paz, Carlos Drummond de Andrade, and João Cabral de Melo Neto—all of whom are key figures evidently absent from this first book. In other words, *Modern*

Poetics and Hemispheric American Cultural Studies is the first of a body of work that will be far more comprehensive than any one book could possibly be.

Even still, I can only ask my reader for compassion. Reading America hemispherically is necessary, but the scale of the hemisphere is, in its way, incomprehensive. Yet by the same token, *incomprehensive* does not mean *incomprehensible*.

Acknowledgments

I would like to thank many people for supporting this project. My graduate advisor Juli Highfill gave me total freedom to explore whatever thread of thought happened to spin through my mind at any given moment while I was a graduate student at the University of Michigan, as did my committee, Jossianna Arroyo, George Bornstein, Santiago Colás, and Marjorie Levinson. I would also like to thank James Dunkerley, Henry Sussman, Caroline Levander, and Charles A. Perrone for providing feedback on the manuscript and, perhaps more importantly, for helping find a way to bring my work to the public. David Castillo and David William Foster were also instrumental in seeing the project along in its final stages. Odile Cisneros, Rosa Sarabia, Jorge Schwartz, Carlos Augusto de Andrade Camargo, Vicente García-Huidobro, Liliana Rosa, and Declan Spring were all instrumental in helping me secure permission to reproduce the bibliographic images in this book. A special note of thanks to the Fundación Vicente Huidobro, the Family of Mário de Andrade, and New Directions for their tremendous work in preserving the legacies of the poets.

Official support for my research was generously provided by the Rackham School of Graduate Studies, the Program in Comparative Literature, and the Global Ethnic Literatures Seminar, all of the University of Michigan; and by the College of Arts and Sciences and the Department of Romance Languages and Literatures of the University at Buffalo (SUNY). Their support has allowed me to conduct archival investigations at the Beinecke Library of Yale; the Fundación Vicente Huidobro in Santiago, Chile; the Instituto de Estudos Brasileiros at the Universidade de São Paulo; the Poetry and Rare Books Library of the University at Buffalo; and the Ransom Library at the University of Texas.

Unofficial support was provided by too many people to remember here, but I would like to pay special mention to Sean Cotter, Bob

Davidson, Scott Gridley, Meredith Martin, Indra Mukhopadhyay, Nirmala Singh-Brinkman, the Academia Carlos e Eliane Andrade of Fortaleza, and the Snail family of Berkeley. I would also like to thank, from the bottom of my heart, my dear *madrina* Celina de Carilla.

My parents Elsbe and Patrick Read—and my brother, sister, in-laws, uncles, aunts, nieces, and nephews across the United States, Canada, Mexico, and Poland—have shown me undying love even when they were not quite so sure what I was up to. My eternal gratitude to them.

Evangelina Rivas de Ibarra, Salvador Ibarra Padilla, Eleanor Read, Lawrence Read, Marjorie Herring, and Emilio Carilla. Spirit Guides.

And finally, to my wife Ania: These words are your words, as well.

Credits

Quotations from *Spring and All* reprinted with permission of New Directions Publishing Corporation. Copyright 1938 by New Directions Publishing Corporation.

Artwork from *Paulicéia desvairada* by Mário de Andrade reproduced with permission of the Family of Mário de Andrade. Quotations from *Paulicéia desvairada* reprinted with permission of the Family of Mário de Andrade and Agir Editora, Ltda.

Pages from print and manuscript editions of *Altazor* by Vicente Huidobro reproduced under the authorization of the Fundación Vicente Huidobro, Santiago, Chile. Quotation from *Altazor* reprinted with permission of the Fundación Vicente Huidobro.

Pages from *The Cantos of Ezra Pound* by Ezra Pound reproduced with the permission of New Directions Publishing Corporation.

Cover art by Julian Montague (used by permission), with many thanks to the Western New York Book Arts Collaborative of Buffalo, NY.

Sections of chapter 3 appeared previously in *Translation Review*, No. 71 (2006): 61–65.

Sections of chapter 4 appeared previously in *CR: New Centennial Review*, 3.1 (2003): 297–327.

Abbreviations

Quotations from primary text will be cited with the following abbreviations followed by page number:

CP: William Carlos Williams. *The Collected Poems of William Carlos Williams*, 2 vols., ed. A. Walton Litz and Christopher MacGowan. New York: New Directions, 1986.

I: William Carlos Williams. *Imaginations*. New York: New Directions, 1970.

SE: William Carlos Williams. *Selected Essays*. New York: New Directions, 1954.

PD: Mário de Andrade. *Paulicéia desvairada*. In: *Poesias completas*, ed. Diléa Zanotto Manfio. Belo Horizonte: Villa Rica, 1993. [Orig. published 1922.] All Portuguese quotations will be followed by my English translation.

A: Vicente Huidobro. *Altazor* [edición facsimilar]. Santiago de Chile: Editorial Universitaria, 1991. [Orig. pub. 1931.] All Spanish quotations will be followed by the English translation of Eliot Weinberger (*Altazor, or, a Voyage in a Parachute* [Hanover, NH: Wesleyan University Press, 2004]).

VC: Vicente Huidobro. *Vientos contrarios*. In: *Obras completas*. Santiago de Chile: Editorial Andrés Bello, 1976.

C: Ezra Pound. *The Cantos of Ezra Pound*. New York: New Directions, 1996 [Paperbound printing].

Chapter 1

Enter the Cannibal: Dependency, Migration, and Textuality in William Carlos Williams's *Spring and All*

The foundation of American culture is migration. The original language of the Americas is only ever translation. But who migrates? Who is the migrant who crosses the border? What does she say? What does her voice sound like to us? What does she think of us? Can we really look at her? Or by writing words (such as "migrant" and "border") am I really creating the *image* of her, creating a thing that can be described in words like so many other things?

In the preface, I began to theorize Hemispheric Americanism with (and in) migration and translation. I suggested that the migration and translation of cultures has direct historical bearing on political and economic configurations of the Americas. But this cultural problematic may itself be fragmented: On one hand, the cultural scholar may hold some ethical obligation to migrating subjects, particularly those whose migration has been spurred by economic exploitation, poverty, or political violence. On the other hand, this ethical obligation to the migrant (but not the migrant herself) may be central to the formation of theories of inter-Americanism. In this sense it is the *image* or *figure* of the migrating subject that assumes critical importance, an image made available for inquiry. The migrant has been transformed into an object (an image-object, figure-object) suitable for use in critical theory.[1]

Such trans-formation (trans-migration?) is far from a comforting act, for it promotes the objectification of the subject, and perhaps also the subjectification of the object, two actions that have often been considered to be politically bad or incorrect. Nevertheless, the process of subject-object movement may hold the key to operating under a Hemispheric American paradigm without monumentalizing the entire hemisphere into a singular (cultural-political-economic) unit.

I would theorize that *all* forms of Americanism stem from historical processes of migration and border-crossing. The border may be international or intercontinental, the intercultural encounter of different societies. It may be linguistic, the translation or (mis)communication across two more languages. Or, the border may very well be *intra*-subjective, in terms of the internalization of subject-object boundaries as a prerequisite for subjective formation. In any event, several critical axioms emerge before any type of American cultural studies can proceed: First, any definition of "American" is always already a priori *deconstructed*, already unhinged or dislocated from itself and its origin, or at least from any final concretization of itself as a "self." Second, that migration is therefore never finalized, but must be understood as a continuing process—American migration is never resolved, but always remains non-conciliated. In political-economic terms, the purpose of the state is to territorialize or ground migration and the cultural translation that ensues from it. Yet the political-economic incorporation of the migrant can only be achieved at the cost of some violence given that the American subject can never be reconciled in such a finalized, grounded way. Even to posit a "hybrid" or "transcultural" subject as a prototype of a national subjectivity may prove oppressive to the extent that the incorporation of hybridity requires a finalized, reconciled subject. This does not mean that transculturation does not occur as a historical process; rather, transculturation and translation do not necessarily reach felicitous ends, if they ever reach an end in the first place.

So who is this migrant of whom we speak? When I began this chapter I had a specific image in mind:

> Unless it be that marriage
> perhaps
> with a dash of Indian blood
> will throw up a girl so desolate
> so hemmed round
> with disease or murder
>
> that she'll be rescued by an
> agent—
> reared by the state and
>
> sent out to work in
> some hard pressed
> house in the suburbs—

> some doctor's family, some Elsie—
> voluptuous water
> expressing with broken
>
> brain the truth about us—
> her great
> ungainly hips and flopping breasts
>
> addressed to cheap
> jewelry
> and rich young men with fine eyes
>
> as if the earth under our feet
> were
> an excrement of some sky
>
> and we degraded prisoners
> destined
> to hunger until we eat filth. (CP 217–218)

The passage is from a poem by William Carlos Williams, "To Elsie," originally published in the 1923 volume *Spring and All*. The image the poem "throws up" is one of dynamic differentiation, individuation: Elsie is an organic body who emerges spontaneously from the land, an individual being who remains tied to the landscape. Yet this landscape is not just natural, but also *national*, political, and economic. The first stanzas of the poem inform us that Elsie is a specifically *American* individual: "The pure products of America / go crazy— / mountain folk from Kentucky // or the ribbed north end of / Jersey" (CP 217). Williams's poem, then, relates a process of *becoming* American—the process by which the individual emerges (produced as a "product") from the landscape as an organic American subject.

But this process is far from heroic, or even organic. Elsie's (national) body is not only "ungainly," but also horrific, disgusting. Her "hips and flopping breasts" are so "hemmed round / with disease and murder" that she appears to saturate the landscape "as if the earth...were an excrement of some sky." Despite the scatological reference to human waste, the poem also grants Elsie a measure of fertility: just as the earth gives birth to Elsie, she herself appears to give birth when her "voluptuous water" breaks. But indeed, the landscape *vomits* Elsie ("throws up") more than it gives birth to her, and if Elsie herself gives birth, she seems to bear a "defective" body, "with broken // brain." If she is to stand as a metonymic extension of the nation (an extension, i.e., not only of the land, but also of the "Homeland"), she is not capable of reproducing the nation in a "healthy" manner. Elsie's body, furthermore, is not only diseased, but also so impoverished that she must relinquish herself to the state ("reared by the state") and is *forced to work by the state*. (Biographical evidence is well established that the real Elsie in question was sent by a New Jersey state agency to work in the house of a physician in suburban Rutherford, a certain Dr. William Carlos Williams.) The "pure product" that emerges from the process of Americanization is homeless—a *rural* subject from Kentucky or the Jersey countryside who has essentially been forced to migrate to the suburbs because of extreme poverty. Her homelessness is redoubled in her vague ethnic background, as a bastardized product of uncertain origin "perhaps / with a dash of Indian blood." She is the product of transcultural encounter, of a dubious origin that goes directly to her *lack* of identity. Elsie is both the cause and effect of total anonymity, one who has either given herself over to some "agent" of the state or has been completely robbed of any agency by the state to make decisions for herself. The poem concludes, "No one / to witness / and adjust, no one to drive the car" (CP 219). The pure product of America is, in the end, a negation. The American subject is "no one." American is ~~American~~.

But even as we speak of these inscrutable contradictions, we have nevertheless been speaking of this American/~~American~~ subject as a spontaneous growth, as if an individual could emerge ex nihilo from the nation's landscape, even though the consolidation of national subjectivity is never a truly "organic" process. Rather, the process of nationhood is one of dynamic social interaction. Or as Benedict Anderson would have it, the national "imagined community" emerges when a mass of individuals who remain anonymous to one another begin to identify themselves as sharing a common national experience—one that they share instantaneously in "empty time."[2] Elsie *cannot* be a pure, organic American product in and of herself, but can only become American in relation to someone else: "American" can only be formed when Elsie and someone else begin to see themselves as *commonly* American. Simply put, the poem substantiates "American" once the poetic voice names Elsie as being American *and* in doing so implies that the poetic voice and Elsie form a national "we." The bonds of national fraternity are only created in the interaction between Elsie and the poet who perceives her (one we will call "William Carlos Williams"), the voice who addresses both Elsie and the poem itself to America. But viewed in this way, the poem works to *subvert* every commonly held belief of national character. Whatever "national fraternity" the poem offers is not a bond of Platonic love between brothers, but a shameful hetero-erotic gaze spurred by the poet's own lust—why else (why Elsie?) does Williams only focus on two "voluptuous" parts of her body, her hips and breasts? If Elsie is a national body, then she is a diseased national body, and her disease spreads to Williams like a communicable virus. Elsie is *antisocial*, whose only desire for human contact stems from her selfish greed for "cheap jewelry." And this antisocial behavior translates into the degradation of the poet who gazes upon her, who is now forced to "hunger until we eat filth." Moreover, it is not clear that *any* common bond of Americanness is shared between them. There is no national destiny ("no one to drive the car"), let alone a destiny of increased freedom ("we degraded prisoners / destined / to hunger"). There is no indication that Elsie actually sees herself as American, or that she has any ability for self-reflection. Indeed, there is no indication of her voice whatsoever—just the words of the suburban physician who employs her labor.

"To Elsie" places us squarely in a dialectic of social inclusion and exclusion—in which the transcultural American subject is *at once* incorporated and disincorporated into the project of American nationhood. Whereas the consolidation of nations is supposed to involve the *incorporation* of people into the national project, Williams's poem shows the incorporation of Elsie as a destructive act of mastication and digestion. America produces Elsie, but it also chews her up and spits her out. The poem therefore asks how the migrant actually participates in the American nation, above and beyond any one ideology of national inclusion. That is, it is one thing to make ideological assertions about what America is, to state that "America" is "multicultural," or a "melting pot," or even "fundamentally Anglo-Saxon Judeo-Christian." It is quite another thing to recognize that for the better part of the past century, all American nations have sought to incorporate various social sectors into the state. American nation-states have sought to "represent" previously unrecognized popular constituencies (symbolized by Elsie in this case) by creating jobs, legitimizing labor, liberalizing opportunities for economic growth, encouraging populations to relocate into urban and (increasingly) suburban housing, or broadening definitions of citizenship. And it is yet another thing to recognize that even though all of these measures have been enacted (at least in part) in the political and economic arena in order to ease social tensions, they have not eliminated exploitation, or even mitigated it necessarily, and have thus not broken the cycle of social exclusion.

Williams's poem opens itself precisely to these sorts of political and ethical dilemmas. Similar to other poems in *Spring and All*, "To Elsie" presents a voice that identifies strongly with the United States, one that also attempts to *give voice* to the U.S.-American subject. The problem, however, is that the poem *does not give voice* to Elsie herself. Elsie never speaks for herself, and the poem operates by marking an absolute difference between the subject who speaks and the subject of the poem who does not speak but who is treated objectively. This problem necessarily carries over into literary-historical judgments we make about the poem. If "To Elsie" typifies all U.S.-American modernist poetry (and in many respects it does), then we would be compelled to admit that modernist literature works to deny and exclude the voice of those marked as different, as "Other." Just as Williams separates himself from Elsie, so too would modernist poetry separate itself from popular cultures in general, even though the poem grants itself privileged knowledge of what is (or is not) American. Given such a climate, to what extent can Williams's modernist poem—or indeed *any* modern poem—be utilized to critique the particularly cruel political, socioeconomic, and cultural dialectics of the Americas?

The Place of the Modernism: Williams and Subjectivity

The question is particularly relevant to Williams's poetry in several respects: on one hand, Williams spent the better part of his life attempting to capture and represent the U.S.-American voice as a concrete, objective fact; on the other, Williams has been subject to debates about what an American voice and an American literature actually are. This latter point has everything to do with the institutional context in which Williams's work has been received. Whatever we may think of multiculturalism in its various revolutionary or reactionary forms, we cannot deny its palpable impact on literary and cultural studies. Prior to the "canon debates" of the 1980s and 1990s, U.S.-American literature was generally understood by academics and educators to be constituted by Anglo-Saxon Protestant English-speakers—the infamous "dead white men." After these debates, there has been much greater awareness of the presence of multiple subcultures, ethnicities, genders, sexualities, languages, and dialects within the umbrella of the national tradition. The question necessarily arises as to whether the Americanism advocated by Williams's modernist poetry has any relevance to the types of multicultural Americanism now favored in the academic world and beyond.

Significantly, much of the work toward multicultural inclusion has occurred by *recovering the voice* of the socially excluded (subalterns) in order to restitute due value and power to them. As José David Saldívar comments quite cogently in *The Dialectics of Our America*:

> Other Americanists, among them Paul Lauter, Juan Bruce-Novoa, Jane Tompkins, and Houston A. Baker, Jr., have centered their "dialectics of validation" on aspects of American literature such as race, class, gender, and difference that had received little attention; such scholars have given a new impulse to the study of subjects ranging from the reevaluation of what constitutes a "classical" American text to the role of a distinctly slave "vernacular" in American discourse in general and in African American literature in particular. The theoretical boundaries within which American literary history and interpretation have unfolded have been redefined in the theoretical works of Fredric Jameson, Frank Lentricchia, Hayden White, and Edward Said. Each has questioned the premises on which the concepts of American hermeneutics, alterity, history and historiography rest.[3]

Writing during the "canon" debates of the early 1990s Saldívar is at the forefront of multicultural efforts, in that he attempts to supplant a univocal (or "classical") notion of American culture and history with a more pluralistic "vernacular" voice as embodied in several literary traditions that at the time were referred to as "minority" (primarily Latino/a and African-American). He thus intends a direct challenge to any cultural institution (in this case the parochial English department) that claims authority to decide what is properly "American" or not. Given the time and place of Saldívar's critique he cannot be faulted for doing so. He is merely attempting to open American studies to what it should be—a study of the many cultures that exist in the hemisphere, and not just a single culture that has been held to be the only valid one. But his challenge also consists of a specific theoretical move in calling for a *Hemispheric* American studies that he begins to elaborate based on the writings of two Cubans, José Martí and Roberto Fernández Retamar. He moves to read Anglo America from the vantage of Latin America and therefore from the vantage of U.S.-Latinos/Chicanos. This is also not a bad move on Saldívar's part, and one that has been called for in one way or another by numerous scholars such as Earl Fitz, Richard Morse, Djelal Kadir, and indeed this present book.

However, the ultimate effectiveness of Saldívar's anti-hegemonic, hemispheric gesture *is* open to question, for he is attempting to recover the voice of the subaltern subject by identifying Martí and Fernández Retamar with the same kind of subalterity as that subject. Such a move does not take into consideration the considerable amount of institutional authority already invested in either Cuban, albeit authority not granted to them by English departments in the United States. The "counter-hegemonic" force of Martí and Fernández Retamar will always be muted by the fact that both are *central* to Latin American studies (largely in Spanish departments), and both are in some sense cultural hegemons. Martí's "Nuestra América" is a direct injunction against *imperial* hegemony specifically—against the hegemony of the Spanish Empire over its colony, Cuba, and even more against U.S.-American hegemony over Latin America as a whole. Yet Martí's response is to call for another kind of hegemony, *national* hegemony, one that we would now find to be more in line with the Gramscian notion of the term: a new national consciousness in Cuba and Latin America enforced over mass populations, led by an enlightened, educated elite (the "Natural Man").[4] Alternately, Fernández Retamar's *Calibán* and *Para una teoría literaria hispanoamericana* call for a new, autonomous Latin American critical theory in distinction to Anglo-American and European models.[5] Yet his theories must always be taken in light of Fernández Retamar's official role in the Castro regime—as head of the cultural organ of the Communist government, la Casa de las Américas. Again, Fernández Retamar may resist the imperial pressures of First World nations, but he also attempts in his early works to consolidate Latin American peoples under the banner of a specific political regimen. Martí and Fernández Retamar, that is, do not give the same voice that Saldívar seeks to recover.

In Saldívar's case and others, the voice of the subaltern migrant may be silenced in the act of recovery—silenced not only by political and economic oppression, but also by institutional pressures on the very cultural scholars who feel most responsible for giving voice to the subaltern. It is not at all clear that the canon debates actually succeeded in "voice-recovery," or whether, as John Guillory would have it, they merely resulted in the creation of new lists of books on new syllabi for literature courses.[6] In any case, we must admit that recovering the voice of the migrant subject in critical theory does not translate directly into political-economic action per se, and that representation within academic disciplines does not directly translate into social representation in the political, economic, or even cultural arenas. Disciplinary representation is not in itself empowerment, as Gayatri Spivak has done well to demonstrate.[7] But this brings us to a set of interrelated problems that I have not yet addressed, which go to the cultural critic's uneasiness with institutional power: How does one work around the institutional authority invested in particular texts and literary movements, otherwise known as the "canon"? And furthermore, how does one work around the kinds of "world system" dynamics that have always fed into the problem of institutional cultural authority in the Americas?

Martí and Fernández Retamar attempt to provide the means to think *as Americans* rather than as Europeans. Carried into the realm of literary textuality, they reject the canonical authority of Dante, Shakespeare, Cervantes, and Camões over American traditions. Yet we should not confuse such anti-canonical gestures as being against the idea of reading any particular canon or canonical author. Rather, Fernández Retamar in particular rejects *the authority* invested in works deemed to be canonical, but not the works themselves. Nevertheless, this seems to create the impression that nothing radically American emerges from *any* canonical author, even the most radically Americanist one. In the case of the present chapter, for instance, we will begin to mine the radicalism of Williams Carlos Williams—in part by reading Williams through another canonical American author, Oswald de Andrade. Yet the success and failure of this chapter depends upon the reader's willingness to accept that any sort of radicalism can emerge from a canonical author, and thus necessitates that I justify the very project of reading modernist poetry before proceeding further. The alternative is no better, though: to choose a noncanonical author without similar justification is merely to invest that author with the same institutional authority one wishes to reject in the rejection of canonicity. Moreover, the migration of ideas from Europe (and Asia and Africa and everywhere else) to the Americas *is constitutive* of American thought. But this is *not* to say that American thought is necessarily Eurocentric as such. That is, it is not merely the case that European culture has migrated to the Americas, but that in doing so American culture has been *subordinated* to the former colonial powers—something that has been as true in Anglo America as it has been in Latin America. Consequently, perceptions of American inferiority, and efforts to overcome that inferiority, *have become central to what it means to be American.* As an American one cannot therefore merely reject Europe and ignore it, since contentious dialogue with Europe is in part what makes one American in the first place. And here I am not fixing Europe (or the Americas) as "original," but rather attempting to focus on dialogic movement as necessary for "America." The colonial mindset is rather perniciously persistent. Indeed, as Fernández Retamar himself wrote in *Calibán* in speaking of Borges, "Aside from a few professors of philology who receive a salary for it, there is only one type of person who really knows in its entirety the literature of Europe: the colonial. Only in cases of dementia could an educated Argentine writer boast of having read nothing more than Argentine authors—or Spanish-language writers. And Borges is not demented."[8] And here Fernández Retamar is surely referring to himself as well.

With Williams's *Spring and All*, we are beginning a series of readings of four highly canonical literary texts by four highly canonical authors. These four texts, furthermore, are exemplary of modern poetry—a period that has been branded, for better or worse, as elitist, antipopular, and Eurocentric. Indeed, if my own anecdotal evidence is worth anything, Williams's poem "The Red Wheelbarrow" (also from *Spring and All*) was the first modern poem I ever read—taught to me as such in my high school English class. "So much depends / upon // a red wheel / barrow // glazed with rain / water // beside the white / chickens" (CP 224). "The Red Wheelbarrow" was given to me to typify what a "modern" and "American" poem was supposed to be, and furthermore I was instructed to follow an American New Critical practice of close reading in order to understand what the poem meant. In this sense, the poem was to exemplify the creation of a distinctly American literature that was only understandable by means of a distinctly American mode of reading. Nonetheless, this type of "American" was merely an extension of a specific type of "modernity" that all concerned tacitly understood to be a European tradition. The modernist poem was selected to exemplify a canon of American literature in which all of "Western" civilization had culminated. I suspect that such an experience of Williams and his poem is entirely common for many who were educated in the United States.

In an effort to counteract the supposed Eurocentrism inherent to modernist literature, concerted efforts have been taken in the past several decades to "give voice" to alternatives—both by recovering literatures previously excluded from consideration and by revising the history of works already included in the canon. This has directly impacted Williams scholarship as critics have read Williams's work in light of his ethnic background, since he was indeed of mixed European and Caribbean background. Williams's mother, Elena Hoheb, was born and raised in Mayagüez, Puerto Rico; his British-born father, William George Williams, migrated to the British West Indies at the age of five. As an adult William George Williams became an "island-hopping" traveling salesman who landed in Puerto Rico in the 1890s, where he met Elena by way of her brother, Carlos Hoheb.[9] After their marriage, William George Williams secured employment in Rutherford,

New Jersey, commuting to Manhattan and traveling extensively on business to the Caribbean and South America.

Given his family heritage, then, William Carlos Williams would seem to make a perfect candidate for historical revision, since his figure provides us a canonical U.S. poet who was the direct result of Latin American migration. From there we would merely need to show how Williams's work cannot help but be read in light of his interstitial position between Americas, and thus we could begin to deconstruct the "United States" as always already "inter-American."

Indeed, much of this work has already been done. At least one full-length book, several scholarly articles, and a handful of doctoral dissertations have been dedicated to tracing the "Spanish" roots of the good Doctor Williams. Julio Marzán's *The Spanish-American Roots of Williams Carlos Williams* is a case in point. Marzán spends hundreds of pages copiously recovering allusions to Hispanic culture and Spanish language scattered across Williams's *obra*, in order to establish a one-to-one correspondence with the author's life. Williams's works therefore may become a product of his biographical stature as an "alternative" American. A key example comes when Marzán attempts to prove that Williams derived "The Red Wheelbarrow" from a lesser-known poem, "Brilliant Sad Sun," in which Elena Hoheb Williams pours water for white chickens. Despite the fact that this connection has not been established elsewhere,[10] Marzán proceeds to make the stunning claim:

> Eliminate the previously discussed leap of the imagination that produced the "red wheel / barrow" image and the poem suddenly loses a power it had gained as paradigm, as well as its signature of Williams' style, the balance of the autobiographical and the aesthetically universal: the "red wheel / barrow" was a tribute to his bloodline twice, first in cryptically evoking Elena on whom so much of his life depended, and ultimately in celebrating his artistic lineage. For the performance of imaginary translation that produced the image was also an application of *conceptismo*, specifically of the lessons that came to him through a major tributary, from whom he discovered early on how wild comparisons in the imagination can bring tremendous inventiveness to the poem on the page. That mentor was Luis de Góngora, cubism's prime literary predecessor and one of several Spanish writers through whom Williams claimed Elena's literary bloodline.[11]

There are a number of questionable claims here. Whatever Góngora's influence may have been on subsequent generations,[12] we cannot deduce that Williams clearly and intentionally inserted himself into a

Spanish literary tradition in order to recover his *Puerto Rican* roots—as if we could conflate Puerto Rican culture with the Spanish literature (*gongorismo*) produced at the time that Spain was effectively committing genocide on its new colony. Such overinterpretations tend to sidestep one of the most basic matters of literary critique: the intentional fallacy. The revisionists assume direct correspondence between Williams's subject-positions (as if these could be located in the first place) and his literary production, in order to recount some essential *latinidad* manifest in Williams and his work.

For his part Williams made no secret of his heritage, as evidenced in his anecdotal essay, "A Memory of Tropical Fruit," in which he remembers his childhood visits to Mayagüez. Williams spends a considerable amount of time in the piece recalling different fruits from the island (mangoes, guavas, guamas, caimito, níspero, corazón, quenepa) as if the very thought of Puerto Rico was reducible to vegetation. Yet he leaves no trace of exoticism in these descriptions, but merely describes them as object-images of his memory. In this context comes the following event, written in free and indirect discourse:

> We never went bathing in the sea. What! take off our clothes where men could see us! No. Once I remember I went with my mother, perhaps at five o'clock in the morning, before anybody was up, to bathe. Then we came back before anybody could see us. When the Americans went there and went bathing in their suits with the men, the people were scandalized but now that there has been time for the children to grow up and get used to it—they are Americans, too. (I 325–326)

Williams records the childhood shame of his own body, transferred through his mother's shame of her body ("What! take our clothes off where men could see us!") And yet, in the description of shame, Williams exhibits no inhibition whatsoever; he merely accounts for what happened. Williams's narration, in other words, is as *objective* as possible even though the narration concerns subjective experience. And this ambivalence between objectivity and subjectivity carries over into the broader cultural politics at play here. "They are Americans, too." Does Williams lament that Puerto Ricans have become *U.S.*-Americans, have become identical to their colonial "protectors," in which case we take the phrase as a cold irony expressing a subjective emotion? Or does Williams merely relate something he accepts as objective fact? "They are Americans, too." If this is the case, is an author who would state that Puerto Ricans "are [U.S.]-Americans, too" someone that historical revisionists would wish to recover into a Puerto Rican tradition in the first place? If I am not mistaken Williams has just *colonized* Puerto Rico, not valorized it.

This is not to say that Williams was antithetical or hostile to his heritage, just as it does not imply that Williams viewed himself as culturally "Latino" in any way. Rather, I merely suggest that relations between subjects and objects (subjectivity and objectivity) in Williams's work are too complex and subtle to be reduced to one-to-one correspondences. Moreover, the views expressed by Williams regarding these matters are too complex to be reduced to a monolithic sense of modernist poetry as being antithetical to the multicultural perspectives that necessitated historical revision in the first place. Indeed, historical evidence clearly demonstrates that U.S. modernism was far more fractured than unified.

In a 1962 article, for instance, Robert Lowell comments on the fissures of modernism just as the modernist era was drawing to its close, writing of William Carlos Williams with a mixture of awe and exasperation:

> Williams enters me, but I cannot enter him. Of course, one cannot catch any good writer's voice or breathe his air. But there's something more. It's as if no poet except Williams had really seen America or heard its language. Or rather, he sees and hears what we all see and hear and what is the most obvious, but no one else has found this a help or an inspiration.... When I say I cannot enter him, I am almost saying that I cannot enter America. This troubles me. I am not satisfied to let it be. Like others, I have picked up things here and there from Williams, but this only makes me marvel all the more at his unique and searing journey. It is a Dantesque journey, for he loves America excessively, as if it were *the* truth and *the* subject; his exasperation is also excessive, as if there were no other hell. His flowers rustle by the superhighways and pick up all our voices.[13]

Lowell's admission that he "cannot enter" Williams or America (a curiously homoerotic, impotent, and homophobic statement all at the same time) is rather stunning, in that Lowell is widely considered among the finest U.S.-American poets of his generation—a poet whose canonicity in the U.S.-American tradition is beyond repute. Lowell's credentials bear this out: educated at Harvard and Kenyon Colleges, student of John Crowe Ransom and Allen Tate, scion of one of the most wealthy and influential of New England families, blood relative to *great* figures in the U.S. literary tradition including James Russell Lowell and Amy Lowell. Aesthetically speaking, one can only characterize Lowell's poetry—especially his early, highly formalistic and "well-wrought" work—as the direct inheritor of Emerson, Longfellow, and Eliot.

At the point he wrote the aforementioned passage, Lowell was departing from the "traditional" poetics favored by the American New Critics (led, coincidentally or not, by Ransom and Tate) in order to lead the so-called Confessional Poets, and then later, to produce highly political poetry centered in protest against the Vietnam War. Nevertheless, even today we cannot avoid thinking of Lowell as a traditionalist. Perhaps we have forgotten such things, but in the 1962 context Lowell is in fact commenting on a somewhat violent division that had developed in U.S.-American poetry between disciples of T. S. Eliot on the one hand and disciples of Williams Carlos Williams on the other. Lowell draws the fault-lines thus:

> A seemingly unending war has been going on for as long as I can remember between Williams and his disciples and the principals and disciples of another school of modern poetry. The Beats are on one side, the university poets are on the other. Lately the gunfire has been hot. With such unlikely Williams recruits as Karl Shapiro blasting away, it has become unpleasant to stand in the middle in a position of impartiality.[14]

As much as he might wish to assume a "position of impartiality," however, Lowell is as much a partisan in the struggle as anyone. By "university poets," Lowell is unquestionably talking about himself. Fresh off the reception of "The Quaker Graveyard in Nantucket" and *Life Studies*, Lowell came to be fashioned (if not by himself, then by his admirers) as a kind of second-coming of Eliot. What Lowell in fact describes, therefore, is not just a battle over what "modern poetry" is and should be, but what the *American* tradition in particular should be—whether continuities with earlier traditions were to be recognized (Eliot), or whether something entirely new had to wipe the slate clean in order to poeticize "from the local ground." But by the early 1960s Eliot had long since renounced America, and had become a devoutly Anglican British subject—a subject who was *more* British than many Britons. Aligned against Eliot and his strident Britannic traditionalism stood Shapiro and the Beats, firing away at their supposed enemies like psychopaths. Lowell is careful to distinguish Williams from his "disciples," and in fact Lowell writes his essay in order to laud Williams—not to demean him. But the damage has been done. By expressing his perplexity at Williams and his voice, Lowell is in fact expressing his inability to grasp his own nation: America is there to be seen and heard, but Lowell has not "found this a help or an inspiration."

Perhaps this is the case because Williams directed much of his efforts over his lifetime toward the dismantlement of the entire tradition of English versification, in order to replace it with acute attention to aural and visual cadence. By doing so Williams intended to create an *American* literature—one designed with the immediate intention of countering the influence of T. S. Eliot on other U.S.-American writers. Indeed, while we may strain to decipher references to Latin American or Caribbean identity in Williams's work, his efforts to create U.S. art, and to capture a U.S.-American voice, are unavoidable in their prevalence over his entire career as a writer. In "The Poem as a Field of Action," for instance, Williams deliberately links versification (what he terms "measure") to the national culture from which it emerges:

> What, by this approach I am trying to sketch, what we are trying to do is not only to disengage the elements of a measure but to seek (what we believe is there) a new measure or a new way of measuring that will be commensurate with the social, economic world in which we are living as contrasted with the past. It is in many ways a different world from the past calling for a different measure. (SE 283)

Several pages later Williams shows this new measure to be an engagement with the "American" voice, and disengagement with England:

> Now we come to the question of the origin of our discoveries. Where else can what we are seeking arise from but speech? From speech, from American speech as distinct from English speech, or presumably so, if what I say above is correct. In any case (since we have no body of poems comparable to the English) from what we *hear* in America. Not, that is, from a study of the classics, not even the American "Classics"— the *dead* classics which—may I remind you, we have *never heard* as living speech. No one has or can *hear* them as they were written any more than we can *hear* Greek today. (SE 289–290)

He then caps his comments off with a direct jab at both the British and, that most treacherous of Anglo-American traitors, T. S. Eliot: "To the English, English is England: 'History is England,' yodels Mr. Eliot. To us this is not so, not so *if* we prove it by writing a poem built to refute it—otherwise he wins!! But that leads to mere controversy. For us rehash of rehash of hash of rehash is *not* the business" (SE 291).

America is the ultimate object for Williams, yet there is no substantial body of American poems nor a way to write "American." Above and beyond lacking a way to write literature, America even lacks a fully formed way of *reading* literature. In another essay, "A Point for American Criticism," Williams contrasts English and American modes of reading:

> And this is the opportunity of America! to see large, larger than England can.
> An appearance of synchrony between American and English literature has made it seem, especially at certain times, as if English criticism could overlay the American strain as it does the English. This cannot be so. The differences are epochal...
> ...We Americans ourselves must still rely on English models. But we must not be misled. We have to realize that an English dictum on any work is, for us, only an approximation. It exists only as an analogous appraisal, as far as we are concerned, to fill *a lack on our part of actual value*. (SE 86–87; emphasis added)

Williams then moves to reject Rebecca West's distinctly English misinterpretation of James Joyce by stating, "What is now left over— Joyce's true significance—his pure literary virtue—is for [West] 'nonsense.' Of literature and its modus showing that she knows nothing. America, offering an *undeveloped* but wider criticism, will take this opportunity to place an appreciation of Joyce on its proper basis" (SE 90; emphasis added). With nothing but nothing and underdevelopment from which to read and write "American" poetry, the only option in Williams's estimation is to listen to American *speech* as an *origin* (a *new* origin?) of history, tradition, and art, much as Joyce had done with Dubliner brogue.

In short, we cannot simply recover *latinidad* within Williams's poetic voice based solely on accidents of Williams's biography, the fact that he happened to be born into a certain heritage. One need not discount biography in literary production, but one does need to be careful in its application to interpretation. We *can* say definitively, however, that Williams strove to treat *subjective* annunciations of the American *objectively*—and from this emerges Williams's sense of his own Objectivism. That is to say, Williams does not seem particularly keen on representing his life-story, narrativizing himself, through his poetic or critical output. Nor does Williams seek to eliminate subjectivity from consideration in poetry and literature—a claim often made against modernism, and objectivist poetry in particular, as if it were bent on some fascistic dehumanization of the subject. To the contrary,

Williams is concerned with how the American voice and American poetry are to emerge given the objective historical parameters in which either occurs—the migration of subjects from one cultural and geographical context to another, from "centers" to "peripheries," which has produced an unbalanced distribution of "development" and "underdevelopment." And we cannot understand these latter concepts—which are political-economic before they are literary—without turning to Latin America.

The Economics of Modernism: Williams, Anthropophagy, and Dependency

In my critique of Julio Marzán, I am not totally discounting Góngora's influence on Williams. In fact it is quite likely that he was influential, given that Spanish *Siglo de Oro* writers (Góngora, Lope de Vega) in general had a rather forceful impact on U.S.-American modernists (Ezra Pound in particular).[15] I am merely stating that the influence of Góngora cannot be proven to be an index of Latin American identity within Williams's work, and that to assume such an index as valid only misdirects the reading of Williams and modernist poetry. The attempt to recover a Latin American voice in such a way, moreover, is doubly unfortunate given that there are such strong and illuminating connections between Williams's Americanism and other forms of (Latin) Americanism, above and beyond the recovery of Latino voice. Indeed, Richard Morse appears to have realized this twenty years ago in rationalizing his comparison of two pairs of U.S. and Brazilian modernist poets (Williams and Oswald de Andrade; T. S. Eliot and Mário de Andrade):

> I committed the heresy of allowing the periphery to interrogate the center and of musing whether the Brazilian mind might help unmask constraints of the "metropolitan" mind. This has forced me to be even-handed in dealing with each of my pairs. I have dismissed the question of influence, which tilts the scale, and examined four persons who simply had different placements in the Western world. This strategy takes us beyond Europe-America or north-south dichotomies and invites shifting triangulations among Europe and the two Americas.[16]

By overlooking influence, Morse does not at all deny history (in favor of, say, a synchronic formalist reading). Rather, he correctly realizes that the *place* of writing and reading in Americas has a necessary relation to the *time* of either activity. Simply put, one may perhaps read Góngora as representative of a suppressed subculture in the United

States, but this is hardly possible when reading a central Peninsular Spanish author in Latin America.

Morse is far more concerned with the ideology of American language and discourse with respect to its location vis-à-vis Europe. Both Oswald and Williams incorporate avant-garde techniques from the other continent: photographic "snapshot," ready-mades, typographic manipulation, cubism, Dada. Yet neither had any interest in the mere replication of Eurocentric discourse as a sign of civility and culture: "They began with the medium itself, language. It was not enough to discard hand-me-down rhetoric and fixed form. That left one still in Europe. One must discover American languages if one is to convey experience directly. Linguistically, modernism began at home."[17] We have already seen how Williams attempted such "discovery," by discarding English versification in favor of a "vernacular" rhythm. In Oswald's case the connection between the emergence of a Brazilian modernism and international order is even more direct and dynamic than in Williams's case, perhaps because Oswald elaborated his aesthetic more explicitly than did his U.S.-American contemporary. Starting with the 1924 "Manifesto Pau-Brasil" ["Brazilwood Manifesto"], Oswald called for a "neological" Brazilian language capable of producing poetry ready-made for export back to Europe, taking his cue from the export product for which the nation was named—brazilwood. In doing so, Oswald attempted to reverse the circuit of intellectual communication and power across the Atlantic: rather than importing ideas from the east, Brazilians would at last forge a more "advanced" culture than their colonizers. This postcolonial gesture was to become yet more acute in the "Manifesto Antropófago" ["Cannibalist Manifesto"] of 1928.[18] In this second, much-discussed and highly influential manifesto, Oswald moves to define *brasilidade* through the figure of the Tupi-Guarani cannibal. Rather than the "noble savage" suitable for European conquest, the "bad savage" anthropophage assumes a position of superiority over the European invader—simultaneously resisting and incorporating the European through a singular act of intersubjective violence: the consumption of another human body. The result is intended to be an alternate narrative of Brazilian nationhood as an "Other": "Brazil" will henceforth be "Pindorama," as Oswald states, using the Tupi-Guarani place-name for his native land.

Of course, as has long been noted, with Cannibalism Oswald in fact calls for a *repetition* of the Eurocentric concept of nation and national identity, albeit from an alternate position—a crucial difference.[19] As Luiz Madureira states in his recent study of Brazilian and

Francophone-Caribbean modernisms: "Indebted to and embedded as it is in the very cultural and philosophical tradition it seeks to displace, *antropofagia* cannot but tacitly (and tactically) acknowledge the extent of its determination by the 'magisterial texts' of the west."[20] In other words, far from obliterating Europe, Oswald attempts to "overwrite" the discourse of Eurocentrism/logocentrism by "rewriting" this discourse from the perspective of the Other. Madureira succinctly captures this peculiar postcolonial logic by referencing the "Manifesto Antropófago" through Homi Bhabha:

> Hence, the Manifesto's shibboleth regarding the inscription of the American indigene in Europe's discourses of republicanism ("Without us Europe would not even have its poor declaration of the rights of man")—as much as it subscribes to the Hegelian logic of *antropofagia*'s effort to reverse Hegel's "course of history"—can also be read in a performative sense, as a "repetition of the sign of modernity [that] is different, specific to its historical and cultural conditions of enunciation."[21]

Here we must specify, then, that Oswald does not necessarily attempt to "recover the voice" of the Tupi-Guarani native as a historical presence, but rather attempts to reinscribe the *absent trace* of the Tupi-Guarani as a disruptive force in the history of European logocentrism. As Haroldo de Campos would famously write of the manifesto: "This last view does not involve a submission (conversion) but, rather, a transculturation, or, even better, 'transvalorization': a critical view of history as a negative function (in Nietzsche's sense), capable of appropriation and of expropriation, of de-hierachization, of deconstruction."[22] The Brazilian, and more generally the American, is the always-already deconstructed obverse of the Western Subject.

Oswald's deconstruction (*avant la lettre*) of Eurocentrism at the level of philosophical and literary discourse also signals a decided shift in political and economic relations between Europe and the Americas, one that ultimately will allow us to unpack the contradictions we have already seen in the Americanism of *Spring and All*. To reiterate, Oswald's Pau-Brasil and Antropófago manifestoes attempt to place Brazilian language and letters in a superior position to France, Portugal, and the whole of Europe—*precisely because Brazil has always been placed in subordinate position to these in the world order*. The place of Brazilian critical theory and literature are therefore tied directly to Brazil's economic and international relations. But what would Brazil's or Latin America's subordinate position in the world economy have to do with U.S.-American literary production, given that the United

States supposedly occupies a place in the "First World" of developed (rich) countries? How exactly are we to link U.S. and Brazilian modernisms through the matter of political-economic positionality, when in fact the United States and Brazil have for so long occupied *different* positions in the political, economic, and even philosophical worlds?

Returning to the comparative reading in his *New World Soundings*, Morse ends his comparison of Oswald and Williams by differentiating them *economically*. In order to show that "Oswald was necessarily more radical than Williams,"[23] Morse compares Williams's "The Red Wheelbarrow" to Oswald's roughly contemporaneous poem, "a roça" ["the farm"], from the volume *Poesia Pau-Brasil*. I will reproduce the poems side-by-side for sake of convenience:

The Red Wheelbarrow	a roça	[the farm
so much depends upon	Os cem negros da fazenda comiam feijão e angu Abóbora chicória e cambuquira	The hundred blacks of the fazenda at beans and cassava gruel Squash chicory and pumpkin-vine stew
a red wheel barrow	Pegavam uma roda de carro Nos braços	They could hoist the wheel of an oxcart In their arms]
glazed with rain water		
beside the white chickens		

Morse begins by noting that each poem emits a photographic image of a farm, although, as we shall see later, this is not a totally accurate comparison. In any case, Morse does correctly characterize Williams's poem as an exercise in economy:

> Visually the stanzas present four identical little barrows composed of words in three-plus-one blocks. They suggest that with the trick of leverage solved, nature becomes infinitely organizable, and the farm infinitely replicable: mass production. The extra short syllables in line one of the first and last stanzas invite us to duck and pick up the barrow to see how light it is, then to set it down. ("Eye it, try it, buy it," said the old Chevrolet commercial.) A child could do it; yet we see no human in the picture. The mechanism "runs itself." At the outset we learn that "so much," perhaps "all," depends on the barrow. Hugh Kenner reminds us of the ambiguity of the word *depend*. It means "hang from," implying vital "dependence" or suspension *from*; yet

idiomatically the verb takes the preposition "upon," implying a load piled *on* the barrow to relieve the owner's shoulders.... Such is the spare and functional vision of the physician, or the Puritan.[24]

In contrast, Oswald's poem does not allow the reader/spectator to think of agrarian production as a self-propelled, self-contained machine. Rather, "a roça" puts human exploitation front-and-center:

> Oswald places a hundred humans at the center of his picture. The "machine," which does not function, comes later. Slaves, or human energies, are the motor power for production and society. Unlike the wheelbarrow, which needs neither food nor fossil fuel—and precious little human exertion—the blacks require constant stoking, although not with meat or white chickens. Luxuriant nature invades the *fazenda* from all sides to offer a host of European, African, and local crops, some wild and some cultivated, some pulled from the vine and some described as already cooked. Enterprise and wild vegetation interpenetrate. Yet the poet never mentions the commercial crop, presumably sugar, but only the foods needed to sustain human labor....
> Here nature is not "managed." Rain, instead of glazing a barrow, creates huge potholes in the road. Therefore the wheel cannot take precedence as a secret of power but comes last as an encumbrance. Sheer human muscle must rescue it.[25]

In this rather brilliant reading, Morse effectively cites the crucial point of difference between the two poets, and thus between the two Americas, as one of economic context. It is as if the U.S.-American poet is given the luxury to posit mechanical production as fully functional regardless of the human, cultural, or historical context in which it operates. By contrast, given that the sugar plantations of Northeast Brazil founded in the sixteenth century were among the first industrialized zones in the world, the Brazilian poet is never allowed to forget the *human* context: the historical roots of industrial production that return to the exploitation and enslavement of the African "Other." Consequently, it is precisely the moment of mechanical *breakdown*, mal-function rather than function, that so concerns the Brazilian modernist.

In fact, the economic context of "The Red Wheelbarrow" is quite a bit different from what Morse suggests, which will give us cause to reevaluate his take on the poem. Nevertheless, Morse is fundamentally correct to relate the subordination of discourse and knowledge to the social division of labor. For Morse is not so much focused merely on a literary comparison between Oswald and Williams as much as he wishes to interrogate more broadly the ideological formations of American language and disciplines of Americanist study. Morse begins his book by outlining the dilemma of American languages in general as *contextual and historical* in nature: "[T]he issue center[s] not on the resources of the mother tongue but on the colonial situation and on sea changes to which that tongue has been subjected."[26] Beyond the inherent structure of American languages, one must pay attention to the historical situations in which they are used—a distinction that seems similar to synchronic vs. diachronic (Saussure), constative vs. performative (Austin), or form vs. utterance (Bakhtin). Morse effectively frames the problem in terms of historical origin: "While the colonization of the Americas effected *transplantation* of European cultures and institutions, it also entailed *re-creation* of conditions reminiscent of the formative period of European history."[27] He then proceeds to frame linguistic transplantation as a reiteration of the Roman *koine*—those speech communities on the peripheries of the Roman Empire with a "common" dialect. Since *koine* were formed by the migration and miscegenation of peoples from different areas of the empire (soldiers, administrators, slaves, workers, etc.), these peoples came to form "homogenous" and "vulgar" speech patterns that tended to erase regional dialects. Eventually these would lead to the distinct Vulgar Latin languages that have evolved into the Romance languages. For Morse, this history is less interesting, however, than the fact that the conquest of the Americas set the stage for the creation of new *koine* communities in Spanish, Portuguese, English, and French colonies, such that relatively "homogenous" dialects of these languages would come to be spoken across wide geographic areas.[28] Most importantly, the formation of these American *koine* was both cause and effect of the peripheralization of the American colonial cultures with respect to the European colonizers: formed on the edges of empires far from the center, *koine* dialects further served to mark colonial communities as un-central and peripheral.

This then sets the stage for a dialectical movement between Europe and the formation of American nations as "solid" or "categorical" realities—a dialectic that is perhaps hardly noticed in Europe (center) but that is omnipresent in the Americas. As a Brazilianist, for instance, Morse comes to interrogate the incomplete or "disordered" formation of the Brazilian nation—the fact that the ideology of "Brazilian nationhood" has served the hegemonic interests of a reduced sector of elites, but has never quite managed to incorporate the entire "people" broadly defined. In essence, it is precisely Brazil's location as a transplanted *koine* that has left the nation in a state of dialectical suspension:

> But what happens if we think of a national society not as a participatory system or as a finely tooled mechanism of domination and control? Suppose we suspend systemic terminology and adopt the qualitative (though not normative) notion of a spectrum ranged from order to disorder? This still leaves "Brazil" in place. But the Brazilian nation becomes a creature of higher and lower degrees not of reality but of realization. It ceases being the systemic unit of the international chess game. Such a view brackets the tortured "marginality" controversy, which in assuming a "system" focuses on whether people are in or out of it. The nonsystemic view assumes, with vague and erratic boundaries, a permanent condition of "disorder" for half or more of the population, but not necessarily a condition of marginality or even oppression. For it is precisely to the realm of "disorder" that one must look for ideological messages.[29]

Morse thus strives to establish the contradictory boundaries of the problem. Given their historical locations as *koine*, American nations perpetually seek definition with respect to the ideological formations of nationhood that have emanated to them from Europe; this never-ending search for national order necessarily implies the persistence of national disorder that the nation perpetually strives to overcome. As a result, we can think of Morse's admittedly "vague and erratic" perspective as *processual* rather than causal: the American nation is always *becoming* itself, but never quite *is*. And as such, he leads us into yet another order of contradictions: the American *koine* may have been peripheralized since its inception, but this is not to say that the American nation is *determined* by its marginalization within a world system.

Morse's view has not been widely adopted in Latin American studies, and indeed would have been roundly attacked if had it been, for it seems to discount real conditions of marginality and oppression that do, in fact, emerge from political disorder. Morse (a traditional U.S.-American Latin Americanist) tends to portray Brazil in terms of incompleteness and instability, against a far more "complete" United States. Nonetheless, Morse operates within a global context that is not unique to him or other Latin Americanists. Works such as Walter Mignolo's *Local Histories/Global Designs* likewise frame the historical constitution of Latin America in terms of its location within the global order. Yet, following from Immanuel Wallerstein's world-systems theory, Mignolo views Latin American history as far more determined by structural constraints of the global economy than Morse would admit. Mignolo quite convincingly demonstrates how Latin America was mapped both geographically and economically after 1500 in accordance with transoceanic trade circuits centered in Europe. Thus, there is no "modernity" in Mignolo's view without "colonization,"[30] so that after the conquest of the Americas modernity is always what he terms the "modern/colonial world." The physical mapping of the modern/colonial world, however, is significant for Mignolo insofar as it led to the hierarchization of societies according to their geoeconomic positions. The economic hierarchy of the world was itself mapped onto various sorts of *cultural* interpretations that were henceforth assumed to be natural—most presciently as hierarchies of race that have resulted in rather nefarious forms of "internal colonization" within Latin American nations, the oppression of indigenous and black peoples by the white *criollo* elite. Moreover, such subordination of entire populations has also resulted in the subordination of non-Occidental forms of knowledge and discourse. Mignolo therefore works to counteract such subordination by advocating what he calls "border thinking" or "border gnosis" based largely in critical discourses from Latin America and indigenous cultures: "Border gnosis emerges as a displacement of this genealogy [of Eurocentric civilization and its academic disciplines] and as an effort toward the restitution of *location* as a geopolitical and epistemological configuration of knowledge production."[31]

With this Mignolo self-consciously positions himself against a postmodern notion of the "flattening" of local cultures into a homogenized globe. But he may also be working against *any* discourse produced by non-Latin American or nonindigenous scholars not operating in the "Third World":

> Historically, and in the frame of the modern/colonial world system, I hear today assertions equivalent to the logico metaphysical "there is no outside and inside." It so happens that such an assertion is pronounced by colleagues who are clearly placing themselves on the "inside" and, by so doing, being oblivious to the "outside." I have heard, on the other hand, colleagues (more clearly colleagues in some corner of the Third World) who do believe in the inside/outside distinctions. Now, one could explain this fact by saying that, it is unfortunate, but they are theoretically behind, underdeveloped, as they do not know yet that the last discovery in the humanities in the metropolitan research centers is that truly there is no such thing as inside and outside. It would be nice to have such an explanation, except that it counters the facts. Colleagues in the Third World asserting vehemently

the distinction between inside and outside (which is made in the form of center and periphery, or center and margin, or First and Third World) are the ones who are most theoretically sophisticated and "developed."[32]

From Mignolo's perspective, then, there is not only a forceful dichotomy between the "inside" and "outside" in world order (a dichotomy that corresponds to other concepts such as "First World" and "Third World"), but also there are clearly identifiable gradations of sophistication and development, especially as concerns critical-theoretical acuity. One can only conclude, therefore, that he would find Morse's critique (and indeed that of Oswald de Andrade) to be locked precisely in the same discursive episteme that Mignolo seeks to dismantle through "border gnosis." That is, both Morse and Oswald still operate within hierarchies of knowledge that establish Europe as "center" and Latin America as "margin," even if they attempt to reverse these polarities dialectically or replace them with some "nonsystematic" order. Mignolo appears confused: harmful inside/outside dichotomies will be eliminated once it is realized that those on the outside are more sophisticated than those insiders who deny that the inside/outside dichotomy exists, the same dichotomy that has been used fallaciously to determine grades of Eurocentric sophistication.

Yet I do not mention this to demean either Morse or Mignolo, for either one presents challenging arguments that push the envelope of Americanist thought. Rather, my purpose is to demonstrate that even Latin Americanists who decamped in opposite sides of the discipline's highly contentious debates will nonetheless concur on a central point: that the *subordinate geopolitical and geoeconomic position* of Latin America vis-à-vis Europe or the so-called First World has proved decisive in the historical processes by which the region has been constituted. Given the persistence of this historical fact, disagreements between Latin Americanists essentially boil down to theorizing to what degree world order has *determined* Latin American history or to what degree Latin America has charted its own history.

This critical focus on "positionality" emerged only relatively recently. Prior to 1960s we can generally say that Latin America's elites chartered a course toward industrialization and urbanization modeled on Europe and the United States, in the hopes that this would "naturally" lead to cultural, civilizational, and/or political "development"—in a word, *modernization*. However, in the wake of the Cuban Revolution (post-1959) Latin American social scientists and critical theorists began to seek "autonomous" (non-First World) explanations for the region's historical predicament. The rise of what came to be known as "dependency theory" as it emerged from the UN Economic Commission for Latin America (ECLA, or CEPAL as its acronym is known in Spanish or Portuguese) after 1960 served to displace earlier theories of modernization that had reached a zenith in the 1950s. Although neither Morse nor Mignolo agree with dependency theory—which by now has been generally discredited in the social sciences and beyond—it is significant that their readings are nonetheless inflected by it. Indeed Mignolo is careful to give dependency theory all due credit:

> A note on "dependency theory" and its mark in the imaginary of the modern/colonial world system is here necessary for two reasons. One, it's the fact that dependency theory was one of the responses, from Latin America, to a changing world order that in Asia and in Africa took the form of "decolonization."... Both [Aníbal] Quijano and [Enrique] Dussel are indebted to the impact of dependency theory in its critique to "development" as the new format taken by global designs once the "civilizing mission" was winding down with the increasing process of decolonization. Although dependency theory has been under attack from several fronts, it is important not to lose sight of the fact that from the perspective of Latin America, it clearly and forcefully put in the agenda the problems involved in "developing" Third World countries. The impact of dependency theory in Latin American philosophy was remarkable too.... It was a crucial moment of self-discovery, of understanding philosophy in Latin America and the Third World as part of a global system of domination.[33]

Despite its flaws, dependency theory succeeded in moving Latin American intellectual thought away from *following* the "developed" Occident, toward a posture of resistance to it. Here we must emphasize that any reading of Latin American modernists or *vanguardistas* of the early twentieth century—artists who corresponded to the rise of modernization and developmentalism—still depends on dependency: Was Oswald de Andrade, for instance, pointing to the *modernization* of Brazil as an historical end? Or was he already demonstrating the fissures in the logic of Occidental modernity several decades before the rest of the world caught up with him?

These questions are significant insofar as the distinction Morse makes between Latin America and Anglo America is one that essentially replays the distinction between modernization and dependency theories. How so? The seminal work of Latin American dependency theory is unquestionably *Dependencia y desarrollo en*

América Latina, coauthored by the Brazilian Fernando Henrique Cardoso and the Chilean Enzo Faletto. In their work, Cardoso and Faletto begin by rejecting several prevalent notions of "function" and "functionality." Functionalist modernization theory rests on a structural sociological dichotomy between "traditional" and "modern" societies, one that assumes that all human societies begin in "tradition" and over time end in "modernity"—as if there were a singular scale by which to measure the "progress" of societies. Indeed the very term "development" (and hence "underdevelopment") derives from this functional dualism between traditional and modern. We can call this "functional," moreover, since in assuming a singular scale of social history, it is also assumed that a singular set of steps might be taken in order to arrive at modernity. To wit, the implementation of certain economic policies and mechanisms (such as, in very broad terms, industrialization or the creation of an internal consumer market) should result in specific social reactions such that the national society would "evolve" in a specific way. The basic claim of Cardoso and Faletto's dependency theory, then, is that such functionalist views are far too simplistic, since they do not take a wide range of other historical and social factors into consideration. At the time Latin America began to industrialize the world market for industrialized goods had already been established, so that the region was forced to compete with industrial powers who already dominated production. Industrialization in such a climate only intensified Latin America's dependence on rich countries for capital and technology. Much more significantly, however, by the incipient phases of industrialization, Latin America already had well-defined political systems, educational systems, and a long history of peculiar class and race relations—relations that were quite a bit more complex than the socioeconomic division of "bourgeoisie" and "proletariat." The authors state:

> If we admit that those factors of differentiation and complexity are intermixed with the above mentioned multiple links with external societies and economic interests, it is not difficult to see the reasons why analyses of dependency need theoretical efforts to stress specificity.
> The social and economic transformations that alter the internal and external aspects of the underdeveloped and dependent societies are actually political processes that, in present historical conditions, do not always favor national development. Our analysis of social development always assumes the possibility of stagnation and heteronomy.... Since [social] forces are interrelated and express a market situation with various possibilities of growth, analysis is complete only

when the economic and the social have their reciprocal determinations defined at the internal and external levels.[34]

With such statements Cardoso and Faletto dispatch reductive, mechanistic "structural-functionalist" models of development, in order to promote a far more dynamic "historical-structural" approach capable of incorporating specific sociohistorical conditions into analysis. Carried into Morse's comparison of Oswald and Williams, we can clearly see that Morse sees "The Red Wheelbarrow" as structural-functionalist, in that the economy of the wheelbarrow (and the poem about the wheelbarrow) operates "functionally" with or without human interference. He therefore contrasts Oswald's "a roça" as a "historical-structural" poem that portrays not only economic production, but also a dynamic network of agro-industrial production, race relations, and indeed gender relations by which a system of severe human exploitation both operates and destroys itself. This does not mean, however, that the concepts of "structure" or "function" must be invalidated; quite to the contrary, both dependency theory and Morse's literary interpretation *require* structure and function as determinants of significance—just as long as structures and functions are *historicized with respect to the locations in which they appear or operate.*

Such historicization, finally, allows us to correct several critical and theoretical problems, especially as concerns reading modernist poetry. First, dependency theory has largely been dismissed in economics, political science, and sociology, because it proved to be far too mechanistic. That is, *dependendistas* after Cardoso and Faletto assumed *all* of Latin America's problems (and the Third World's) to be the result of structural impediments to success fostered by the First World. All problems could then be blamed on the rest of the world, not on historical conditions specific to each context. It seems to me, however—and Cardoso himself would still agree with me on this point[35]—that dependency theory proves far more valuable as a means to understand specific historical processes of social movement within Latin American nations, rather than to comprehend the entire world-system. Second, dismissing functionalism does not at all dismiss structural or formal interpretation, but rather alters the parameters of such interpretation. Translated into literary and cultural studies, formalism and structuralism have by and large fallen into disrepute as ahistorical, and therefore as blinded to social conflicts of race, gender, and sexuality. This has been particularly detrimental to the image of modernist poetry—of poetic movements defined by their emphasis on poetic form and structure. To complain, for instance, that modernist poetry "dehumanizes" social questions through formalism, and is therefore an elitist or reactionary brand of literature, misses the point entirely. One must pay attention to the historical contexts in which poetic forms appear as well as the forms themselves.

We can therefore posit Oswald's *Pau-Brasil* and *Antropófago* poetics as an historical result of a Third World condition. Oswald reacted to Brazil's dependent and subordinate position in a world political-economic order, to the extent that the nation's dependency had served to position its culture and intellectual production in a similarly subordinate position. Yet this belies the fact that Oswald may have been far superior in terms of the quality of his intellectual production than many of his European contemporaries; this is impossible to prove, of course, but we must hold it open as a possibility. Just as we must also consider that Oswald's own political and economic position—as a member of the landed oligarchy of São Paulo state—likewise placed him in a position to move freely between rich and poor Worlds, much more freely than many of his contemporaries elsewhere. In other words, Oswald can be a First World *and* Third World writer without ever having to leave São Paulo, and this double "worldliness" is the predominant mark of his *brasilidade*. There *is* a palpable difference between First and Third Worlds, but these are not necessarily continental categories. Indeed they may be local: a single city, let alone a single nation, may have its own First and Third Worlds; accordingly, a Third World writer may in fact operate in the First World, just as a First World writer may operate from a Third World embedded in the First. To be certain, Williams Carlos Williams produced *Spring and All* from what we can now consider a First World location (the United States), but more specifically he produced from the periphery (Rutherford, NJ) of the commercial center of the capitalist world (New York, NY). Thus, the mark of Williams's "American-ness," just as Oswald's *brasilidade*, may be its dependent location in-between First and Third Worlds. Even though the United States may be in the First World, this does not at all mean that it is not simultaneously in the Third World—for the literary economy of Williams's poetic formalism (the "historical structure" of his poetry) coincides with the economy of brutal poverty.

The Formal Economy of *Spring and All*

A quick glance at Webster's dictionary informs us that "economics" is the "science that deals with the production, distribution, and consumption of wealth." But any economist will also tell us that measuring the production, distribution, and consumption of wealth only matters insofar as the world is marked by a *scarcity* of resources. Indeed, the *lack* of resources becomes the very reason for *being* economical, in order to embody a secondary definition of "economy": "a) careful management of wealth, resources, etc.; avoidance of waste by careful planning and use; thrift or thrifty use; b) restrained or efficient use of one's materials, technique, etc., esp. by an artist."[36] In this sense, "The Red Wheelbarrow" *is* economy—not metaphorically or otherwise figuratively, but literally:

> so much depends
> upon
>
> a red wheel
> barrow
>
> glazed with rain
> water
>
> beside the white
> chickens (CP 224)

The full range of Williams's poetic technique is on display in this poem. It begins in abstraction with the *idea* that something depends on something else, though these "somethings" are not defined concretely. As it proceeds, the poem begins to populate its world with material objects: we have the "wheel-barrow," which predicates two dependent clauses that modify and specify it ("glazed with rain / water" and "beside the white / chickens"). We might further note how the *idea* of abstraction in the first stanza transforms into a *concrete image* of abstraction in subsequent stanzas, with stark contrasts drawn between a machine (wheelbarrow) and an organism (chicken); between the natural (water, chickens) and the artificial (wheelbarrow); between animate (chickens), inanimate (water), and simply moveable (wheelbarrow) objects; and between the colors red and white (by way of a translucent "glaze"). The poem thus plays with abstraction and figuration, as it is a kind of painterly still-life portrait of a real scene, but one that emerges by way of an abstract formal composition. But, of course, the poem itself *is* an abstraction, insofar as it *is not* a portrait, but rather a poem made of words—words that, following Saussure, we tacitly hold to be arbitrary signs referring to object-images.

By the same token, we can reverse this reading by noticing that the words are ordered spatially down the page in order to form a sequence of shapes that resemble wheelbarrows, a mimetic figuration earlier noted in the discussion of Richard Morse. Yet this is only the case if we take words to be objects in themselves—that words do not merely *refer* to other things, but *are* things themselves. The objectivity of words would thus create tension with what these words reference: words-as-objects in opposition to their semantic meanings. If we take words in the poem to be word-objects, however, we cannot fail to notice the modulations of their formal arrangement. Each stanza consists of four words, three in the first verse, one in the second; and each stanza consists of three accented beats, two stressed beats in the first verse and one in the second. Yet in terms of accentuation, the poem's arrangement creates a rather stunning sense of movement: the first stanza is entirely iambic ("sŏ múch dĕpénds / ŭpón"). The second stanza also begins with an iamb ("ă réd"), but the short-long iambic pattern stops with the unisyllabic "whéel" to form a bacchius, and then becomes reversed by the long-short trochee "bárrŏw." The "bacchic" (short-long-long) pattern of "ă réd whéel" is transposed in the next stanza into cretic (long-short-long), "glázed wĭth ráin," although both stanzas end in trochees ("bárrŏw" and "wátĕr"). The final stanza terminates the poem by combining metrical elements from the previous stanzas, beginning with the iambic "bĕsíde thĕ white" and ending with the trochaic "chíckĕns." To reiterate the scansion of the poem in more cohesive fashion:

sŏ múch dĕpénds	(4 syllables, 2 iambs, short-long-short-long)
ŭpón	(2 syllables, 1 iamb, short-long)
ă réd whéel	(3 syllables, 1 bacchius, short-long-long)
bárrŏw	(2 syllables, 1 trochee, long-short)
glázed wĭth ráin	(3 syllables, 1 cretic, long-short-long)
wátĕr	(2 syllables, 1 trochee, long-short)
bĕsíde thĕ white	(4 syllables, 2 iambs, short-long-short-long)
chíckĕns	(2 syllables, 1 trochee, long-short)

In sum, the poem *distributes* and *circulates* value (i.e., accents, stresses) *as if* in circular fashion, perhaps mimicking the way the wheel of the wheelbarrow might spin (although, of course, the wheel does not actually spin in the poem).

However, the circulation of value is not marked by wealth, but scarcity: the poem *only* consists of 16 words (22 syllables), or 15 words if you factor in that "wheelbarrow" has been split into "wheel" and "barrow." As a result, the poem becomes something that is easily expendable and consumable: it is so short (and therefore easy to type) that I can quote it in its entirety multiple times, and so short that you can read it multiple times with minimal effort. It is thus a rather *cheap* poem from the standpoint of economy. Such poverty is only redoubled by the image the poem presents: the poem populates its world with objects, but we must concede that the world it populates is exceedingly poor—*only* consisting of a wheelbarrow left out in the rain to rust next to a few chickens. Even if we wish to imagine that these things pertain to the real world, the scene is nonetheless that of a poor farm or a poor backyard, with simple, disused implements, and chickens—the most economical of foodstuffs, the cheapest meat in the meat section, "the poor man's beef," "a chicken in every pot," and so forth.

If "The Red Wheelbarrow" is an exercise in economy; in other words, its economy is that of privation. Because there are so precious few words in the poem, each word seems to hang upon the bare bones of the others. As soon as we reach "depends" the first verse ends abruptly, and we have to wait for the next word "upon," which does not complete the phrase but just hangs from "depends" like a pendant. Enjambment creates a sense of linguistic suspension, so that the semantic and phraseological incompleteness of the first stanza increases our expectations for what is to follow. Yet what follows is nothing more than a mundane object, the wheelbarrow. The entire poem hangs from, depends upon, the opening stanza "so much depends / upon." Yet conversely, the opening stanza *also* depends upon "the red wheel / barrow" and its subsequent dependent clauses "glazed with rain / water // beside the white / chickens" for any sense of completeness or closure. Such closure cannot be reached, however, because the poem only gives us chickens, a few drops of water, and a wheelbarrow, things that the poem tells us are important ("so much") but that do not tell us much at all. If you doubt that this poem is economical, then you should consider the fact that despite its scarcity of substance—or rather, *because of its scarcity of substance*—the poem has proven time and time again to generate excessive commentary. My own exegesis is a case in point, itself being quite a bit longer than 22 syllables.

Perhaps "The Red Wheelbarrow" has proven so compelling—above all among Williams scholars—because it condenses the prevailing poetic attributes of *Spring and All* as a whole: attention to formal function, positional or spatial function, and ultimately social function, all of which functionalities themselves stand in direct relation to scarcity. The poem "To Have Done Nothing" is a case in point. In "To Have Done Nothing" language appears to operate as a nullification of historicity—an operation, however, that functions in a decidedly "Baroque" arabesque that ornately weaves together historical presence and absence. The first stanza begins in a mode that is strikingly negative:

> No that is not it
> nothing that I have done
> nothing
> I have done (CP 191)

These verses create ambiguity as to the nature of dependent or independent clauses: "nothing that I have done" is clearly a dependent clause waiting for a verb; yet it is followed by "nothing / I have done" which may be a repetition (i.e., "nothing [that] I have done") or an entirely new sentence (an independent clause we could rephrase "I have done nothing"). Such ambiguity may be read back onto the first line, "No that is not it," which at once reads directly ("No, that is not it") but which also approximates a Latin or Latinate construction of negativity. This is perhaps best seen in a rough translation into Portuguese. "Não é isso" would be a succinct translation of "No that is not it," but it is also ambiguous: "Não é isso" could mean the negative "Não, não é isso" ["No, that is not it"] or it could mean the positive "Não, é isso" ["No, that *is* it"]. In other words, the appearance "No" and "not" within an unpunctuated statement creates the impression of a Latinate *modal negativity* ("Não é nada"), and simultaneously appears to be an Anglo-Saxon double-negative (that is, a positive).

In this semantic sense, the first stanza would seem to read as a corrective to the title.[37] Although the stanza insists on the negative with the selection of "No," "not," "nothing," and "nothing," the poem is *not* about "having done nothing," but states instead, "Nothing (that) I have done." This latter statement implies that the "I" *has* done something, but that this "something" is irrelevant or will not be spoken of. Furthermore, the action of doing something (even if it remains unspoken) seems to be in the past, as something that *was done*. However, the grammatical tense of the stanza is the present, or more precisely the present perfect of "nothing / I *have* done." The poem in fact makes this grammatical distinction explicit:

> nothing
> I have done
> is made up of
>
> nothing
> and the diphthong

> ae
>
> together with
> the first person
> singular
> indicative
>
> of the auxiliary
> verb
> to have (CP 191)

"Nothing I have done" does not actually *say* anything in this context, but is held in the abstract as a metalinguistic token—a sample grammatical clause that consists of the word "nothing" and the "first person singular indicative" verb-form of the infinitive "to have." With this classification, however, we begin to encounter several temporal dilemmas. Grammatical categories are used to show how the clause "is made up," which in turn may imply a present-ness (that the clause "consists of" or "is made up of" something in the present), or may imply a futurity (that the clause has been "dreamt up" or "made up" for some future). In another sense, the clause is also "made up" of a negation of history, through the (supposed) inclusion of the "diphthong / ae" that *does not* appear anywhere in the clause or elsewhere in the poem. This "ae" unmistakably alludes to a vague Latinate etymology, as in the words "aether" or "aesthetic," or even in the feminine plural suffix of "alumnae." Yet this historical allusion (or illusion) is fractured by the fact that "ae" is not a word, but merely a component (diphthong) of some unmentioned lexeme. The poem thus establishes rather confusing antagonistic relationships between its language and history: the linguistic history of etymologies dating to *imperial* Rome has been elided or made *absent* by the *presence* of an *empirical* categorization of linguistic terms in the past, present, and future tenses.

That is not to say that history or etymology has been eliminated. The very terms of empirical classification are in fact Latin derivations: "person," "singular," "indicative," "auxiliary," and of course "verb." Moreover, the "Baroque" effect of the poem is achieved in the vertical-temporal succession of words from one stanza to the next. For example, moving from the passage just cited we read:

> of the auxiliary
> verb
> to have
> everything (CP 191)

At this point, "to have" seems to move both upward as the metalinguistic example of an auxiliary verb, and downward as a statement that would begin "to have everything." This latter reading, however, runs contrary to the meaning expressed in the stanza in which "everything" is inscribed, which we realize once we read the stanza in its entirety:

> of the auxiliary
> verb
> to have
>
> everything
> I have done
> is the same (CP 191)

At this point, it becomes evident that "everything" actually begins an entirely new sentence unrelated to that of the previous stanzas, although this sentence is not demarcated by punctuation or capitalization. The vertical disposition of one word *after* the next ("*after*" being a temporal disposition as well) thus permits the generation of multiple horizontal combinations: "of the auxiliary verb 'to have'"; "to have everything"; "to have everything I have done"; "everything I have done is the same." A similar movement occurs in the latter half of the poem:

> if to do
> is capable
> of an
> infinity of
> combinations
>
> involving the
> moral
> physical
> and religious
>
> codes
>
> for everything
> and nothing
> are synonymous
> when (CP 192)

As we read downward, we can begin to form an "infinity" of combinations: "involving the moral physical and religious codes"; "...physical and religious codes for everything"; "...physical and religious codes for everything and nothing"; "...codes. For 'everything' and 'nothing' are synonymous." The subtle differences between each of these phrases (all contained within a single poetic phrase) are sufficient to generate a wealth of philosophical discourse. This "poetic function" of vertical selections projecting into horizontal combinations, however, only serves to manifest confusion regarding the relation of language to history. All of the "horizontal" phrases we have just generated work well as metalinguistic tokens of phraseology, but only if we ignore the semantic content of what such phrases might actually *say*. Likewise, the *infinitive* "to do" may be transferred to the *infinity* of linguistic combinations that, because they are "infinite," are therefore timeless and ahistorical; yet these combinations nonetheless involve historically laden institutional practices of "moral physical and religious" codification. That is, the action of "to do" (apart from "to say" or "to be"), even in its aspect as grammatical token, still carries historical weight in discursive practice as the metaphysical platform for the elaboration of codified social-institutional control. The more the poem moves to operate outside such codes through the categorical repression of historicity, the more history reemerges as a negative force:

>   for everything
>   and nothing
>   are synonymous
>   when
>
>   energy *in vacuo*
>   has the power
>   of confusion
>
>   which only to
>   have done nothing
>   can make
>   perfect (CP 191)

The *empire* of history becomes a powerful vacuum that leads to semantic/symbolic confusion; moreover, the presence of the etymologically preserved Latinism, "*in vacuo*" appears as the palpable expression of historical vacuity. Confusion can therefore only be transcended by the *empirical* imposition of signs stripped of timeliness or historicity. As mentioned earlier, "something" and "everything" may be conflated with "nothing" in phrases such as "nothing that I have done," since such negative phrases still imply grammatically that something (or everything) *has been done* at some point in the past. The final stanza thus re-corrects "nothing I have done" as "to have done nothing" so that the past may be evacuated by the grammatical perfection of the *present perfect*. The sign may now (potentially) proceed to act upon a "new world" freed from the transient confusions of time. Yet clearly, this itself is a hopelessly confused statement: for if the poem makes "nothing" perfect or "perfects nothing," it also says "perfectly nothing."

"To Have Done Nothing" thus plays with an economy of *nothing*: "nothing" as the evacuation of everything, but also as an "energy" *in vacuo* or *in potentia*. In terms of quantification, "nothing" in the poem equals "0"—the cipher that is the placeholder for absence, but without which no mathematics (and hence economics) could proceed. But by bringing in the mathematical allusion, we may be tempted to think of "nothing" as merely formal and abstract, even though the poem never totally elides history and society. To the contrary, the various dispositions—placements—of nothing open vast possibilities for sociohistorical critique, which are perhaps best viewed elsewhere in the volume. The eponymous first poem of *Spring and All* begins within a geographic margin:

> By the road to the contagious hospital
> under the surge of the blue
> mottled clouds driven from the
> northeast—a cold wind. Beyond, the
> waste of broad, muddy fields
> brown with dried weeds, standing and fallen
>
> patches of standing water
> the scattering of tall trees (CP 183)

Like "The Red Wheelbarrow," this first poem "paints" an image of natural (or quasi-natural) scenery through formal contrasts: blue against brown; the "blue / mottled clouds" against the "muddy fields / brown"; blue sky against brown earth and dead brown vegetation; and thus an ethereal, gaseous atmosphere in contrast to a solid earth. Taken in this way, moreover, we will also see that the contrast of sky and earth is immediately relayed into one of abundance and scarcity: the "mottled" clouds do not merely float, but "surge" as if overflowing; meanwhile, the ground is a "waste" of evidently useless mud, dead weeds, and puddles of excess water.

Such contrasts are only significant insofar as the poem treats a moment of climatic change, from "cold" to "hot," or more precisely the equinoctial transition from winter to spring. As such we receive an initial image of death:

> All along the road the reddish
> purplish, forked, upstanding, twiggy
> stuff of bushes and small trees
> with dead, brown leaves under them
> leafless vines—
>
> Lifeless in appearance, sluggish
> dazed spring approaches (CP 183)

As spring approaches, however, "lifeless appearance" is transformed into rebirth:

> Now the grass, tomorrow
> the stiff curl of wildcarrot leaf
>
> One by one objects are defined—
> It quickens: clarity, outline of leaf
>
> But now the stark dignity of
> Entrance—Still, the profound change
> has come upon them: rooted they
> grip down and begin to awaken (CP 183)

The poem is therefore one of *natural* regeneration, cycles of life in concert with cycles of the seasons, such that the central dichotomies (functional dichotomies?) are not just formal-physical (blue vs. brown) or astrophysical (sky vs. earth, gas vs. solid), but much more significantly biological (life vs. death).

Yet to what extent are such movements and dichotomies relegated only to the natural world? In certain respects, the final lines of "Spring and All" also recall Oswald de Andrade's "a roça" analyzed earlier. Just as Williams lists "grass" and "wildcarrot leaf," so too did Oswald list beans, cassava, squash, chicory, and pumpkin. However, as Morse rightly notes in his reading of "a roça," Oswald actually lists *social* products of agriculture, which are cooked and processed so as to "fuel" the human labor needed for industrial production. By contrast, Williams leaves his leaves of grass rooted in the soil, evidently out of contact from the human world. The proof is in the grammatical structure of the description: objects "are defined" in the passive impersonal tense, followed by another impersonal construct "It quickens."

Vegetation regenerates spontaneously of its own accord, not only "organically" but also "impersonally."

But such a reading will prove erroneous given the context in which this regeneration occurs. The central formal dichotomy of the poem is not merely life vs. death, but in fact *natural* cycles of life/death in contrast with *social* cycles of life/death. All action in the poem passes "By the road to the contagious hospital," thereby setting the shapes of natural objects against a backdrop of human architecture. The two architectural structures in the poem, moreover, are hallmarks of civilization: the road by which movement, economic commerce, and therefore political interaction become possible between one locale and another; and the hospital—not only a site of "panoptical" control in the Foucauldian sense but also one where science is mobilized in order to extend the longevity of individuals and the community at large. In the practice of the poem, however, such civilizing missions are in fact evacuated from either construction. The road (as far as we know) is not utilized by any human/social actor, but merely demarcates a margin beside which plants die and regrow. Meanwhile, the hospital is merely a repository for viral or bacterial infection, rather than a defense against it; the contagious hospital is a zone of death and the spread of more death. While not explicitly delineated by the poem, the rebirth of vegetation therefore acquires historical and political-economic resonance by its proximity to artificial structures. Natural cycles appear *marginal* to social structures that *do not function properly*, and thus promise the possibility of some "renaissance" for the centers of civilization. And this may be a distinctly American promise, for the reborn plants "enter the *new world* naked, / cold, uncertain of all / save that they enter" (CP 183; emphasis added). Nakedness is an attribute exclusively of those who wear clothes,[38] since those who have no concept of clothing have no clothes to lack. Likewise, a "new world" can only be an invention of sixteenth-century cartographers and colonizers who viewed their own world as "old."

Each in its way, both "To Have Done Nothing" and "Spring and All" present us contrastive or dichotomous formal arrangements, whether of color, texture, or grammar. But we must begin to call such arrangement "economic," to the degree that these poems operate as *social and historical* distributions of scarcity and abundance, whether in terms of abstract quantification (nothing/everything) or life itself (alive/dead, or rebirth/contagion). By the end of *Spring and All*, such "formal economy" comes to acquire racial- or ethno-cultural aspects. "The Wildflower" begins by painting a portrait of a bunch of flowers:

> Black eyed susan
> rich orange
> round the purple core
>
> the white daisy
> is not
> enough (CP 236)

Like "The Red Wheelbarrow" (and to a lesser extent "Spring and All") the immediate mode of "The Wildflower" is an impressionistic disposition of colors. Where do these flowers reside? Are they in a field or a vase or in someone's hand? Such questions are irrelevant because the immediate concern of the poem is merely the contrast of orange next to purple against a backdrop of white. Yet this colorful disposition foregrounds a contrast between floral species, the black-eyed susan and the white daisy, which creates a gestalt between them in name only—a *false* black-and-white gestalt given that "black" is merely part of the flower's name, not one of its actual colors as mentioned by the poem. Nevertheless, and rather unexpectedly, the gestalt among plant species is immediately transferred over in the social realm of race and gender relations:

> Crowds are white
> as farmers
> who live poorly
>
> But you
> are rich
> in savagery—
>
> Arab
> Indian
> dark woman (CP 236)

The masses of farmers appear as little more than "white noise" ("white trash"?) in the poet's field of vision. For he disregards them in order to engage in conversation with the metaphor he constructs. Overlooking the crowds with whom he cannot or does not communicate, the poet personifies the wildflower and addresses "her" as "you." The contrast of black-eyed susan and daisy is therefore transfigured as *social difference*—social Otherness—demarcated in a gestalt of presence and absence. By addressing a second-person "you," we automatically become aware that there is a first-person "I" speaking (rather than, e.g., an impersonal third person), even though "I" never names itself as such. The "I," furthermore, speaks to a "woman," thereby suggesting that the "I" is a "he." The first-person poetic voice therefore works to fix the object of his gaze—objectifying the female figure through masculine perspective. This is doubly problematic given that the male-gaze also works to objectify racial categories in terms of civilizational stature. The poem in fact aligns gender ("woman"), skin features ("dark"), ethnicity ("Arab" and "Indian") with "savagery." And in doing so, the poem tacitly endorses a parallel normative alignment in its unspoken negative space: man, light, Occidental, and civilization.

Significantly, such syntagmatic alignments occur within an economy of scarcity and wealth. The white daisy "is not enough" in direct opposition to the "rich orange" of the black-eyed susan. Likewise, the white farmers "live poorly / But you / are rich / in savagery." The various contrasts in "The Wildflower" are not just an abstract play of gestalt, but have a distinctly economic character of wealth and poverty. However, the transformation of natural objects into social and economic objects only occurs by means of profound *confusion*. The poet affords wealth to his object, but only to grant her a wealth of "savagery." In doing so he therefore *deprives* her of any cultural (or even perhaps behavioral) validity—she is beyond the control of an unnamed "civilization" and codes of proper behavior, the lack of which is precisely the source of the poet's attraction to her and his need to objectify her. The "white crowds" may live poorly, but the unnamed "white poet" tends to horde wealth and culture. But of course he does none of these things, because he is operating within a poetic conceit. *There is no economic exchange* in the poem, unless we confuse the color of flowers with the color of people. Indeed, the entire poem is an exercise in confusion in that the poet personifies the flower by confusing the improper name of a species of plants ("black-eyed susan," lowercase) with the proper name of an individual woman ("Susan," uppercase). The poetic structures he utilizes only reinforce this confusion. For the most part, the poem consists of two- or three-stress accentuated verses, either in loose trochees ("Bláck ĕyed súsăn") or iambs ("Bŭt yóu / ăre rich"). The sole exceptions are two antibacchial lines: "rích ŏrănge" and "dárk wómăn." In terms of rhythm and meter, therefore, the poem itself conflates the richness of a color as such with the skin color of a woman who is wealthy in barbarity and poor in everything else. This is the way the poem *functions*; but in fact all that is produced by the poem is *malfunction*—a false set of socioeconomic meanings ascribed to human bodies that do not actually exist.

Williams has just done nothing to us. And this is everything.

No Name No. 22 (or, the Economics of Bibliography)

But everything we have been discussing in *Spring and All* may be nothing—and therefore quite a bit more than everything.

Significantly, the (formal) economy of poems such as "The Red Wheelbarrow," "Spring and All," and even "To Elsie" has made them suitable, not only for repeated quotation but also for repeated republication. From this standpoint, the canonicity of Williams's poetry is not just a question of the critic's ideology of Americanism, but rather the somewhat more mundane interests of pedagogy. In covering U.S.-American modernist literature, teachers are much more inclined to favor a compact poem such as "The Red Wheelbarrow" over more unruly works such as Pound's *Cantos* or even his "Mauberley." The poem can be read quickly by novices, and its words readily understood by them. This can then allow the instructor to raise interpretative questions of a higher order than whether or not students have understood the poem: Why would someone write about wheelbarrows and chickens? What is so important about them? Is it even a poem at all? Moreover, Williams's brief poems can be neatly included in anthologies and textbooks, lowering the end-cost of these books to students or school districts. We might therefore call this an "informal" economy of the poems—the extratextual context that, by an almost accidental collusion of diverse interests over time, has served to guarantee their persistence in the culture.

One cannot expect a high school teacher or a graduate student instructor of introductory literary studies to relay *everything* about the texts read in class. At a certain level, novices *must* begin by dealing with the text itself, and as a result poems such as "The Red Wheelbarrow" that can be read quickly and discussed in the span of a 50-minute period become attractive options for instructors. The problem is not with novices, but rather with what happens to novices when they emerge as experts later on in life still thinking of "The Red Wheelbarrow" as a text unto itself to be read "on its own terms." I have respect for Richard Morse's literary interpretations in general, yet Morse makes a fundamental error when he states that "The Red Wheelbarrow" depicts a farm. In fact the poem makes no mentions of farms or any external landscape, and indeed bibliographic evidence only magnifies this fact. Writing in 1933, Williams relates the genesis of the poem:

> The wheelbarrow in question stood outside the window of an old negro's house on a back street in the suburb where I live. It was pouring rain and there were white chickens walking about it. The sight impressed me somehow as about the most important, the most integral that it had ever been my pleasure to gaze upon. And the meter though no more than a fragment succeeds in portraying this pleasure flawlessly. Even if it succeeds in denoting a certain unquenchable exaltation—in fact I find the poem quite perfect.[39]

The author provides us a rather stunning admission of historical and socioeconomic circumstance. Historically, the poem is by no means pastoral or georgic; not only does the poem give us no indication of a landscape, but now we learn that the images of the poem were derived from a decidedly *urban* setting—or more precisely a *suburban* setting, one marked by its transitional location between the urban (New York City in this case) and the rural (the Jersey countryside).

But who exactly would be raising chickens in an urban or suburban setting? Obviously, we have several options: this person whose chickens Williams viewed in the rain is someone who has recently arrived from the agricultural countryside, or has had his previously rural land overtaken by the suburb, or has not given up on the old ways of raising one's own food. In any case, this is someone who does not always buy his meat or eggs in the grocery store, but grows his own. Like Elsie in the earlier reading, this is someone who has either recently arrived to the suburbs or has had the suburbs arrive to him—but someone who has not yet been fully "suburbanized." Tacitly or not, this is a sign of Williams's sense of difference, differentiation, from the "negro" in question, who is thus marked, above and beyond the rural/urban argument just made, by *racial* difference. And based on this racism can we not also infer, given the epoch in which he writes the poem and the anecdote (the 1920s and 1930s), that by "negro" Williams automatically implies "*poor* negro"? This would not be such a radical inference, for even though Williams should not be judged as a racist (the opposite in fact), like anyone else he was nevertheless subject to the paternalism of his time. Williams would, after all, offer this lament of "colored" men and women in his prose treatment of American history, *In the American Grain*: "For sheer sordidness we never touch them, the desperate drunkenness, upon foul stuff, in which they nearly die under a heap of rags under the eaves in the attic of some revolting, disease-ridden, female's dump—fly-covered, dazed—."[40]

On the other hand, the problem with this inference is that it is precisely that, an inference, and one made by way of an anecdote no less. If the poem itself gives us no indication of the external landscape, we must also admit that the poem gives us no indication of any historical context whatsoever, much less the one we just analyzed. In fact, the very purpose of the poem is to remove any external connotation from language in order to arrive at a new or renewed sense of language's objectivity in itself. As James Breslin famously wrote, Williams "strips objects bare of all acquired associations and it is this neutralization of things that makes it possible for him to accept *any* thing as suitable for poetry."[41] And with this we can understand words themselves as among such "objects." In fact, looking back at Williams's anecdote regarding the genesis of "Red Wheelbarrow," the author either does not see poverty in the scene or he does not find poverty to be absolutely important. What he does find "most important," rather, is the scene's structural or formal arrangement, and he states directly that he finds *a wealth of pleasure* in the sight of such an arrangement. In this sense, the meter and form of the poem coincide "flawlessly" with what Williams gazed upon at the "negro's" house, thus maximizing pleasure for both author and reader. The scene and the poem are further marked for the author by infinite *excess*—or what he calls "unquenchable exaltation." Thus, on the one hand, "The Red Wheelbarrow" is an impoverished poem originating from a scene of poverty and providing us nothing more than a scene of poverty; on the other hand, taken from the vantage point of formality, of structure, of "poeticity," the poem is perfect, infinite, exalted, unquenchable.

In terms of its genesis, "The Red Wheelbarrow" presents a *transitional* or *marginal* image: the movement of poor rural people and their cultures to the edge of urban agglomerations (and furthermore a "backstreet" in this suburban setting, doubly marginalized). Even though such movement and marginalization is the historical *origin* of the poem, it no longer seems *necessary* to it. Nevertheless, such tacit "excision" of marginality or historical context—now deemed unnecessary to the poem—runs contrary to what the poem itself states: "so much / depends." By not specifying what this "so much" is we can only assume that there is a whole world just beyond the poem itself that hangs upon its every word. Indeed, context is fundamental to the interpretation of the *Spring and All* poems. In addition to noting Williams's bare objectivity, Breslin also emphasizes that *all* the poems of *Spring and All* must be read in the context of one another as a kind of singular "serial" poem: "The point is that the serial poem genre enables Williams to create a special kind of poetic field.... There is no articulated surface of connections that a narrative or explicit argument would provide; instead, there is a buried coherence—of recurrent words, images—which the reader himself [sic] must uncover."[42]

It would appear that such contextual, or otherwise "informal, extra-textual," considerations have not been deemed significant for critical readers, pedagogues, or textbook editors. An index of this may be found in the ways the poems of *Spring and All* have been anthologized. When I was taught the poem in the 1980s and into the 1990s, my textbooks—including the *Norton Anthology of Poetry* and the *Norton Anthology of American Literature*, the most widely used college textbooks in the United States—re-presented (republished) the poems with no mention of their bibliographic provenance. As such, a poem such as "The Red Wheelbarrow" appeared as a self-realized and self-contained work of art, and therefore was left open to interpretation "on its own terms" with little external considerations. More recent Norton Anthologies as well as the Oxford *Anthology of Modern American Poetry* make some mention of the original context of *Spring and All*, in the form of footnotes. Nonetheless, all such anthologies provide what amounts to a radical decontextualization of Williams's work—a displacement of a poetic work that so deeply questions matters of place, location, and disposition. For instance, all the textbooks just mentioned fail to note that they have, directly or indirectly, taken "The Red Wheelbarrow" from a single source-text: *The Collected Earlier Poems* (New York: New Directions, 1951), the contents of which were drawn from the earlier *The Complete Collected Poems, 1906–1938* (New York: New Directions, 1938), which was itself drawn from the even earlier *Collected Poems, 1921–1931* (New York: Objectivist Press, 1934). Yet most anthologies *do not* take as their source-text the most current critical edition of Williams's poetry, *The Collected Poems of William Carlos Williams*, 2 Vols., edited by A. Walton Litz and Christopher MacGowan (New York: New Directions, 1986). We have verifiable proof of this for a very simple reason: anthologies always entitle the poem, "The Red Wheelbarrow."

"The Red Wheelbarrow" per se did not appear in print, however, until the 1923 pamphlet, *Go Go*, which Williams literally cut-and-pasted into the 1934 *Collected Poems*. This statement most likely comes as a shock to anyone familiar with Williams's poetry, since everyone (except for me apparently) knows that "The Red Wheelbarrow" first appeared in another 1923 book *Spring and All* (published several months before *Go Go*). But I must insist. It is true—the 1934 *Collected Poems,* and every other "collected works" volume thereafter (including the 1986 critical edition) *correctly* lists "The Red Wheelbarrow" (and all the other poems read in the present chapter) as part of the book entitled *Spring and All*, and make no mention of anything called *Go Go*. And indeed, all the poems we have considered *did* appear first in *Spring and All*, a volume published at Williams's own expense in France through Charles McAlmon's Contact Publishing Co. with a one-time run of 300 copies. Yet the poem's title, "The Red Wheelbarrow," *did not* appear in this first edition of *Spring and All*, but only arrived several months later when *Go Go* was published (New York: Monroe Wheeler, 1923) as the second installment of a serialized pamphlet called *Manikin*. In the Table of Contents of their 1986 critical edition, Litz and MacGowan list the poem as "XXII. The Red Wheelbarrow," but within the body of the edition, the poem only appears as "XXII"— which is to say, the twenty-second in a series of 27 poems. This is because the *original* poems of *Spring and All* did not carry titles, but instead were numbered I–XXVII. (To make matters a bit more complicated, the version of *Spring and All* in the *Complete Collected Poems* of 1938 [and the 1951 *Collected Earlier Poems*] has 28 poems, adding one, "The Hermaphroditic Telephones," that did not appear in the original *Spring and All* although it does appear in *Go Go*; these versions also place "The Red Wheelbarrow" as the twenty-first poem in the sequence, switching positions with "Quietness," previously known as "XXI.") In other words, anthologies and collected volumes lend the impression that "The Red Wheelbarrow" is an original work of art. Yet at its origin, the poem was *not* "The Red Wheelbarrow," but merely "XXII."

Why, then, were some of the *Spring and All* poems not taken from *Spring and All* for subsequent publication, but rather from this *Go Go*—a minor publication that has largely been excised from Williams's bibliography, or at least from the "bibliography" presented by the various Tables of Contents of his collected works? The answer is largely *economical*, and will require us to dissect a rather complex network of authorial intentions. We should make no mistake that Williams obviously intended "XXII" to appear as "The Red Wheelbarrow" in subsequent editions, and for all the other numbered poems of *Spring and All* to appear with the titles later given to them, for this is how he *chose* to entitle his poems in editions most widely available during his lifetime. From 1923 to 1970, furthermore, close to no one read *Spring and All* in its original form for the very simple reason that it was essentially a vanity print of 300 copies, all of which are now only held in Rare Books libraries or private collections. Williams himself would state of the original *Spring and All*, "Nobody ever saw it, it had no circulation at all—But I had a lot of fun with it."[43] Wide distribution of the *Spring and All* poems would not occur until 1938 when Williams prepared the *Complete Collected Poems* for J. Laughlin at New Directions, and a reproduction of the first edition *Spring and All* would not be widely available until the 1970 collection, *Imaginations* (New York: New Directions).

In the matter of Williams's preparation, Litz and MacGowan make an extremely interesting comment in their "Note on the Text":

> We have used the text of the 1951 *Collected Earlier Poems* for the poems included in that volume, since this was the last printing of these poems that Williams supervised; but we have eliminated the numerous errors in the 1951 text caused by the circumstances of its preparation. Williams prepared the 1951 text for the printer in two stages. The first was a combination of re-typed poems and pasted-up poems from earlier printings that followed the sequence of the 1938 *Complete Collected Poems*....In all 60% of the poems were pasted in. Most of the pasted-up versions came from the *Complete Collected Poems*, but Williams occasionally used an alternative printed text. His correspondence makes clear that these alternatives were not chosen for textual reasons, but because they were more easily available or prevented the cutting-up of rare editions. In the case of some of the *Spring and All* poems, for example, Williams preferred to cut up the 1923 *Go Go* text rather than the more valuable *Spring and All* volume.[44]

Here Litz and MacGown adhere fairly closely to the so-called Greg-Bowers school of critical editing, a "method" especially prevalent among English scholars in the latter half of the past century.[45] The editors choose a "copy-text" that best represents the "most authoritative text" available—giving more weight to the "final intentions" of the author by choosing the final edition prepared during his lifetime. Once they have done so, they clear up discrepancies between different versions (i.e, 1934, 1938, and 1951 collected volumes, as well as alternate printings and manuscripts if available) by distinguishing "substantive" from "accidental" variations—in other words, by correcting only "accidental" printing errors, spelling and punctuation mistakes, and so forth. Most editors, however, will inevitably encounter cases in which the difference between an accidental and a substantive is not quite clear. In the case of "The Red Wheelbarrow," for instance, Litz and MacGowan undoubtedly noticed that in almost every version published after the original, the poem terminates with a period; in the original *Spring and All*, "XXII" has no punctuation. The discrepancy, especially in such a compact poem, is significant, since it raises the question of whether this is an "open-ended" or "closed" work of art.[46] This matter of punctuation was no accident of the printer, but a specific alteration mandated by Williams himself. For reasons that will become apparent later in this chapter, Williams wished the original "XXII" to remain open to what followed it, but in preparing subsequent printings he wished "The Red Wheelbarrow" (and other poems from *Spring and All*) to stand on their own as discrete works of art.

Yet Litz and MacGowan also uncover certain economic choices that interfere or intersect with the strictly aesthetic choices made by the author. In preparing the 1938 *Complete Collected Poems*, Litz and MacGowan note that Williams had to retype his poems. But this proved to be a *costly* task in terms of time and money: since Williams (the practicing physician) had no time to do so, he hired one of his neighbors in Rutherford, Kathleen Hoagland, as his typist. And, in order to save time (and presumably money) on that front, Williams "pasted-up poems from earlier printings"—meaning just this, that he literally cut out pages from earlier printings (did he use his physician's scalpel?) and pasted them onto new pages sent to the printer, pages now archived at Yale University's Beinecke Library. The chain of causation is impressive: the original *Spring and All* was precious and scarce, but Williams needed extant printed versions of the poem for his publisher; since there were only 300 copies in existence, Williams opted for the next best option available—the pamphlet (not book) pages of *Go Go* that gave us not only "The Red Wheelbarrow" as a title, but also a period at the end of the poem.

This will have tremendous impact on the way we read Williams's work, because *Spring and All* is *not* a book of 27 poems, but rather (as is well known) a book of poems *interspersed with prose*. The poems are not just meant to be read as a "serial" (in Breslin's terms), but also in conjunction or continuity with prose. The *lack* of periods at the end of poems, as well as the lack of titles prior to them therefore marks a sense of flow or connection throughout the work. Nothing is self-contained or totally individuated in *Spring and All*; to the contrary, each element flows into and out of one another without marking an end or beginning. But for most of the work's existence, a reading practice of ends and beginnings—or means-and-ends—has prevailed. On one hand, it must not have been economically viable to republish the prose of *Spring and All*, which is rather difficult to read. Readers—book-buyers—wanted Williams's poetry, not his quasi-philosophical ramblings, or at least this must have been the determination of Williams and his editors. Moreover, the prose must not have been considered as aesthetically or culturally "serious" as poetry, as evidenced by Williams own assertion that the original *Spring and All* was something of a "playing-around book." In either case, the work's prose at some point became dross—compared to the poems they seem to be second-order. Which is to say, some implicit power-differential between prose and poetry immediately comes into play.

Despite the evident primacy of poetry, however, the prose sections of *Spring and All* are rather indispensable to a reading of the poems they surround. Poem "III" (later titled "The Farmer") presents the farmer as an "artist figure... / —composing / —antagonist" (CP 186). That is, the farmer "composes" the landscape, pushing back nature in order to objectify a new reality for the land. The prose following poem III (and IV) then serves to expose the "pragmatic" philosophical implications of reading poetry:

> So long as the sky is recognized as an association
>
> is recognized in its function of accessory to vague words whose meaning it is impossible to rediscover
>
> its value can be nothing but mathematical certain limits of gravity and density of air
>
> The farmer and the fisherman who read their own lives there have a practical corrective for—
>
> they rediscover or replace demoded meanings to the religious terms
>
> Among them, without expansion of imagination, there is the residual contact between life and the imagination which is essential to freedom (CP 187)

The new, objective poem models a new way of perceiving and interpreting reality. Thus, the interpretative actions "the farmer and the fisherman" (poet-figures who are presumably armed or influenced by the new poetic objectivism) may serve as a corrective to the demoded metaphysics of religion, so long as the associational function of modern (nearly scientific or "mathematical") words can be recognized properly. Williams's objectivist poetry does not really reduce words to a nonsubjective reality, but rather provides *social* functionalities designed to provide the means to create a new sense of life and freedom—which are ultimately *political* aims. The farmer is not merely an artist/antagonist to nature, but in a certain sense represents the Jeffersonian ideal of citizens forging a new reality—a novelty that *requires* a poetic imagination. Such political content, however, is only available by reading the poems in context with the prose.

The sense of connection between prose and poetry, however, does not discount the fundamental difference between them. As may be perceptible in the passage just cited, the prose of *Spring and All* often appears to be composed of disconnected phrases and fragments that, in contrast to the orderly composition of the poems, tend to break off in mid-sentence as if reaching a dead end. One should not be confused by this apparent lack of resolve. The discursive difference created between forms of prose and forms of poetry establishes a textual power-dynamic, with the prose continually returning us to the material condition of the text as printed, typographic object. Standing in marked contrast to the poems (ordered numerically from I to XXVII), the prose of *Spring and All* begins in a series of chapters that follow no apparent order: we begin with "Chapter 19," followed by chapters "XIII," "VI," "2," and "XIX." "Chapter I" does not appear until several pages into the volume. Since there are no capitular demarcations after "Chapter I," we may conclude that the majority of the text (including all the poems) has been subsumed into the first chapter, as if most of *Spring and All* were a "beginning" that paradoxically appears as the "final" chapter in the work. We will also notice that chapter numbers are given in both Arabic and Roman numeration for no particular reason (with "CHAPTER XIII" appearing upside-down) thus emphasizing the arbitrariness of typographic symbols with respect to the abstract numerical values they represent.

As physical material, moreover, the prose iconically frames the poems. Prose typography covers the page from margin to margin, yet when the prose sections end, they "carve" out a negative space or "blank field" for the typographically reduced, imagistic poems to inhabit. The movement between the overabundant typography of prose and a "deprived" typography of poetry creates what Donald Wesling has called a "gestalt" effect in the physical appearance of the volume, between black space and blank space.[47] In short, the very layout of poems in the original *Spring and All* emphasizes absence and presence, serving to mark poetry as a zone of textual deprivation.

I would call this "gestalt" a kind of "discursive diglossia" in which two distinct discourses collide into one another. The prosaic "framing" of poetic discourse is as critical and conceptual as it is visual. For instance, much of the volume's prose provides critical definitions of the concepts "prose" and "poetry." In the prose immediately following poem XXII: "Poetry is something quite different [from prose]. Poetry has to do with the crystallization of the imagination—the perfection of new forms as additions to nature—Prose may follow to enlighten but poetry—[...] There is no confusion—only difficulties" (CP 226). Earlier Williams defines prose and poetry separately, apparently to weed out any potential confusion

> or better: prose has to do with the fact of an emotion; poetry has to do with the dynamization of emotion into separate form. This is the force of the imagination.
>
> prose: statement of facts concerning emotions, intellectual states, data of all sorts—technical expositions, jargon, of all sorts—fictional and other—
>
> poetry: a new form dealt with as a reality in itself.
>
> The form of prose is the accuracy of its subject matter—how best to expose the multiform phases of its material
>
> the form of poetry is related to the movements of the imagination revealed in words—or whatever it may be—the cleavage is complete...
>
> To enter a new world, and have there freedom of movement and newness. (CP 219)

In a sense, prose seems to hold a parasitic relationship to poetry, a discourse that merely "follows" poetry "to enlighten" it. In contrast poetry does not "mimic" or "copy" nature, nor does it represent some extraneous "subject matter" no matter how accurately. Without naming it as such, Williams's prose appears to characterize poetry as capable of synthesizing new categories of thought, emotion, and perception in a quasi-Kantian manner. Poetry brings new forms into reality. Prose therefore follows poetic synthesis in order to explain its consequences, but prose itself is not capable of creating or objectifying anything new. The poetic imagination alone produces new meanings in language, and hence it alone allows men to imagine a "new world...with freedom of movement and newness." Yet such work nevertheless appears to be incomplete. If the poem does achieve an objective reality, it ceases to be self-defining or self-articulating. Whereas the poem creates the imaginative illusion of "freedom of movement and newness," this illusion cannot produce knowledge of itself in the "multiform phases of its material." The poem now requires nonpoetic prose—a form of writing that is by its own self-definition extra-poetic—in order to be defined *as poetry*. The recognition of "poeticity" in the "original" context is therefore stripped from the poem itself, only to be relocated between the objectivist thing and a reflexive prose response, between poetic objectification and a nonpoetic prosaic frame that explains how poetic objectification is supposed to function.

The original *Spring and All* therefore establishes a sense of constant *migration* between discourses and languages ("discursive diglossia"), yet this is not a subjective journey—and certainly nothing like a *bildungsroman* where the subject emerges at the end of history fully realized. Rather, discursive diglossia only results in back-and-forth movement marked by material privation and dependency. The poems depend upon—"hang" upon—the prose fragments that frame them. Yet the prose also depends upon the poetry, in parasitic relationship to the new categorical forms poetry provides. In fact, we might dare to call such parasitism a form of colonization in which the prose creates visible *margins* (zones of blankness or deprivation) in which the prose *extracts or reproduces* value from the raw material of poetry—poetry that, according to my earlier readings, we saw to be *economically* reduced to nothingness. Significantly, the poems never explicitly comment upon the prose, even though the prose constantly comments on poetry. That is, poetry has no value in itself until a prosaic description *gives it value*. And this textual gestalt (as Wesling terms it) or diglossia (as I do) has a deliberate political and cultural effect. As Wesling explains: "...Williams uses all the rhetorical and gestalt effects I've mentioned, and goes further to use sequence as a political logic. He relates poverty of sense-making to poverty of emotion, and both of these to actual, brutalizing poverty, his and the reader's emotions deriving from sequence is something like despair."[48]

Williams's prose defines poetry as anti-symbolic, as a part of nature, and—problematically—as the mark of (human) culture. The prose that leads into poem V emphasizes this point: "The word must be put down for itself, not as a symbol of nature but a part, cognizant of the whole—aware—civilized" (CP 189). By becoming free from the sycophantic relation of being a "symbol of nature," the poetic word serves to create "civilization." The prosaic statement thus creates the impression of an unbounded or totalizing civilization to be instantiated by the poetic word, an impression that will prove false by the very terms of the statement. The prose defines an historical shift in the use of language, from merely symbolic language to some sort of "self-cognizant" language that will be civilized. Evidently there is some prior uncivilized quantity against which civilization may be recognized. Yet, the poetry in *Spring and All* appears to be incompletely aware of this entire context; the word "civilized" itself only appears *outside* of the poetry, in a discourse that gives definition to the poetic. If the poems work to synthesize or imagine new categories of thought and reality, the prose functions to give the poetry a more expansive purpose: a "civilizing mission."

This mission, however, only results in almost unimaginable barbarity. From the very beginning of *Spring and All*, the prose works to dislocate and relocate history, and specifically American history. The opening prose section, for instance, situates the original energy of the New World as emerging from total holocaust and plagiarism:

> o meager times, so fat in everything imaginable! imagine the New World that rises to our windows from the sea on Mondays and on Saturdays—and on every other day of the week also. Imagine it in all its prismatic colorings, its counterpart in our souls—our souls that are great pianos whose strings, of honey and of steel, the divisions of the rainbow set twanging, loosing in the air great novels of adventure! Imagine the monster project of the moment: Tomorrow we the people of the United States are going to Europe armed to kill every man, woman, and child in the area west of the Carpathian Mountains (also east) sparing none. (CP 178)

Here we have a declaration of American *in*dependence that alludes, no less, to the 1776 U.S. Declaration of Independence ("We the people..."). Caught between "meager times" and a "fat" imagination, the unleashing of the New World enacts a global holocaust where all humans, both east and west, are murdered, including the very "people of the United States" doing the killing. This total annihilation of the human species only leads, in the ironized narrative laid out in Williams's prose, to a new evolution that repeats the old exactly:

> ...Through the orderly sequences of unmentionable time EVOLUTION HAS REPEATED ITSELF FROM THE BEGINNING.
> Good God!
> Every step once taken in the first advance of the human race, from the amoeba to the highest type of intelligence, has been duplicated, every step exactly paralleling the one that preceded in the dead ages gone by. A perfect plagiarism results. Everything is and is new. Only the imagination is undeceived. (CP 181)

In theory, then, the novelty of the "New World" can only come about through the radical and violent erasure of all human history—here framed as the erasure of natural evolution of the species. This "newness" suggests independence from Europe and from historical time as such—such that time itself becomes characterized as "meager," even "unmentionable." In practice, however, these biological and historical elisions only serve to reintroduce a decidedly "inauthentic" historical time—only to produce a "new evolution" that stands as a simulacrum of the old, an evolution that because verisimilar can only be described as plagiaristic.

Plagiarism therefore becomes the very tradition of the New World, as Williams outlines in a section entitled "The Traditionalists of Plagiarism":

> In that colossal surge toward the finite and the capable life has now arrived for the second time at that exact moment when in the ages past the destruction of the species Homo sapiens occurred.
> Now at last that process of miraculous verisimilitude, that great copying which evolution has followed, repeating move for move every move that it made in the past—is approaching the end.
> Suddenly it is at an end. THE WORLD IS NEW. (CP 182)

Here is the crux of the American problem. The New World must repeat the evolution—that is, the *development*—of the Old World exactly. As such the history of the New World can only result in an inauthentic plagiarism of the original, even though its inauthenticity may only be perceived as originality. New World history is therefore not merely a "miraculous verisimilitude," but will also come to require *new* forms of life finally capable of bringing the "miraculous verisimilitude" of historical development to an end, so that an "original" may finally come to be. But this search for originality will only set in motion another repetition of the same developmental cycle. The end of history is never an end of history, but only a repetition of an historical cycle oriented to the development of an end. Heidegger may have called this process "*Dasein*." But we have another word it—*holocaust*.

~~Bárbaro e Nosso~~

As I mentioned earlier dependency theory inaugurated a radical shift in Latin American thought. Through dependency theory, Latin American intellectuals came to recognize fully that, although Latin American societies were no longer colonies of foreign powers, nations in the region still had to contend with colonization, since these nations had been located in a subordinate position in the world's political-economic order. Perhaps more forcefully, colonialism had historically shaped relations between communities, social movements, economic forces, and political structures, all of which relations had persisted in their way into the industrial (and postindustrial) era.

Perhaps the most stunning achievement of dependency theory was therefore to direct critical attention—not to the position of Latin America in a "world-system" but rather to modes of "internal colonization" by which the state attempted to incorporate populations and consolidate its power.

In this chapter, I have attempted to extend dependency into the First World through *Spring and All*. When read without its prose sections ("cleansed," as it were, of prose "messiness"), the poems of *Spring and All* may be said to *function objectively*, almost mechanically, with minimal human or historical interference. In fact, the poems always refer to the fact that the human element *has been* stripped away from them; the prose of the original context further works to place the poems in sociohistorical context. Nonetheless, when Williams's poems are reproduced individually, devoid of their typographical-material context, it appears that they promote a U.S.-American culture exempt from all the corrosive problems relegated to the "Third World." The Williams poem appears to operate as a depersonalized machine working to objectify anything—and anybody—that comes its way. Such a view can therefore be extended into "canonical" or "high modernist" Anglo-American poetry as a whole: canonical modernist poems become tiny self-contained *oppression-machines*.

Nothing could be more true. Poem XXVI of *Spring and All* later came to be entitled "At the Ball Game." It objectifies a crowd at a ballgame as a kind of "mass ornament" as Siegfried Kracauer[49] would have called it:

> The crowd at the ball game
> is moved uniformly
>
> by a spirit of uselessness
> which delights them—
>
> all the exciting detail
> of the chase
>
> and the escape, the error
> the flash of genius—
>
> all to no end save beauty
> the eternal—
>
> So in detail they, the crowd,
> are beautiful (CP 233)

Despite overt appearance, "the crowd" here has no shape, no uniformity, and no detail. Indeed, crowds are the very negation of these things, and as such will prove to be rather useless. The crowd only *becomes* something meaningful once it is given some thing—some detail—to which its collective attention may be directed as a newly formed *collectivity*. The escape and the chase of the baseball player stealing second base is perfectly useless, a delightful diversion, but it nevertheless serves to focus the crowd, transforming it into a unified mass. In a word, baseball *aestheticizes* the crowd, forming it into an object capable of action, capable of being thought of as active. The crowd is *not* "in detail," then, since a massive crowd overwhelms any single particularity; rather, it is "in the detail" of the spectacle that the crowd may be objectified as such. Such objectification serves to create force or power; as the poem states, "This is / the power of their faces" (CP 234).

Poem XXVI, written and published before the advent of fascism per se, nevertheless envisions the means by which fascistic oppression legitimizes itself—robbing individuals of their inherent political rights and power by forming crowds into a unified mass through aesthetic spectacle—"the situation of politics which Fascism is rendering aesthetic," as Walter Benjamin famously wrote.[50] In the sense of such aestheticization, Williams's objectivist poem does not merely *describe* the aestheticization of a crowd into a "useful" though "thoughtless" mass. We must recall that poetry is, for Williams, uniquely capable of creating new forms and categories—new worlds—ex nihilo. As such, it is Poem XXVI itself that is the detail—the focus through which a crowd may be incorporated as a political body. The "new world" produced by the poem would feed directly into "internal colonization" by the state.

However, the poem itself works to frustrate such a reading on multiple fronts. On the one hand, the poem exposes danger posed by the aestheticization of the crowd "in detail":

> for this
> to be warned against
>
> saluted and defied—
> it is alive, venomous
>
> it smiles grimly
> its words cut—
>
> The flashy female with her
> mother, gets it—
>
> The Jew gets it straight—it
> is deadly, terrifying—
>
> It is the Inquisition, the
> Revolution (CP 233)

As a kind of warning, the poem "gets it" as to what is happening. That is, the phrase "gets it" is utilized a vernacular (*koine?*) expression meaning "to understand." The flashy female and the Jew therefore understand why the crowd is to be "warned against / saluted and defied." But why? Both individuals also "get it," by which we can also understand that they "receive" the attention of the crowd. In other words, either the female or the Jew may serve as the "detail" to which—and against which—the collective power of the crowd may be directed as a threat. The "detail" becomes a stereotypical object of sexual or sectarian aggression. Either may become the sacrificial scapegoat of the "Inquisition" or the "Revolution," through which the crowd's power may be objectified and harnessed. On the other hand, as we saw in the previous section of this chapter, as much as the poem may objectify subjects into a national mass, the poem's objectification is never self-contained, but rather requires prosaic description in order to have any force whatsoever. It so happens that the prose of *Spring and All* works to model poetic objectification as a form of national dependency and social violence, thereby *exposing* rather than *beautifying* the terrors of objectification. The crowd "without thought" (CP 234) in fact exists just beyond the ability of the poem to contain or understand it. Or rather, the crowd—in its thoughtless excess in relation to the poet—can only be objectified by the poem through violence, either real or imagined.

If "At the Ball Game" works to aestheticize the masses, *Spring and All* responds by exposing such aestheticization as an historical plagiarism, a veritable falsity. If modernist poetry renders the people aesthetic, *Spring and All* responds by *politicizing and economizing* art. But this will only become evident if *Spring and All* is read in the broader context of itself—which is to say, in the context of migration from states-of-scarcity to states-of-abundance, migration marked by violent social antagonisms—the fundamental movement of the American hemisphere.

Chapter 2

The Reversible World: America as Dissonance in Mário de Andrade's *Paulicéia desvairada*

The French philosopher Jean-Luc Nancy has theorized the possibility of radical politics from the posture of what he calls *finitude*. If the individual is a *finite* being, then the community—the collectivity of individuals—may well be infinite, in a particular sense. While Western philosophy affords the individual *being* an immanent power, the community—or what Nancy calls the *"being-in-common"*—can never be formalized or substantiated in the same way. The individual always exists in connection to the community, of course, but the community is never reducible to any individualized form. We can see this in the futility of applying close-ended, essentialized characterizations to whole societies: Is the United States uniformly "democratic" as certain proto-authoritarian neoconservatives would have it? Are Catholics uniformly "authoritarian" as Hegel stated on several occasions? Nevertheless, political regimes *can* try to force such limits upon the community, and efforts to shape the community into a singular body usually amount to totalitarianism. In Benjaminian terms, the "aestheticization" of the community under the metaphor of "body" is a mode of fascism. For his part, Nancy does utilize the "body" metaphor with relation to community, albeit in an entirely different direction. At the moment the individual realizes that its body ends (is *finite*), the individual begins to realize that others outside itself also exist; "community" occurs in the exposition of one finite face to another finite face. Or as Nancy writes,

> ...having access to what is *proper* to existence, and therefore, of course, to the proper of *one's own* existence, only through an "expropriation"

whose exemplary reality is that of "my" face always exposed to others, always turned toward an other and faced by him or her, never facing myself. This is the archi-original impossibility of Narcissus that opens straight away onto the possibility of the political.[1]

Little did Nancy know, however, that his theories of politics had *already* been articulated—and thoroughly mocked—a century earlier in an American nation. In Machado de Assis's *Memórias póstumas de Brás Cubas* (1881), the titular narrator stops narrating at one point to contemplate the nose. Brás Cubas first considers mystical middle-eastern *fakirs*, who gain sight of the "celestial light" by focusing their eyes upon their own noses:

> When he sets his eye on the point of the nose, [the *fakir*] loses all sense of outside things, becomes enraptured with the invisible, learns the intangible, becomes detached from the world, dissolves, is aetherialized. That sublimation of the being by the tip of the nose is the most lofty phenomenon of the spirit, and the faculty for obtaining it doesn't belong to the *fakir* alone: it's universal. Every man has the need and power to contemplate his own nose with an aim to see the celestial light, and such contemplation, whose effect is the subordination of the universe to just one nose, constitutes the equilibrium of societies. If noses only contemplated each other, humankind wouldn't have lasted two centuries, it would have died out with the first tribes....
>
> The conclusion, therefore, is that there are two capital forces: love, which multiplies the species; and the nose, which subordinates it to the individual. Procreation, equilibrium.[2]

Cubas's terms are more or less those of Nancy. When the individual becomes enraptured in his own being, being-in-common through sexual intercourse is quite impossible; and if noses only became enraptured with one another, individuals would pay no mind to other parts of their bodies. The individual has the immanent *right* to stare at his own nose, but doing so not only makes the individual cross-eyed, it also negates the possibility of copulation or community. The whole history of humanity for Cubas thus boils down to two bodily protuberances: the nose and the penis. Besides being phallocentric and sexist, this view is utterly narcissistic since the only two things that really matter to the narrator are *his own* nose and penis. All the same, the narrator's narcissism is tempered by the fact that he is already dead when he writes his memoirs. In other words, we are always to understand his words—the ridiculous philosophizings of a corpse—as utterly *silly*, a frothiness that allows one to see past narcissism by means of its own parody.

In this sense, parodic *silliness* provides a means to surpass the "impossibility of Narcisssus." But does it also "open straight away onto the possibility of the political"? In other words, in what ways can we think through the political entity of the nation, and particularly Machado's Brazilian nation, as *silly*? This is no laughing matter I assure you. In the preface, I *did* mention Brazilian nationalism by way of a joke: "O Brasil é o país do futuro...e sempre será." But to my credit, this was followed in chapter 1 by a reading of the U.S.-American nation as *dependent* upon Brazilian readings of the nation. I characterized (at least in part) the ways William Carlos Williams *exposed himself* to a community: In objectifying an American language, Williams ultimately shows how the objectification of the masses as "U.S.-American" depends upon the objectification of other individuals. Yet throughout these multiple levels of objectification Williams does not totally endorse objectivity as political platform for the nation, but rather lays bare how the differences between individuals, ethnicities, genders, and typographies remain continually non-conciliated. In order to understand the United States as a nation/community in this (paradoxical) way, we therefore had to turn to another ("an Other") nation/community, Brazil, via Oswald de Andrade and Fernando Henrique Cardoso.

Yet in turn, the question of the Brazilian nation is particularly vexing, not quite constituted. Of course, *no* nation is ever totally, absolutely constituted as a thing in itself, except in the ideologies of those who seek dominance. Nonetheless Brazil does not fit into a "typical" pattern of American independence, insofar as Brazilian independence did not result from a protracted armed conflict against an empire, but rather occurred by imperial decree.[3] While the rest of America nation-states were busy struggling to dismantle monarchies, Brazil just as quickly established one. Of course, there were only two Brazilian emperors, both named Pedro, although the reign of Pedro II was positively Victorian in its duration (1831–1889). When the end of empire came in 1889 it came by a swift coup d'etat and a peaceful abdication, as the devoutly positivist Dom Pedro II felt the age of monarchies had ended and the age of bourgeois republics had just begun.

If the modern (bourgeois) nation-state begins, as Benedict Anderson claims, with the "imagined community," we will be pressed to find how Brazil conforms to the concept. To be sure, from 1822 onward there was a small, highly literate class of lettered-*crioulos* (Brazilian-born whites) who constituted a public sphere, both in terms of writing literature and running the affairs of state. Among this *letrado* class, concentrated primarily in Rio de Janeiro, the circulation of printed materials surely helped to construct a *Brazilian* imaginary. Yet it was also an extremely circumscribed class. The vast majority of the Brazilian populace throughout the nineteenth century was black slaves or indentured servants, many of whom continued to be "imported" from Africa well after the supposed end of the trans-Atlantic slave trade, and *all* of whom were officially powerless. Furthermore, literacy—and thus the very possibility of a print-based national imaginary—has always been quite low in Brazil. The Portuguese crown banned the printing press and the university in the colony, such that neither appeared in Brazil until after the transfer of the royal court to Rio de Janeiro.[4] According to the official census of 1920, Brazil had an illiteracy rate of some 75 percent even at that late date; official estimates suggest that illiteracy rates in the large cities were much lower, although we could extrapolate that illiteracy in São Paulo remained around 40 percent. Among those who could read at that time, it is doubtful that they would have had sufficient expendable income to buy books; the average white-collar wage for professions such as book-keepers would have been the equivalent of U.S.$22 per month, while casual laborers garnered a paltry U.S.$10 per month.[5] Perhaps no broad-based imagined community really emerged until after the positivist military officers and bourgeois oligarchs of the First Republic (1889–1930) had fallen into decadence by the 1920s, giving way to the populist dictatorship of Getúlio Vargas. And the "imagined community" under Vargas's Estado Novo was not circulated in print, but rather broadcast over radio, forging identifications with popular forms such as samba and Carnival.[6]

"Nation" may not have definitively emerged in Brazil until *modern* state efforts to shape the character of the Brazilian community in the twentieth century. Throughout the nineteenth century, the monarchical, quasi-feudal political-economic order did not necessitate such efforts. Until the end of empire, wealth and power were almost entirely based on sugar and cotton production, and to a lesser degree mining, all of which were slave-based economies. This meant that the plurality of Brazilians were "property" not "citizens." Given the clientalism of Brazilian politics, moreover, any truly democratic suffrage was subverted by the oligarchy's control over their rural subjects. The vast divergences between regions—political, economic, *and* cultural divergences—were sutured over only by the oligarchic elites' allegiance to the emperor, which may explain why Brazil did not splinter into separate countries as happened in the rest of Latin America. After 1889, however, the situation changed dramatically. Since government transformed (at least nominally) into a constitutional democracy, blacks suddenly became a potential power base, although there is little to suggest that their interests have ever been truly represented. Perhaps more significantly, as slave-based production centered in the Northeast declined, the wage-labor production of coffee ascended in the Southeast—first in Rio de Janeiro state and then São Paulo state. Wage-laborers were drawn not only from internal migrations from north to south, but to a greater extent from foreign immigrants from Italy, Poland, Iberia, Japan, and elsewhere.

All told, regional and ethnic cultural differences became much more complex by the start of the twentieth century—as the Northeast lost power, wealth, and people to the Southeast, and as the countryside lost power, wealth, and people to the cities. This eventually emerged as a political problem, as the state had to find means to overcome popular differences and consolidate a singular nation. Rather fortuitously, this occurred just as the country mechanized itself. Brazil's first rail lines were built to move coffee from the interior of São Paulo state to the coast. Profits from coffee and other agricultural products were reinvested into industrial manufacturing, primarily in São Paulo where a good number of educated immigrants had settled, and also in Rio and Porto Alegre. Much of this mechanization was financed by foreign interests, as was the case with the rail system (British) and the Canadian-owned São Paulo Light Co. Nevertheless, with increasing numbers of urban dwellers, it became possible to distribute radios rapidly and reach a mass audience, many of whom, remember, were illiterate. Vargas's various regimes, then, were the first to exploit new technologies politically, as both state-sponsored and private transmitters (who were nonetheless reliant on government favors for licensing and operation) began to broadcast popular "images" of the "Brazilian." For its part, print-based "high" literature also played a significant role in defining the "new" Brazil, particularly with the rise of *modernismo* in São Paulo.[7] In key respects, the *modernistas* of the 1920s prefigured certain cultural trends toward nationalism that would only come to fruition politically in the 1930s and 1940s. However, the "Brazilian community" did not truly emerge until "illiterate" aesthetic texts such as recorded/broadcast music and the proto-fascistic "mass ornament" of Carnival could be transmitted to the public by machines. As Tulio Halperín writes:

> ...Vargas eliminated all traces of partisan politics and introduced, for the first time in Latin America, mass propaganda and indoctrination of the style recently invented by European fascist states. Such tactics

were not required to protect the regime from political enemies who, in reality, no longer posed a threat. Instead, they aimed to create a central state powerful enough to carry out integrating functions at which the oligarchical republic had so egregiously failed.[8]

Yet it would be quite a mistake to think that "community" was totally contained and controlled by the state, as evidenced by the emergence of São Paulo as the economic and cultural center of the nation. It is impossible to imagine modernity in Brazil without São Paulo; indeed it is rather impossible to imagine São Paulo at all. Currently, São Paulo is the largest city in South America, the second-largest in the Americas, and the center of finance capital for most of Latin America. Its population hovers around 16 million, with perhaps 25 million in the greater metropolitan area. It is also a zone of unspeakable poverty, largely concentrated in the expansive Zona Leste (East Zone)—home to some 4 million residents, a quarter of whom are totally unemployed (i.e., not employed in either the formal or informal economies), and many of whom live without paved roads, running water, or proper sewage.[9] In this light, the sheer size and amorphousness of São Paulo do not suggest any sort of official control at all.

The history of the city only bears this out. Although founded in the sixteenth century by Jesuit missionaries, São Paulo remained something of a provincial backwater for much of its history until the coffee boom at the end of the nineteenth century. The correlative population growth of São Paulo is simply staggering: from 23,243 people in 1872, to 129,409 in 1893, to roughly 240,000 in 1900, 500,000 in 1917, to 1,000,000 in 1933—a rise in gross terms of some 4,350 percent in but 60 years.[10] Given the present population of 16 million, the aggregate growth of São Paulo is some 65,000 percent in 150 years. Such dramatic expansion after 1870 led to the creation of a fundamentally *shapeless* city. Once the original settlement of São Paulo—now called the *Centro Velho* [Old Center], around the Praça da Sé—became impacted, upper- and middle-class urbanization spread to the west and north, toward what is now called the *Centro Novo* or República, where São Paulo's city hall is now located. The rise of the bourgeois capitalist class financed the importation of French (and French-inspired) designers for public architectural projects, such as the beaux-artes Teatro Municipal (1911, a derivative of the Paris Opera) and the Anhangabaú Parks in the valley below the Teatro. Anhangabaú, in turn, would be crossed by a steel bridge (à la Eiffel), the Viaduto do Chá, built in 1892. In sum, the construction of the New Center served as a kind of "release valve" permitting high-end construction that fundamentally erased any cohesive sense of style. As Richard Morse writes:

> One of the most dramatic developments has been the progressive occupation of the high land by the *haute-bourgeoisie*: an advance after 1890 through Higienópolis up to Avenida Paulista on the crest, then down to the southwest slopes into the "Gardens" [the neighborhoods known as "Jardins"]. This movement, correlates with the rise of the tradition-less industrial-commercial elite. It is reflected architecturally in a shift from the modified fazenda-type dwellings of the coffee barons to the ostentatious hodgepodge of styles—including classical, Florentine, English, Near-Eastern, and neocolonial of Avenida Paulista.[11]

But beyond these rather tacky, *nouveau riche* importations of "high" yet traditionless style, São Paulo grew according to short-term economic exigencies that have contributed to a good amount of social chaos. Factories were built close to the Tietê and Pinheiros Rivers, and later near transportation ways, and poor immigrants to the city began to concentrate in slum dwellings close to these factories. Almost all of this construction (both commercial and residential) was unregulated since São Paulo lacked *any* official urban plan until 1930, by which time it was about to top 1 million people.[12] Adding to this confusion, the majority of residents were not Brazilian, or even Portuguese-speakers. As Morse writes in his biography of the city, "of the proletariat [ca. 1890], 75 to 85 percent were foreign"—a move spear-headed by "...the influx of Italians, who were by 1897 to outnumber Brazilians two to one in the capital."[13] In the space of a single lifetime, then, São Paulo moved from the economic periphery to economic dominance; it lost all trace of its previous architectural style; and it switched from a Lusophone city to an Italophone one—or shall we say, a multilingual one. Thus, it makes perfect sense for the historian Nicolau Sevcenko to state:

> In the end, São Paulo was not a city of blacks, nor of whites, nor of *mestiços*; not of foreigners nor of Brazilians; neither American, nor European, nor native; nor was it industrial, despite the growing volume of the factories, nor an agricultural emporium, despite the crucial importance of coffee; it was not tropical, nor subtropical; it wasn't even modern, yet it still didn't have much of past. This city that sprouted suddenly and inexplicably, like a colossal mushroom after the rain, was an enigma for its own inhabitants, perplexed, attempting to understand it as much as they could, while fighting to not be devoured.[14]

Clearly, the São Paulo of the 1920s was part of a *new* Brazil. But how were Brazilians to ascribe meaning to this new Brazil? Ironically, São Paulo's avant-garde *modernismo* emerged as a response to precisely this question. I say "ironically" ironically: on the one hand, in order to solidify a "new Brazilian" tradition, *modernistas* imported antihierarchical avant-garde tendencies from Europe oriented to the destruction of tradition; on the other hand, given the nature of the avant-garde of the time, the primary modes of *modernismo* were to be irony and parody. We will see all this most forcefully in Mário de Andrade's 1922 *Paulicéia desvairada*, widely considered the first great work of *modernista* literature. Returning to Nancy's differentiation of *being* and *being-in-common*, the particular problem of *Paulicéia desvairada* is how the individual poet (being) is to represent the collective space of São Paulo (being-in-common)—to contain the city aesthetically as a singular work of art. As the volume's title suggests, such containment will prove quite impossible. São Paulo (the "*Paulicéia*"[15]) exceeds the poet's rational capabilities, and instead becomes a delusional spectacle ("*desvairada*"). The result is *literally* schizophrenic, "double-headed," as São Paulo, and by extension Brazil, doubles over into a parody of itself. For our purposes, furthermore, we will have to come to terms with how Mário's work *induces* schizophrenia in the reader, in how the delusions of the literary texts "break containment" and spill over into reality. In order to understand this, we will have to contend with *Paulicéia desvairada* as a kind of "illiterature" ("ill literature"?). By this I mean that *Paulicéia desvairada*, though presenting itself *as literature*, nonetheless strives to unravel the social function of literature through a poetics based on the "subliterary" structures of sound and music—a poetics that will ultimately set our heads *ringing*.

Harmonics: A New Brazilian Poetics

By "subliterate" or "illiterate" I do not at all mean "unintelligent." Song-forms such as samba and forró, for instance, may have been created by illiterate people, but to think of either form's complex polyrhythms, melodies, lyrics, or dances as lacking intelligence would be ridiculous. Rather, by "subliterate" I merely refer to aesthetic modes that have traditionally been considered lower or less than literary. Music—at least popular music—usually falls under this definition, as it pertains to a lyrical "oral tradition" historically considered inferior to the written lyric. Even "high" orchestral music has been labeled "subliterary," however. In his *Aesthetics*, Hegel ranks music just below poetry in its proximity to Spirit, music not being quite as sublime as poetry. In terms more prescient to an "underdeveloped" nation such as Brazil, subliteracy may nonetheless carry strong connotations of "uneducated" and "uncivilized," and indeed it is precisely these connotations that became so attractive to the emergent *modernistas* of the 1920s. Anita Malfatti's primitivist paintings or Oswald de Andrade's poems and manifestoes "return" to Tupi-Guarani natives as a means to counter Eurocentric civilization—providing a shock to the educated *letrado* sensibilities, in order to "uneducate" them of Eurocentrism by means of native intelligence. And in due course the literate intelligentsia reacted against such primitivism by rejecting any notion that the Tupi-Guarani figure could be superior; certainly this was the case with the Verde Amarelo group who opposed itself to Oswald's *antropofagismo* by stating, "The Tupis came down to be absorbed, to dilute their blood in the new population."[16]

In Mário de Andrade's work, the subliterate subject is not so important as a symbolic figure of Brazilian-ness as is the actual *practice* of subliteracy, often as a musical or poetic performance. This is evident in Mário's performance at the opening salvo of *modernismo*. Unlike most avant-garde movements worldwide, Brazilian *modernismo* has a definitive starting point: the *Semana de Arte Moderna* (Modern Art Week) organized by Graça Aranha, Di Cavalcanti, Oswald de Andrade, and others in São Paulo's Teatro Municipal in February 1922. Consisting of art exhibitions, musical performances, and literary readings, the *Semana de Arte Moderna* announced not only the new art but also São Paulo as Brazil's new cultural capital. For his part, Mário declaimed poems from his soon-to-be published *Paulicéia desvairada*, including "Ode ao burguês":

> Eu insulto o burguês! O burguês níquel!
> O burguês-burguês!
> A digestão bem feita de São Paulo!
> O homem-curva! o homem-nádegas!
> O homem sendo francês, brasileiro, italiano,
> É sempre um cauteloso pouco-a-pouco!
>
> Eu insulto as aristocracias cautelosas!
> Os barões lampeões! os condes Joões! os duques zurros!
> Que vivem dentro de muros sem pulos;
> E gemem sangues de alguns milréis fracos
> Para dizerem que as filhas da senhora falam o francês
> E tocam o *Printemps* com as unhas! (PD 88)

> [I insult the bourgeois! The nickel-bourgeois!
> The bourgeois-bourgeois!
> The well-done digestion of São Paulo!
> The curve-man! the asscheek-man!
> The man who being French, Brazilian, Italian,
> Is always a cautious little bit-by-bit!
>
> I insult the cautious aristocracies!
> The lantern-barons! the Counts João's! the braying dukes!
> That live within walls without jumps;
> And howl bloody hell for a few weak bucks
> So as to say that the daughters of the lady can speak French
> And play the *Printemps* with their fingertips!][17]

According to lore, Mário was booed off the stage by the audience after reading this rant, although this appears to be more legend than fact. What *is* clear is that Mário's "Ode"[18] veers sharply from the normative etiquette of lyrical poetry, both formally in its lack of melodiousness and substantively in its blatant attack on those who consume the *beaux-artes* and understand nothing of them.

Yet Mário's performance of the "Ode," taken historically, opens whole other political and economic registers of subliteracy. Shortly after the *Semana de Arte Moderna*, Mário would lose his position as a piano teacher at the Conservatório de São Paulo (where he was hired in January 1922) and he spent most of 1922 in financial duress. Here it is absolutely essential to consider the socioeconomic status of the author. In concrete terms, Mário was professionally and financially beholden to the bourgeois families who sent him their daughters to learn music, such as the *Printemps*. Mário literally bit the hands that fed him by reading his poetry at the Teatro Municipal. Unsurprisingly, these "asscheek-bourgeoisie" stopped sending their daughters (and money) to Mário after the event.[19] But this is only an index to a larger set of issues. As a piano teacher—and also as a mulatto[20] and (closeted) homosexual—Mário did not pertain to the traditional class of *crioulos-letrados*, who historically have been white, wealthy landed oligarchs such as Oswald de Andrade. Benedito Nunes confirms this: "While his generational companions came, in large part, from the Faculties of Law, Mário de Andrade had, as a title in advanced studies, one course in piano at the Conservatório de São Paulo, which gave him the unusual condition for the epoch of musicologist, *avis rara* among graduates emerging from Juridical Letters."[21] Extrapolating from Nunes's observations we might say that music was *inferior* to poetry, in that the piano teacher usually lacks the time and disposable income of a lawyer, politician, or *fazendeiro* to dedicate his life to letters. This is central to our present purposes insofar as the poetry of *Paulicéia desvairada* is based almost entirely on novel theories of harmonic structure that govern any and all readings of the work.

Paulicéia desvairada is somewhat strange in that it not only contains short lyrical poems, but also an interpretative guide to reading in manifesto form. *Paulicéia desvairada* is downright *silly*, furthermore, in that it contains not one, but *two* manifestoes which bookend its 21 lyrics. The first of these, the "Prefácio interessantíssimo" ["Very Interesting Preface"], is an exercise in self-effrontery. Like all good avant-garde manifestoes, the "Prefácio" begins by announcing the creation of a new school of art, "*Desvairismo*" or "Delusionism"; but it ends by calling for the dissolution of "Delusionism" stating: "E está acabada a escola poética. 'Desvairismo.' / Próximo livro fundarei outra. / E não quero discipulos. Em arte: escola = imbecilidade de muitos para vaidade dum só" (PD 77). ["And the poetic school is now finished. 'Delusionism.' / Next book I'll start another. / And I don't want disciples. In art: school = imbecility of many for the vanity of one alone."] In calling for a "new" poetry and art, Mário likewise rejects any characterization of his work as "futurist" or "avant-garde." Instead, he retreats (apparently) into impressionism, or what he calls "passadismo" ["past-ism"]. Not for nothing, then, does the second line of the manifesto read, "Este prefácio, apesar de interessante, inútil" (PD 59). ["This preface, although interesting, useless"] This deliberately ironic, *silly* posturing should be taken as somewhat defensive in that Mário positions himself above the *crioulo-letrado* politics of founding aesthetic schools and literary circles. Mário's clear intent is not to move from one form of poetry to another, and certainly not from one poetic school to another. Rather, with the "Prefácio" he is attempting to overthrow the entire class structure of "high" poetry. He accomplishes this (or at least strives to) by subordinating poetry to music. Mário finds poetry to be much less advanced historically, more "underdeveloped," than music:

> Sei construir teorias engenhosas. Quer ver? A poética está muito mais atrasada que a música. Esta abandonou, talvez mesmo antes do século 8, o regime da melodia quando muito oitavada, para enriquecer-se com os infinitos recursos da harmonia. A poética, com rara exceção até meados do século 19 francês, foi essencialmente melódica. (PD 68)
>
> [I know how to construct ingenious theories. Wanna see? Poetics is much more backwards than music. Music abandoned, even perhaps before the eighth century, the regimen of melody when overly octavated,

in order to enrich itself with the infinite resources of harmony. Poetics, with rare exceptions until the nineteenth century in France, was essentially melodic.]

With its "backwards" dependence on melody, poetics can only be univocal, similar to the way Mikhail Bakhtin—writing several years later in "Discourse in the Novel"—would characterize poetry as "monologic" in distinction to the novel's "heteroglossia." In contrast, music had already dumped univocal melody a millennium ago, opening up the polyphony of multivocal harmony. Thus, the subliterate art form is not at all "primitive," but rather "super-literate," superior to literature.

With this historical distinction in place, Mário then proceeds to define and expand upon the differences between melody and harmony, which I quote at length:

> Chamo de verso melódico o mesmo que melodia musical: arabesco horizontal de vozes (sons) consecutivas, contendo pensamento inteligível. Ora, si em vez de unicamente usar versos melódicos horizontais:
>
> "Mnezarete, a divina, a pálida Phrynea
> Comparece ante a austera e rígida assemblea
> Do Areópago supremo...."
>
> fizermos que se sigam palavras sem ligação imediata entre si: estas palavras, pelo fato mesmo de se não seguirem intelectual, gramaticalmente, se sobrepõem umas às outras, para a nossa sensação, formando, não mais melodias, mas harmonias.
>
> Explico milhor:
>
> Harmonia: combinação de sons simultâneos.
>
> Exemplo:
>
> "Arroubos...Lutas...Seta...Cantigas...Povoar!"
>
> Estas palavras não se ligam. Não formam enumeração. Cada uma é frase, período elíptico, reduzido ao mímimo telegráfico.
>
> Si pronuncio "Arroubos," como não faz parte de frase (melodia), a palavra chama a atenção para seu insulamento e fica vibrando, à espera duma frase que lhe faça adquirir significado e QUE NÃO VEM. "Lutas" não dá conclusão alguma a "Arroubos"; e, nas mesmas condições, não fazendo esquecer a primeira palavra, fica vibrando com ela. As outras vozes fazem o mesmo. Assim: em vez de melodia (frase gramatical) temos acorde arpejado, harmonia—o verso harmônico.
>
> Mas, si em vez de usar só palavras soltas, uso frases soltas: mesma sensação de superposição, não já de palavras (notas) mas de frases (melodias). Portanto: polifonia poética.

Assim, em *Paulicéia desvairada* usam-se o verso melódico:

"São Paulo é um palco de bailados russos"; o verso harmônico:

"A cainçalha...A Bolsa...As jogatinas..."; e a polifonia poética (um e às vezes dois e mesmo mais versos consecutivos):

"A engrenagem trepida...A bruma neva..."

Que tal? Não se esqueça porém que outro virá destruir tudo isso que construi. (PD 68–69)

[I call melodic verse the same as musical melody: horizontal arabesque of consecutive voices (sounds), containing intelligible thought.

Now, if instead of only using melodic horizontal verses:

"Mnezarete, the divine, the pallid Phrynea

Appears before the austere and rigid assembly

Of Areopagus supreme..."

we had it that words without immediate connection would follow: these words, by the very fact that they do not follow intellectually, grammatically, are superimposed one upon the others, for our sensation, forming, no longer melodies, but harmonies.

I will explain better:

Harmony: combination of simultaneous sounds.

Example:

"Ecstasies...Fights...Arrow...Ballads...To populate!"

These words are not connected. They do not form an enumeration. Each one is a phrase, period ellipses, reduced to the telegraphic minimum.

If I pronounce "Ecstasies," as it does not form part of a phrase (melody), the word calls attention to its own insulation and stays vibrating, waiting for a phrase that would give it meaning and THAT DOES NOT ARRIVE. "Fights" does not provide any conclusion whatsoever to "Ecstasies"; and, in the same conditions, not forgetting the first word, remains vibrating with this word. The other voices do the same. Thus: instead of melody (grammatical phrase) we have an arpeggiated chord, harmony—the harmonic verse.

Yet, if instead of using only lone words, I use lone phrases: the same sensation of superposition, now not of words (notes) but of phrases (melodies). Therefore: poetic polyphony.

Thus, *Paulicéia desvairada* uses the melodic verse:

"São Paulo is a stage of Russian dances"; or harmonic verse:

"The dogpack...The Market...The wagers..."; and poetic polyphony (one and sometimes two or even more consecutive verses):

"The fearful gear...The dusty snow..."

How about it? Do not forget however that another will come to destroy everything that I have constructed.]

For Mário, words and phrases are not sufficient unto themselves, but rather depend upon the other words around them for their vital force, their resonance. It bears casual notice here how closely his conception of words therefore resembles several more-or-less contemporary theories of language of which he could not have known in 1921: Saussure's structural theories of syntagmatic and paradigmatic selection, in which one sign always stands in differential relation to all others in the system; and Bakhtin's conception of the socio-ideological word that shoots through the language-system like a ray of light that "weaves in and out of complex interrelationships, merges with some, recoils from others, intersects with yet a third group: all this may crucially shape discourse, may leave a trace in all its semantic layers, may complicate its expression and influence its entire stylistic profile."[22] Mário's invention is to frame similar ideas in terms of harmonic *simultaneity* in which the structural differences between words are exploited aesthetically—word layered upon word to create peculiar phonic and semantic vibrations. "Harmonic verse" or "poetic polyphony" would expand the possibilities of normative language and poetry by adding multiple concurrent dimensions of semantic range. To a certain extent it would test the reader's linguistic proficiency by utilizing odd syntactic arrangements of words and phrases in a way that disrupts conventional grammatical patterns of subject-verb-object—grammar that has served to lock linguistic phrases into a more unidimensional melodic regime. At the same time, harmonic verse would maximize the associational semantic conventions of the linguistic sign; Mário's theories emphasize the power of the signified mental image represented by conventional word-forms on the page, and the power of the psyche to superimpose disparate signifieds into some sort of collective, unified image.

It bears noting in this light that Mário's theories are really nothing new. Indeed, Mário cites both Victor Hugo and Olavo Bilac as precursors to this kind of poetic harmony; and one need only think of Stéphane Mallarmé (also cited in the "Prefácio"), especially "Un Coup de Dés" with its graphic dispositions of different typefaces, as being in a similar vein of harmonic verse. Mário has simply formalized these precedents into a novel theory. However, what distinguishes Mário's theories as a *modern* poetics in distinction to these precursors is the poet's attention to dissonance as a form of harmony. In other words, "harmony" here is not limited to "euphony," but is merely the juxtaposition of sound frequencies, a type of atonality. Mário's sense of poetic harmony rests on the abrupt—even *violent*—movement from one word or phrase to the next word or phrase.

In this sense, "harmony" is a decidedly physical activity (a physical violence?) since, in contradistinction to mere "juxtaposition," any notion of harmony ultimately emerges from the mutual reinforcement of sound waves made by the compression of air.

By the same token, however, the particular problem of such a theory is that the harmonies presented on the page—such as "Arroubos...Lutas...Setas...Cantiga...Povoar"—are *on the page* and therefore *not spoken* physically. Harmony, when applied to (printed) language, thus appears to be a *psychological* effect of multiplied thought-patterns, rather than a tactile effect (as in music) of mutually reinforced sound waves, and herein lies a significant problem tacitly addressed by Mário's theorization. Harmony cannot be directly translated from music to poetry since the two media are fundamentally different, both conceptually and physically. The mere superimposition of sound-patterns would not be sufficient to create poetic harmony or polyphony, since the fundamental aspect of language (and linguistic sound-patterns) is *meaning*: the psychological-semantic association of sound and thought-image. Moreover, the materiality of "modern" poetry as opposed to music (the physical parameters of the printed page, as opposed to sonic frequencies) would not seem to permit the types of superimposition called for in Mário's harmonic verse. In print, harmonic superimposition could not be achieved by merely printing one word on top of others; rather, words *need* to be arranged consecutively (not simultaneously) in order to be understood. Mário attempts to solve this problem by use of ellipses ("...")—punctuation marks that cannot actually be spoken, but that nevertheless signal the presence of multivoiced harmony.

Mário thus quite overtly positions printed poetry as incomplete. On the one hand, in harmonic verse the word vibrates only to the extent that it "wait[s] for a phrase that would give it meaning and THAT DOES NOT ARRIVE"; vibration between words occurs when two words/phrases that *should not be conjoined* suddenly are. On the other hand, because words can only be printed in succession, the simultaneous harmonization of words cannot be achieved on the page itself, but only in the mind of the reader. Harmonic verse is necessarily *psychological* as words are reduced to a "telegraphic minimum," before being transmitted into nonphysical impressions for the reader. It is in this sense that Mário refers to his own work as "impressionistic." Indeed, harmonic verse shares key traits with nineteenth-century notions of the mind and poetic inspiration. For Mário, all lyricism stems from libidinal urges of the subconscious, similar to the ways that the Symbolists—and earlier Romanticists for that matter—began to plumb the *stürm und drang* of subjective experience to find "pure" poetry. The abrupt, fragmented movements of harmonic verse are therefore appropriate means of expressing the fundamental violence of all lyricism. The problem here is that Mário is not living in the nineteenth century in which subjective experience might be potentially "unified" by poetry. *Ironically*, harmonic verse requires a poetic "Eu" (a poetic "I") to order the fragments of words and phrases into a phonic-semantic harmony, yet this "Eu" is never framed in *Paulicéia desvairada* as a singular first-person, but is always thoroughly fragmented.

Much of the "Prefácio" stands as a testament to the author's own subjective position, as Mário plays with the fragmentation of the "Eu." The author constantly and consistently asserts his own ego by speaking directly to the reader in the first person, and he theorizes the position of his own subjectivity within the process of creating verses and theories. He states, for instance:

> Todo escritor acredita na valia do que escreve. Si mostra é por vaidade. Si não mostra é por vaidade também.
>
> *
>
> Não fujo do ridículo. Tenho companheiros ilustres.
>
> *
>
> O ridículo é muitas vezes subjetivo. Independe do maior ou menor alvo de que o sofre.
>
> Criamô-lo para vestir com ele o que fere nosso orgulho, ignorância, esterilidade. (PD 62–63)
>
> [Every author believes in the value of what he writes. If he shows it, it is out of vanity. If he does not show it, it is out of vanity as well.
>
> *
>
> I do not run from the ridiculous. I have illustrious companions.
>
> *
>
> The ridiculous is oftentimes subjective. It does not depend upon the greater or lesser target of he who suffers it.
>
> We create it in order to dress it with that which damages our pride, ignorance, sterility.]

Here the author *does* speak in the first person as a unified speaking-subject to proclaim the vanity he has infused into his work. As a unique "Eu," he does not shy away from painful ridiculousness or irony. Rather he conceptualizes the ridiculous (the *silly*, if you will) as a means of projecting oneself, as projecting one's own "pride, ignorance, and sterility" out onto the pain and suffering of the person being ridiculed. The author thus clearly conceptualizes poetry as a projection of the subjective self, replete with the subject's unconscious strategies for avoiding pain and displeasure. Poetry and poetic theorization, in other words, appears a means of asserting the self in totalizing ways, as both the conscious *and* unconscious self. The poet states, "Prefácio: rojão do meu eu superior. Versos: paisagem do meu eu profundo" (PD 74). ["Preface: firecracker of my Superego. Verses: landscape of my Id."] Furthermore, poetry (or poetic publication) promotes and completes the search for one's own self:

> Por muitos anos procurei-me a mim mesmo. Achei. Agora não me digam que ando à procura de originalidade, porque já descobri onde ela estava, pertence-me, é minha. (PD 75)
>
> [For many years I searched for my self. I found it. Now they cannot tell me that I walk around in search of originality, because I have already discovered where it rests, it belongs to me, it's mine.]

"Originality" is an immanent force of the individual that Mário "discovers" through poetic creation; as such, "originality" shields him from those critics (the unnamed "they," presumably the arts community of São Paulo and Brazil) who would attack him. The individual stands in stark, even antagonistic, relationship to the community at large.

This is all well and good, except that throughout the "Prefácio" we *do not* always witness Mário de Andrade speaking for himself. To the contrary we witness the poet's near-obsessive compulsion to incorporate others into his thought via obsessive quotation. The author incorporates direct citations from Epstein, Shakespeare, Musset, Renan, Wagner, Fock, and other anonymous sources in Portuguese, Italian, and French; he also alludes to Watteau, St. John the Evangelist, Walt Whitman, Mallarmé, Verhaeren, Marinetti, Hugo, Virgil, Homer, Gourmont, and Cocteau, among others. The preponderance of external voices serves to defer the author's own sense of originality to the originality of outside sources. The subjective-self in this sense is not only the subject who speaks, but also a subject who finds himself through intersubjective relations accreting into a "multiple self." As the critic João Luiz Lafetá states:

> The fact is that, if Mário de Andrade's poetry constitutes an exploration of his "I" and, as Álvaro Lins affirms, tells the story "of a multiplied man who seeks to encounter himself" (and this would explain the text's plurality of themes and techniques), it constitutes as well an

attempt to explore the multiplicity of Brazilian culture and to relate the history of an intellectual looking to find the identity of his country (and this explains better the social determinations of plurality). The movement is simultaneous and solid: the search for national identity...attaches itself "to the more intimate problem of the discovery of *one's own* identity."[23]

The "multiple self" is therefore thoroughly ironicized. That is, the "self" in the "Prefácio interessantíssimo" speaks to a question of national identity, but does so from a subject-position of solitude—unity, but also solitary confinement. Indeed the piece ends with an allusion to citation and imprisonment: "I could have cited Gorch Fock. I would have avoided the Prefácio interessantíssimo. 'Every song of freedom comes from prison'" (PD 77). Yet by the very act of citation and quoting, the "self" in question strives to disburse itself into a *community*, or nation, of other selves. Or better yet, the "Eu" thinks itself to be a "Nós," a "We"—as an "Eu" speaking through the voices of other (mostly dead) authors whom "Eu" has read, but whom he has not actually met.

This irony doubles back into the work printed on the page itself. The poet quite consciously begins by stating he *knows* how to create very ingenious theories, but in the context of a manifesto that proclaims itself "useless" *we know* that his theories are a joke. Mário presents the psychologistic theory of lyricism just mentioned, for instance, by means of an incredibly *silly* allegory:

> Dom Lirismo, ao desembarcar do Eldorado do Inconsciente, no cais da terra do Consciente, é inspeccionado pela visita médica, a Inteligência, que o alimpa dos macaquinhos e de toda e qualquer doença que possa espalhar confusão, obscuridade na terrinha progressista. Dom Lirismo sofre mais uma visita alfandegária, descoberta por Freud, que a denominou Censura. Sou contrabandista! E contrário à lei da vacina obrigatória! (PD 73)

> [Sir Lyricism, upon disembarking from the Eldorado of the Unconscious, upon the shores of the Conscious, is inspected by the attending physician, the Intelligence, who cleanses him of all the little monkeys and each and every illness that sprouts confusion and darkness in this little land of progress. Sir Lyricism suffers one more customs inspection, discovered by Freud, who called it Censure. I'm a smuggler! And against the law of obligatory vaccination!]

Through irony and humor (why the "law of obligatory vaccination"?) the author does not afford his own work, nor any reader who pretends to take it seriously, any measure of seriousness at all. As a result the whole project becomes a double of itself. Mário's theories *are* serious to the extent that they provide an innovative poetic practice that expands the possibilities of the medium; indeed Mário himself utilizes his own harmonic verse throughout the lyrical poems immediately following the "Prefácio interessantíssimo." *At the same time*, however, Mário's theories are exercises in *silliness*, such that the "Prefácio interessantíssimo" necessarily resonates against the oh-so-serious avant-garde manifestoes and theorizations it systematically dismantles through parody. Thus, we can begin to see the "Prefácio" as double-headed, at once a manifesto in its own right, and a manifesto that is not complete unto itself unless it vibrates against other texts in its historical milieu. If this is the case, then the multivocal harmonizations effectuated in the mind of the reader reading harmonic verse amount to nothing less than multiple voices inside one's head. Mário hears voices, and I who read Mário hear myself hear the voices Mário hears in his head. The only psychology of Delusionism is, unsurprisingly, insane delusion.

The Performance of Two São Paulos

If it is psychological, harmonic verse is only ever *social psychological*. By alluding to the "law of obligatory vaccination," for instance, Mário opens his "delusionist" harmony to broader social questions. Given the nation's location in the tropics, epidemiology has long been central to conceptions of Brazilian national culture. Machado de Assis's work, for instance, is littered with characters who succumb to small pox, or whose faces are scarred by pox marks. Likewise, Gilberto Freyre's masterwork *Casa-grande e senzala*—the first modern anthropological account of Brazilian ethnicities—contains countless descriptions of widespread syphilis and gonorrhea, as if the Brazilian subject were born in a pool of sexually transmitted diseases: "They say that civilization and syphillization go hand-in-hand: Brazil, however, appears to have syphillized before it had civilized."[24] Whether or not this is true, hygiene and public health became increasingly powerful, and increasingly problematic, preoccupations of the state and the ruling elite. Not for nothing was one of the first upper-class suburban developments beyond São Paulo's *centro velho* named "Higienópolis"— the city of hygiene. All the same, official efforts to mandate vaccinations among the population at large were often met by public resistance—at times *armed* resistance as was the case with Antônio Conselheiro and the Canudos uprising (depicted in such exhaustive detail in Euclides da Cunha's *Os sertões*) who fought to protect God's kingdom from the state's imposition of the metric system and obligatory vaccination. But of course, Mário is making a direct reference to the *Lei da Vacina Obrigatória* passed by Brazil's National Congress in 1904. This law allowed public-health workers to enter private homes uninvited (with the aid of the police) to vaccinate residents by force if necessary, or to destroy homes deemed to be public-health risks. Rio's reactionary and inflammatory press responded by calling all vaccines dangerous, often because vaccines would allegedly need to be administered to the private parts of women. A popular *Liga Contra a Vacina Obrigatória* (League against Obligatory Vaccination) was quickly formed in Rio de Janeiro, whose actions led to a mass violent uprising now known as the "*Revolta da Vacina*" in which large sections of the city burned from November 10 to November 16, 1904 (with some 30 people killed), and which in turn led to the subsequent imposition of martial law. In short, public health in Brazil has often resulted in public chaos, public inferno, and public death.

Mário's work does not make the situation appear any less ridiculous. The second of *Paulicéia desvairada*'s two manifestoes, "As enfibraturas do Ipiranga," represents a *public* display of the subjective/psychological/demented harmonic theories of the "Prefácio interessantíssimo." If *Paulicéia desvairada* opens with a theory of harmonic verse in the "Prefácio," the "Enfibraturas do Ipiranga" with which it closes represents the performance of said theories, dramatizing linguistic and psychological dissonance that *Paulicéia desvairada* takes as its point of departure. For this reason, Vicky Unruh has correctly termed the latter piece a "performance manifesto":

> [V]anguardist writers produced manifesto-style creative texts that simultaneously built on the manifesto's performative qualities and developed the narrative seeds that it enclosed. The hybrid creative texts that I call performance manifestos prescribe for concrete public display the new aesthetic relationships and practices espoused in the more straight-forward manifestos.... These works enact the stories of adversarial encounters between conflicting views of culture and art, and while the manifesto incorporates the spectator into its communicative scheme, the performance manifesto recasts the spectator as a character in its story. Not surprisingly, one can often discern explicit connections between these creative works and the authors' more expository writings on art. Generally, however, these performative texts are artistically richer than the average manifesto, and, resisting strict formal or generic classification, they frequently combine poetry, music, dance, narrative, or ritual display. The purpose of these

multimedia performances is to spin a palpable tale of cultural encounter that enacts, through metaperformative strategies and metaphors, specific artistic views. In Latin America, moreover, these ostensibly antimimetic works are strikingly culturally specific and make reference to the specific national historical contexts within which modern artistic activity was to emerge.[25]

"As enfibraturas do Ipiranga" encapsulates all these tendencies outlined by Unruh. The text is site-specific and culturally specific, grounded (literally) in São Paulo and *paulistana* sociocultural divisions, in order to mobilize a nationalistic consolidation of "new" Brazilian culture. It also marks a literary-historical rupture from (what it perceives as) a decadent, outmoded, and elitist traditionalism, to a modern and moder*nist* aesthetic geared to the reevaluation of Brazilian culture on its own terms.[26] And lastly, the piece achieves all of this through the "multimedia" mixing of poetry, music, and dramatic staging.

"As enfibraturas do Ipiranga" is not, however, a manifesto in itself, which is why Unruh correctly emphasizes its performative nature. Rather, the piece labels itself a "Profane Oratorio," to be sung by five distinct voices/choruses, each of whom carry rather ridiculous names:

OS ORIENTALISMOS CONVENCIONAIS—(escritores e demais artificies elogiáveis)—Largo, imponente coro afinadíssimo de sopranos, contraltos, barítonos, baixos.

AS SENECTUDES TREMULINAS—(milionários e burgueses)—Coro de sopranistas.

OS SANDAPILÁRIOS INDIFERENTES—(operariado, gente pobre)—Barítonos e baixos.

AS JUVENILIDADES AURIVERDES—(nós)—Tenores, sempre tenores! Que o diga Walter von Stolzing!

MINHA LOUCURA—Soprano ligeiro. Solista. (PD 103)

[THE CONVENTIONAL ORIENTALISMS—(writers and too many laudable artifices)—Large, imposing, and very well-tuned chorus of sopranos, contraltos, baritones, and bassos.

THE TREMULOUS SENECTUDES—(millionaires and bourgeoisie)—Chorus of sopranos.

THE INDIFFERENT SANDAPILLARIES—(workers, poor people)—Baritones and bassos.

THE GOLDENGREEN JUVENILITIES—(us)—Tenors, always tenors! No matter what Walter von Stolzing says!

MY MADNESS—Light soprano. Soloist.]

The author uses operatic, dramatic, and musical staging to subvert and critique a range of social and cultural divisions in the city. The Orientalismos Convencionais, for example, unmistakably allude to the small cliques of *literati* in Brazil's major cities—formalized as a national institution by the *Academia Brasileira de Letras*—who tended to enforce strict standards of "civilized" culture modeled exclusively on European trends; it is precisely such groups that are the immediate target of *Paulicéia desvairada* and *modernista* movements in general.[27] The name Mário attaches to them, for instance, serves to reverse power-positions of traditional/modern and colonizer/colonized: since Europe is in reality located to the *orient* of Brazil, the name renders the Eurocentric ideal enshrined by such writers as an exotic commodity. Yet even if they are "orientalists" in this way, the Orientalismos are utterly conventional, singing mostly in thoroughly redundant rhymes:

>Somos os Orientalismos Convencionais!
>Os alicerces não devem cair mais!
>Nada de subidas ou de verticais!
>Amamos as chatezas horizontais!
>Abatemos perobas de ramos desiguais!
>Odiamos as matinadas arlequinais!
>Viva a Limpeza Pública e os hábitos morais!
>Somos os Orientalismos Convencionais! (PD 106)

>[We are the Orientalisms Conventional!
>The foundations any more must not fall!
>Nothing of risings or of verticals!
>We love the boredoms horizontal!
>We cut down trees of branches unequal!
>We hate the sunrises harlequinal!
>Long live Public Health and habits moral!
>We are the Orientalisms Conventional!]

Similarly, the Senectudes Tremulinas—the rich, senile, and palsied men who support the Orientalismos at every turn—sing in an entirely clumsy "minuet tempo":

>Só admiramos os célebres
>E os recomendados também!
>Quem tem galeria
>Terá um Bouguereau!
>. . . . .
>Preferimos os coros

Dos Oriental-
ismos Convencionais.... (PD 107)

[We only admire celebrities
And also the recommended!
He who has a gallery
Must have a Bouguereau!
....
We prefer the choruses
Of the Oriental-
ismos Convencionais...]

The tastes of the Senectudes Tremulinas are only defined by the celebrities they are told to collect, such as the French Parnassian/Academic painter William-Adolfe Bouguereau. By maintaining their strict minuet cadence, the Senectudes trip rather stupidly even in enunciating their preferred cultural group, the "Oriental-" and then "-ismos." Yet Mário's venom is not reserved only for the rich. The poor, working-class Sandpilários Indiferentes are literally characterized as idiots. As Benedito Nunes has shown, "The noun *sandeu* ["idiot"], plus the verb *pilar* (to grind or crush), with the suffix *–ário*, gives the pejorative *Sandapilário* (those idiots who grind and regrind stupidities)."[28] The disrespect is compounded by the fact that the Sandapilários are only given five lines of dialogue at the beginning of the piece, and remain dumb thereafter.

Against these negative types, the Juvenilidades Auriverdes serve (or rather, should serve) as heroes of the oratorio. Wrapped in the gold and green colors (*ouro* and *verde*) of the Brazilian flag (see figure 2.3), the Juvenilidades Auriverdes are clearly identified as "we"—that is, the youthful *modernistas* with whom the author has joined. Here, then, Mário is setting forth a new concept of a national voice, an imagined community of "nós"/"we" who are promoting the new, modern nation. All of this is bolstered by the fact that the Juvenilidades Auriverdes are to be buried up to their knees in the soil of the Anhangabaú parks, in the soil of the nation, in a musical piece that is to be performed at "The Dawn of the New Day" (PD 104) heralding the coming of the modern age. Yet paradoxically, this "Nós" of the Juvenilidades Auriverdes is differentiated from an "Eu." The final voice listed in the distribution of voices is the only soloist in "As enfibraturas do Ipiranga," *Minha* Loucura (or *My* Madness), who flits about the Juvenilidades Auriverdes but never actually joins them. In this way, "As enfibraturas" is marked by an impossible subjective stance: the first-person singular "Eu" is *not* grouped into the first-person plural "Nós," so that we have two first-persons in dialogue with one another—a "two-headed" first-person. And in this sense, we must also note that with "My Madness" Mário de Andrade self-identifies as a fairy who sings in a register (soprano) reserved only for females. In other words, the author fashions a cross-gendered, and perhaps homoerotic or autoerotic, fantasy of himself—a fantasy that he himself labels mentally ill, deviant, and even perverse. This labeling is echoed in the final lines sung by Minha Loucura, with which "As enfibraturas" closes: "Eu... os desertos... os Caíns... a maldição" (PD 115). ["I... the deserts... the Cains... the damnation"]—a verse that harmonizes "I" with the immoral, hell-worthy perdition of "deserts," the Biblical "Cain," and "damnation."

All told, the distribution of voices unifies distinct harmonic range (tenor, soprano, baritone, contralto, basso) and distinct socioeconomic classes, with the sociocultural modernization of the nation. But by the same token we should not be fooled by words such as "unifies" and "harmony," for "As enfibraturas do Ipiranga" amounts to little more than a shouting match between dissonant choruses who despise one another, bark at one another, and refuse to communicate. As I mentioned, for instance, the Sandapilários Indiferentes sing only once:

> Vá de rumor! Vá de rumor!
> Esta gente não nos deixa mais dormir!
> Antes "E lucevan le stelle" de Puccini!
> Oh! pé de anjo, pé de anjo!
> Fora! Fora o que é de despertar! (PD 105)
>
> [Enough of this noise! Enough of this noise!
> These people don't let us sleep!
> Before Puccini's "E lucevan le stelle"!
> Oh! foot of the angel, foot of the angel!
> Away! Away from that which is to awake!]

The reference to Pucini could indicate that they are Italian (not quite Lusophone), and therefore distanced culturally from the rest. In any case when the working class does finally open its mouth, it is only to tell the others to shut up so they can sleep.

In reality, though, "As enfibraturas" is a fight between the Orientalismos Convencionais who sing from the balconies and windows of the Teatro Municipal, and the Juvenilidades Auriverdes who are literally set into the valley below Teatro Municipal in the grounds of the Anhangabaú Parks. As the Juvenilidades push for aesthetic and cultural change, the Orientalismos resist them. The *modernista* youth, for instance, sing:

> E a pátria simples, una, intangivelmente
> Partindo para a celebração do Universal!
> Ventem nossos desvarios ferverosos!
> Fulgurem nossos pensamentos dadivosos!
> Clangorem nossas palavras proféticas
> Na grande profecia virginal! (PD 109)
>
> [And the simple homeland, unite, intangibly
> Parting for the celebration of the Universal!
> Let our fervent delusions bellow!
> Let our generous thoughts sparkle!
> Let our prophetic words ring out
> in great virginal prophecy!]

The Orientalismos respond by yelling, "Submetei-vos à metrificação! / A verdadeira luz está nas corporações!" (PD 110) ["Submit thyselves to metrification! / The true light is in the corporations!"] To such sentiments the *haute-bourgeois* Senectudes do little more than add their stupid assent. At one point the Orientalismos sing of their own sexlessness: "E a riqueza! O nosso anel de matrimônio! / E as fecundidades regulares, refletidas.../ E os perenementes da ligação mensal..." (PD 110). ["And wealth! Our wedding ring! / And regular fecundities, reflective.../ And the perennials of *monthly* intercourse...."] The Senectudes reply with a Freudian slip, unwittingly desexing themselves even further: "Bravíssimo! Bem dito! Sai azar! / Os perenementes da ligação anual!" (PD 110). ["Bravisimo! Well said! How appropriate! / The perennials of *yearly* intercourse!"]

As the Oratorio speeds along to its conclusion, the battle between the two aesthetic groups literally reaches a crescendo. In their final exchange, the stage directions inform us that the Orientalismos roar fortissitissimo (*fff*), to which the Juvenilidades respond in a yet louder fortissitissitissimo (*ffff*), to which the Orientalismos fire back an even louder fortissitissitissitissimo (*fffff*), after which the Juvenilidades fall delirious, "mad, sublime, falling exhausted" (PD 113). Significantly, at this point "As enfibraturas" pushes its own operatic allegory of Brazilian culture to a breaking point. As we mentioned earlier, any operatic or symphonic qualities of the piece are already debilitated by the disunified discord enacted between its mal-tuned voices. Once the discord becomes impossibly loud (*fffff*), the piece suddenly ends without any firm conclusion. After all the cacophony Minha Loucura sings a soft lullaby, and then both she and the Juvenilidades Auriverdes (i.e., both "Eu" and "Nós") are to "sleep eternally deaf." By this point, the rest of the performers have already vanished into thin air and the orchestra conductors all die at once. The audience, finally, is to respond with derision, with "whistles, cat-calls, and feet-stomping." The oratorio champions *modernismo* and modernization, but never actually shows a triumph of *modernismo* and modernization. Quite to the contrary of triumph, the oratorio is *supposed* to be a critical and popular disaster.

Unruh and others have rightly noted that the inconclusiveness of "As enfibraturas" is decisive. The culture-war depicted in it does not reach definitive closure, but instead the reading/viewing public is invited into the piece itself. The lack of closure thus allows space for the public to participate in creating a new aesthetic order, a new national order, a new world—goals that the piece can only promote, but not achieve of its own accord. This is quite a good reading. But we cannot fail to remember as well that the public's participation is as much a parodic farce as anything else in the oratorio. The public participates only by *hating* the oratorio. The sense of derision also pervades other instances of audience participation in which the piece breaks down the "fourth-wall" of dramatic staging. In the final rant of the Juvenilidades Auriverdes, the youth scream "Seus .... !!!" (PD 113). ["You .... !!!"], to which the reader is to insert "a maior palavra feia que o leitor conhecer"—"the ugliest word the reader knows." A similar move is made just prior to this, a half a page earlier, when the Orientalismos Convencionais roar, "E as .... cidades, as .... cidades, / as .... cidades, as .... cidades, / e mil .... cidades..." (PD 112). ["And the .... cities, the .... cities, / the .... cities, the .... cities, / and a thousand .... cities...."] The footnote directs us that:

> Aqui o leitor, se for partidário dos ORIENTALISMOS, porá nomes de escritores paulistas que aprecia e das JUVENILIDADES, os que desesta. Exemplo com meu próprio nome: E as mariocidades. Não existe esse sufixo: quero assim bater melhor ou ritmo. (PD 112)
>
> [Here the reader, if he is a partisan for the ORIENTALISMS, will place the names of São Paulo writers he appreciates, and if for the JUVENILITIES, those who he detests. Example with my own name: And the mariocities. This suffix does not exist: I want it this way to better beat out the rhythm.]

The audience, in other words, is to contribute by creating new words (if not new worlds necessarily), but these words are sheer nonsense. Indeed, Mário includes himself in this same nonsense-creation ("mariocities"), as I can do to myself ("justinicities"). In the final toll, such neologisms are totally self-serving and ineffectual. Unlike the "worst word the reader knows," "justinicities" is entirely ambiguous: if you adore me it is praise, but if you detest me it is an insult. But either way, whether you have used it as praise or insult, its use only speaks to your good or bad judgment as a reader, saying nothing of the exceptional quality of my own work.

Significantly, these last examples (mariocities, justinicities) are totally insubstantial. Mário himself states that "cidades" does not exist; he only uses it to better beat out a rhythm, and in a certain respect he is absolutely correct. As Charles Perrone has noted well, "-cidades" is not a suffix in the Portuguese language, although "-idade" (without the "c") certainly is.[29] On the other hand Mário is lying, in the sense that "cidades" *does* exist in the Portuguese language, although not in the ways Mário's own (rather duplicitous) diction would immediately suggest. When we first read "E as .... cidades, as......... cidades, / as......... cidades, as......... cidades, / e mil......... cidades...," we are apt to read the term "cidades" as if it were referring to real "cities." But "cities" *is not a word* in this case; it is only used as a suffix, an incomplete part of a word. "Cities" is literally duplicitous, then, inviting the reader to think that "cities" have meaning; until we realize "cities" is not a *they*, but only an *it*—not a word in the plural referring to multiple places, but only a singular suffix.

This is important insofar as "As enfibraturas" performs a similar double cross on the real city, São Paulo. The choruses are not only organized by harmonic range and socioeconomic status, but they are also distributed spatially, geographically, throughout the city. As I noted earlier, the Orientalismos Convencionais sing out from the balconies and windows of the Teatro Municipal, with the Juvenilidades Auriverdes and Minha Loucura below them with their feet buried in the soil of Anhangabaú. The Sandapilários Indiferentes scream from the Viaduto do Chá, the steel bridge (now concrete) crossing Anhangabaú just in front of the Teatro Municipal. And the Senectudes Tremulinas are disseminated throughout various places of business and power in the Centro Novo: "pelas sacadas do Automóvel Clube, da Prefeitura, da Rôtisserie, da Tipografia Weisflog, do Hotel Carlton e mesmo da Livraria Alves, ao longe" (PD 104) ["from the balconies of the Automobile Club, City Hall, the Rotisserie, Weisflog Typography, the Hotel Carlton, and also the Alves Bookstore, in the distance"].

Here we must not fail to notice the musicians. The singers are to be accompanied by both bands and orchestras, close to 5,000 musicians in all, who are directed by conductors imported "from abroad" (PD 103). The *maestri*, however, have no control over the musicians who often remain mute, and who at other times play out of tune. As the prelude begins, the musicians "entre largos silêncios reflexivos, enunciam, sem desenvolimento, nem harmonização, o tema" (PD 104) ["between long reflective silences, announce, with neither development nor harmonization, the theme"]. At this point, the stage directions inform us that the singers are to number 550,000 in total—or roughly the entire population of São Paulo in 1922.

In this way the stage directions mandate the allegorization of the city. The entire city performs the performance, even if they are beyond the control of the directors. The allegory is totalizing: *all* working-class people in São Paulo are the Sandapilários Indiferentes, *all* bourgeoisie are the Senectudes Tremulinas, and so forth. This also means that no one could be left in São Paulo to form an audience, unless of course everyone in São Paulo were to serve simultaneously as members of the chorus *and* as a public witnessing the chorus singing. Like all good allegories, "As enfibraturas do Ipiranga" is thus marked by doubling, since *everyone* is to live in the real São Paulo as an audience *and* perform in the aesthetic spectacularization of São Paulo. The action of the oratorio thus takes place in a theater, but *not* on a stage inside the theater. Rather, the interior of the Teatro Municipal literally explodes out into its exterior environment, such that São Paulo itself becomes the theater of its own performance as *opera bouffe*. The staging of "As enfibraturas," including any audience participation in it, is totally impossible—not mimetic representation, but necessarily anti-mimetic and anti-ontological. That is, "As enfibraturas" offers us *two* São Paulos—the real one and its own impossible one, and thus exploits the *distance between* the two "cities" for humorous effect.

What the...

The 21 short poems of *Paulicéia desvairada* therefore occupy a middle ground *in-between*—between one manifesto and another, between theory and performance, between the idea of harmony and the practice of dissonance, between concrete reality and aesthetic representation. Thus, although the volume contains (at least) three distinct sections, these sections cannot be read in isolation, but rather must always be read "harmonically" in-between one another.

And although the three sections appear in sequence, the volume as a whole offers "precious few overviews or images of unity, preferring to weave a fabric made of numerous constituent parts" as one scholar recently put it.[30]

Paulicéia desvairada does not build chronologically toward some grand philosophical or aesthetic conclusion. Rather, one must learn to read the volume rather holistically, in terms of how each aspect of the work resonates intertextually and *intra*-textually. A "movement in-between" structures Mário's lyricism, as is evident in the very first poem we actually read in the volume. In "Inspiração," the poet frames both poetic inspiration and São Paulo in terms of constant commotion:

> São Paulo! comoção de minha vida...
> Os meus amores são flores feitas de original!...
> Arlequinal!...Trajes de losangos...Cinza e ouro...
> Luz e bruma...Forno e inverno morno...
> Elegâncias sutis sem escândalos, sem ciúmes...
> Perfumes de Paris...Arys!
> Bofetadas líricas no Trianon...Algodoal...
>
> São Paulo! comoção de minha vida...
> Galicismo a berrar nos desertos da América. (PD 83)

> [São Paulo! commotion of my life...
> My loves are flowers formed from the original!...
> Harlequinate!...Suits of diamonds...Ash and gold...
> Light and dust...Oven and tepid winter...
> Subtle elegances without scandals, without jealousies...
> Perfumes of Paris...Arys!
> Lyrical slaps in Trianon...Cottonfield...
>
> São Paulo! commotion of my life...
> Gallicism screaming in the deserts of America.]

Beyond simply terming the city the "commotion of my life," the poem itself operates through a series of displacements on various levels. Notably the ellipses (...) alert us to the fact that the entire poem is harmonic/polyphonic verse, designed to achieve sharp semantic contrasts as in the movement between hard and soft in "bofetadas" ["slaps"] and "algodoal" ["cottonfield"]. To a certain extent we see a similar movement between "original" and the neologism "arlequinal" ["harlequinal"] in the juxtaposition of originality next to the buffoonery of the ironic court jester (harlequin). The semantic resonance of "original...arlequinal" is bolstered by the subtle orthograph-phonetic duplication of the two terms: or-ar, i-li, gi-ki, nal-nal.

Indeed, from the standpoint of phonetics, "Inspiração" is not just about commotion, but *is* itself a commotion of swirling sounds and letters. The sound of "são" in "São Paulo" is replicated three times in the poem's opening: in "como*ção*" in verse 1, the verb "*são*" in verse 2, and indeed the title "Inspira*ção*." The second verse, in turn, also reiterates "-ores" in "am*ores*" and "fl*ores*," and alliterates *f* in "flores feitas," just prior to "original.../ Arlequinal." Likewise, in verse 4 the terms "luz e bruma" are linked by *u*, even though "light" and "mist" would seem connotationally opposed (the light does not shine on a misty day, the mist blocks or disperses light). The latter half of the fourth verse, "forno e inverno morno" modulates "or"-"er"-"or" (f*or*no e inv*er*no m*or*no) against a constant "no"-"no"-"no" (for*no* e inver*no* mor*no*), all of which is preceded by a declining movement from the hard dentilatibial *f* to the soft dentilabial *v* to the yet softer bilabial *m* (*f*orno e in*v*erno *m*orno). And as a final example, in the next verse we have another modulation in the iterations of "elegâncias" and "escândalos," both of which have similar cadences marked visually by the circumflexed *â*. These modulated terms stand in contrast to the repetition of "sem"-"sem" ("Elegâncias sutis *sem* escândalos, *sem* ciúmes..."), while "sutis" and "ciúmes" are marked by reversal: the "-*is*" that terminates "sutis" is mirrored in the "*ci-*" of "ciúmes," as is the order of "u-i" ("s*uti*s") mirrored in the "i-u" of "c*iú*mes," even though the terms form an assonant rhyme.

The phonetics of the poem parallel the pervasive sense of movement and translation the poem conveys. In the end, São Paulo is nothing more than a Gallicism—a French word brought directly into a foreign language—one that is only capable of screaming as if lost in the "deserts of America." The metaphor of the Gallicism may itself be taken as a metaphor for international economic trade, indexed by the presence of the Parisian perfume named Arys—which must have been the mark of distinction for São Paulo's wealthy. Interestingly, the two actual Gallicisms in the poem are proper names, "Arys" and "Trianon." This latter name, however, does not refer to the small palace built for Marie Antionette at Versailles, but rather to the São Paulo park located amidst the mansions of the Avenida Paulista where it was customary for the rich to take Sunday strolls and meet for tea.[31] The "Trianon" of "Inspiração," that is, has lost all vestiges of French monarchy, but is now a rather cheap, bourgeois, *paulistana* imitation of Gallic splendor. By criticizing the wealthy in this way, the poem stages a violent confrontation between rich and poor (or at least between the rich and not-so-rich)—which it calls a "lyrical slap" in the face of those in Trianon, before pulling its punches somewhat with the soft "algodoal." In other words, "Inspiração" enacts socioeconomic encounter between the New World bourgeoisie and poor as the interaction between an Old World king and court jester, the poor lunatic who attacks "original" power through duplicitous wit. Phonetic commotion thus duplicates contentious (if inconclusive) movement between rich and poor, urban and rural, sovereign and subject, France and Brazil.

The moment of poetic "inspiration" in this context is *not* original, not an origin, but rather a translation. Inspiration occurs only after language and customs have been transferred across the Atlantic. And from this moment onward, the 20 poems that follow "Inspiração" assume similar postures of commotion and contentious linguistic and social encounter. "Anhangabaú," for instance, treats two images "frozen" in motion in the Anhangabaú parks: one is of classical bronze statues of nudes "correndo eternamente, / num parado desdém pelas velocidades" (PD 92) ["eternally running, / in halted disdain for velocities"]; and the other (Other), "E o contraste boçal do lavrador / que sem amor afia a foice" (PD 93) ["And the black-slave contrast of the reaper / who lovelessly sharpens the scythe"]. The former, classical (read: European classical) representation strives to halt the course of time and history into a state of permanence; yet this stands in uneasy contrast to the latter image, which could be either another statue or an actual person, of a poor black garden worker preparing to mow the lawns of the park with a scythe. In any event, the poem juxtaposes black and white people, rich and poor, European "originals" (classics) and African/American slavery upon which Europe obtained its state of "originality" and "historical permanence." In the end, the poem gives way to utter ambiguity: the parks could be either "Anhangabaú ou Paris" (PD 93); and within the parks, either two frogs or two children (the poem does not specify) engage in infantile arguments: "Meu pai foi rei! / —Foi.—Não foi.—Foi.—Não foi" (PD 93). ["My father was king! / —Was.—Was not.—Was.—Was not."] But by the final stanza, ambiguity itself become definitive: "Meu querido palimpsesto sem valor! / Crônica em mau latim / cobrindo uma écloga que não seja de Virgílio" (PD 93). ["My dear worthless palimpsest! / Chronicle in bad Latin / covering an eclogue not written by Virgil."] São Paulo is not just a copy of Paris, but a palimpsestic copy lacking substance, an inscription pressed into negative space, with no value of its own, that could be classical in its own right (but is not). "Anhangabaú" is nothing but a translation in "bad Latin"—a Tupi-Guarani name translated directly (like a Gallicism) into a vulgar derivative, Brazilian Portuguese.

Paulicéia desvairada is similarly littered with exotic terms—"exotic" in the sense of being foreign terms (principally Tupi, French, Italian, and English) brought directly into Portuguese discourse. Such "exoticism" is clearly an index of transculturation—the meeting of disparate migrant groups within the space of the city. Yet such transculturation is never quite heroic, in the sense of seamlessly creating a "great" *mestiço* Brazilian subject. Instead, transcultural encounter is often framed in terms of poverty and privation, of unequal distributions of worth and power. In another poem, "Tu," Mário sings a love song to the city, fondly calling it "Costureirinha de São Paulo / ítalo-franco-luso-brasílico-saxônica" (PD 98) ["Little seamstress of São Paulo / italo-franco-luso-brazilic-saxonic"]. Even though the city stitches these cultures/languages together, it is nonetheless the work of a *poor* worker, a diminutive seamstress.

Likewise, the "processions" of another poem, "Os cortejos" ["The Processions"], are not those of royalty, but rather common workers on commuter trains who greet each other in Italian, "Bon giorno, caro" (PD 84). São Paulo then becomes a delusion of horror ("Horrivéis as cidades" (PD 84)) splayed across the retinas of the poet: The city becomes a "great mouth of a thousand teeth" (PD 84) devouring its citizens; the trains become a serpentine "trifid tongue" that spurts "pus and more pus..." (PD 84). In this sense, "Os cortejos" uses phonetic modulations similar to "Inspiração" to enact the mastication, digestion—in a word, *cannibalization*[32]—of the workers: "Giram homens fracos, baixos, magros.../ Serpentinas de entes frementes a se desenrolar..." (PD 84). ["Men whirl by, weak, short, gaunt.../ Serpentines of frementine beings unrolling...."] Here, the phonemes "ente" [/en'tɾi/] appears thrice, in "serp*ent*inas," "*ent*es," and "frem*ent*es," yet the progression of "en" to "es" in "*ent*es frem*ent*es" is reversed in "d*es*enrolar," as is "es" into the reflexive pronoun "se" ("ent*es* frement*es* a *se* d*es*enrolar"). In this way, the poem literally chews up syllables and mixes them around, which again is only significant to the extent that the central image of the poem is that of men being chewed up by the city and sent down the digestive track of the serpentine train. In the end:

> Estes homens de São Paulo,
> todos iguais e desiguais,
> quando vivem dentro dos meus olhos tão ricos,
> parecem-me uns macacos, uns macacos. (PD 84)

[These men of São Paulo,
all equal and unequal,
when they live within my eyes so rich,
seem to me just so many monkeys, just so many monkeys.]

The men's poverty—they are only "equal" to one another in that they are all victims of social "inequality"—is contrasted to the wealth of the poet, who seems only rich in poetic inspiration (not money). Yet the poetic vision of the city only serves to debase the men into just so many monkeys, just so many monkeys—the sound of which in Portuguese ("uns macacos, uns macacos") onomatopoetically mimics the sound of the trains clacking across the tracks. Although the poem presents a hallucination, the city transforming into a jungle of snakes and monkeys, it nonetheless yields the *real* vibration of the train.

If anything, the São Paulo of *Pauliceia desvairada* is a meeting ground between socioeconomic classes, above and beyond the meetings of cultures. "Colloque sentimental," for instance, imagines a dialogue between rich and poor that begins in Higienópolis, in an elite *fête* marked by decadence: a "colored" jazz-band, perfumes, naked shoulders, "lips laden with adultery" (PD 99). Into this scene enters the poet whose poverty is indexed by shoelessness, as his bare feet have been "lacerated on the thorns of the sidewalk" (PD 99). The poet meets a count at the party who has "all the perfumes of Paris" (PD 100) and who offers the poet a bribe not to say anything about his philandering. The poet asks the count whether he knows of Brás or Bom Retiro—both poor, working-class neighborhoods of São Paulo—and steals the count (who "only knows Paris") away from his lady friends and into the darker corners of the city. The count's movement away from female interlocutors to a male one perhaps indicates a movement from heterosexual adultery to an illicit homoerotic encounter. In any case, as the count holds his handkerchief to his nose to mask the stench, the two see "a thread of nameless tears" (PD 100) pouring out from under the doors of the poor areas and into the sewers. The poem thus conflates socioeconomic encounter with filth, luridness, perversion, and with "lacerated feet," bloody (and perhaps sado-masochistic) violence.

On the whole, however, the volume brings together disparate social factions through sharp juxtaposition rather than physical contact or dialogue—in a way modeled on harmonic verse. Harmony/dissonance, that is, clearly becomes a *social structure* in the volume as much as a poetic one. A clear example of this is the poem, "Domingo." Each of the poem's four stanzas presents a scene in four discrete locations in São Paulo on a given Sunday, each of which culminate with the refrain, "Futilidade, civilização" ["Futility, civilization"]: (1) A Catholic mass in which parishioners flirt with one another with "olhares acrobáticos" ["acrobatic glances"] like "Tantos telégrafos sem fio" (PD 91) ["So many wireless telegraphs"]; (2) A soccer match in which two male fans "adore" players such as Bianco and Bartô; (3) A street scene in which two other males mooch cigarettes and admire women such as Marília and Filis, "Que vestido: pele só!" (91) ["Whatta dress: only skin!"]; and finally (4) A moviehouse showing Tom Mix films today, and German films tomorrow, so that the little girls "mordem os beiços pensando em fita alemã" ["bite their cheeks thinking of German film"] and "sonham masculinidades" (PD 91) ["dream masculinities"] from their virginal beds. Besides the fact that they occur on a Sunday, each scene is linked by unrealized desire: church flirtations, a desire for a goal or for the body of the goal-scorer, desire for cheap women and free cigarettes, ardent teenagers yearning for matinee idols. By finishing each scene with the same refrain ("Futilidade, civilização"), moreover, the poem strives to equalize them in some way, to impart a particular sense of social simultaneity (an imagined being-in-common, civilization) to them, even though each scene appears in different times and spaces down the page. In terms of what actually appears on the page, we must read each stanza of "Domingo" chronologically, just as we do "Arroubos...Lutas...Setas...Cantigas...Povoar!" Yet just as the goal of harmonic verse is to have each word superimposed upon the next, the clear intention of the poem is to have us consider each event as simultaneous, as if each discrete scene of subtly deviant sexuality were to amass into an entire "civilization" of body piled upon body orgiastically. Significantly, "Domingo" foments *civilization* in terms of intersubjective erotics—but erotics that are only fantasized, and therefore *futile*, a point to which we will return shortly.

The sense of mass orgy is not at all uncommon in the volume. In "Noturno," (PD 95–96) the poet guides us through a night in the lower-class Cambuci district "pelas noites de crime" [on nights of crime"]: prostitutes from Turkestan; moths flittering "na epiderme das árvores" ["on the skin of the trees"]; a golden mulatto (whom the poet clearly adores) smelling of vanilla; "guerreiros blancos" ["white warriors"] frequenting brothels in search of blossoming "Iracemas."[33] All of these scenes are united by the refrain of an Italian street vendor selling hot, phallic yams in thick dialect ("Batat' assat'ô furrn!..." as if to say "Batata assada ao forno," oven-baked yams). With this last image of the vendor's cart, we may want to consider a similar image in a poem by Oswald de Andrade, "pobre alimaría," (1924) which provides a snapshot of another scene in São Paulo, in which a horse-drawn cart gets jammed into streetcar tracks and stops traffic, much to the chagrin of lawyers and professionals riding the tram. In a well-known analysis of the Oswald's poem, Roberto Schwarz reads the scene in terms of an uneasy, yet simultaneous, coexistence of "development" and "underdevelopment," progress and backwardness:

> The city in the poem is modern, since it has trams, and backward, since there is a horse and cart stuck in the tramlines. Another sign of modernity are the lawyers, though it is only a relative modernity—a tramful of legal men suggests a rather simple society, whose professional gamut remains idyllically, comically small.... The progress is undeniable, but its limited nature, which allows it to be placed in the same context as the backwardness in relation to which it can be defined as progress, is no less undeniable.[34]

A similar coexistence of "limited modernity" and "persistent tradition" appears in Mário's poem. "Noturno" has two distinct sets of refrains: that of the yam-seller ("Batat' assat'ô furrn!..."); and another set of refrains enacted by the motion of streetcars:

> Gingam os bondes como um fogo de artifício
> Sapateando nos trilhos,
> Cuspindo um orifício na treva cor de cal...
> ....
> E os bondes passam como um fogo de artifício,
> Sapateando nos trilhos,
> Ferindo um orifício na treva cor de cal...
> ....
> E os bondes riscam como um fogo de artifício,
> Sapateando nos trilhos,
> Jorrando um orifício na treva cor de cal...(PD 95–96)
> [The streetcars sway like fireworks
> Tapping their feet on the tracks,
> Spitting an orifice in the whitewashed gloom...
> ....
> And the streetcars pass like fireworks
> Tapping their feet on the tracks,
> Wounding an orifice in the whitewashed gloom...
> ....
> And the streetcars trace like fireworks,
> Tapping their feet on the tracks,
> Spurting out an orifice in the whitewashed gloom...]

Here, then, the cart and the streetcar collide in the form of duplicate sets of refrains. And this meeting of yam-cart and streetcar, poverty and progress, may be further transposed into violent (violative) sexual copulation—the phallic yam and the "orifice" of burning metallic sparks that spit, wound, and then spurt/ejaculate.

The São Paulo of *Paulicéia desvairada* literally explodes into scenes of mass bacchanalian sex, or at least that is what the poet seems to *desire*. All the scenes just described are not unified holistically merely by our perspectives as readers, but rather by the lyrical expressions of the poetic "Eu"/"I" who organizes visions of the city so that we may perceive them. And this same "Eu" is a poetic voice who clearly identifies himself as mad, schizophrenic, and lonely at various points in the volume. "Eu" *sees* various erotic encounters in the city, but never actually participates in them. He is a voyeur, and a bisexual one at that, and the scenes are presented so luridly that we can only assume that the poet considers his own bisexual voyeurism to be deviant, with profound consequences for the broader national-cultural argument of the work. That is, lyrical expression performs the work of building civilization, of simultaneity—or what Benedict Anderson calls "empty time"—linking São Paulo's diverse cultural groups into a singular whole. Yet to reiterate, this "Eu" is thoroughly fragmented, occupying an impossible subject-position *in movement between* "Eu" and "Nós"/"We"—finding himself only by projecting his desire into and out of others so that he becomes only a dialogic movement (a translation) between a first-person "Eu" and what is essentially (and paradoxically) a third-person "Nós." The "Eu," that is, willfully disembodies himself, desiring to disappear into the desires of *other* subjects who constitute a "Nós," transforming himself into a rather spectral phenomenon. São Paulo is not merely a *place* in which "Eu" produces language. São Paulo *becomes dis-placement* itself, and spectral dis-placement at that.

I would argue, then, that spectral disembodiment, displacement, occurs precisely at the moment when we expect the *reading* of phenomena, and not just the *perception* of phenomena, to begin. The reading of *Paulicéia desvairada* depends not just on the words on the page, but literally upon the empty space between them. To reiterate, according to the *new, modern* harmonic scheme Mário devises, the word in itself is only partially significant until it vibrates against other words and phrases; reading can only occur at the point of interrelation between words, in the unspoken spaces that the work manifests as ellipses ("..."). But when this poetic logic is carried over to the social relations represented in the volume, we must conclude that individual subjects and the sociolinguistic communities to which they belong do not exist *except* in (harmonic-dissonant) interrelation to others. São Paulo can only be represented, therefore, as an empty space "in-between" ("..."): in-between the singular "Eu" and plural "Nós" perceived as deluded phenomena, and in-between different social groups engaged in irreconcilable (dissonant) vibration against one another. Or rather the *new, modern* city and civil society being created by these cultural harmonics can only be read as a palpable non-conciliation, a spectral subject-position, which *Paulicéia desvairada* ultimately attempts (and fails) to dub the modern "Brazilian."

The Punch Line: The Harlequin Banner

There is little debate among Brazilianist scholars that *Pauliceia desvairada* works to *represent* the city of São Paulo, and thus to represent modern Brazil. As Charles Perrone has written, "Analysts' approaches to *Pauliceia desvairada* invariably involve the treatment of the city *per se*—its physical spaces, configurations of people and places, the outward traits of groups, notable activities, etc.—particularly in relation to the poems' lyrical subject."[35] He then moves away from this "physical" interpretation to a less tactile mode:

> In contrast to potentially hermetic cartographic details, the sequence of poems in *Pauliceia desvairada* does effectively configure linguistic and ethnic multiplicity in the city. English and French phrases and authors are heard and cited as befits captured moments satirizing aristocrats and bourgeois folks attuned to European high culture, a clownish inventory of high-brow cultural opportunities in town, or nods to the novelty of film. On the popular level, the dominant Other tongue is Italian (together with Italianized Portuguese), treatment of which specifically concerns the representation of Italian identity in this and other literary works by Mário de Andrade.[36]

In a more recent reading, David William Foster objects to such conceptual configurations of the city, citing Perrone by name in his objection, and instead strives to move the discussion back to the physical or material level:

> What is not at issue is merely the way in which the city is thematized or "represented" (Perrone 2002), as though the individual poems (there are twenty-two in all) were pictures in an exhibition of landscapes, local-color settings, and typical occupations and pastimes. Rather of concern are the material aspects of the city as they become

the stuff of poetry: its semiotic process, rather than its meaning effects; the urbanization of poetic language, rather than the poeticization of the cityscape as Suárez and Tomlins assert.[37]

As an example of Foster's materialist reading we can turn to his reading of the poem "Paisagem No. 1," which names São Paulo "Minha Londres das neblinas finas..." ["My London of the fine mists..."] as a vagrant ("São Bobo" ["St. Cuckoo"]) passes by the poet (PD 87):

> I would suggest that what is going on here is that the middle of the summer in São Paulo (January and February) is the middle of winter in England, the period, of course, of the deep fogs of London (at least before current air pollution controls). So that what the poet perceives is that the São Paulo summer, with its combination of temperatures averaging in the mid-90s and its equally high index of humidity, produces a shimmering atmosphere as though it were the equivalent of the fabled London fog.[38]

Thus the two scholars have reached an impasse: one critiques the other for reducing the volume to local-color depictions; the other would critique the next for reducing the volume to hermetic cartographic details.

In all fairness to Perrone and Foster, neither is really that far from the other. Whether the representation of São Paulo is conceptual, linguistic, semiotic, topographical, or meteorological, the fact remains that *Paulicéia desvairada* cannot be separated from São Paulo. Where I would fault both, however, is that neither adequately stresses that the connections between the "Eu lírico" and the city of São Paulo in the work are formed by way of schizophrenic spectacle—by a voice who hears voices and becomes the voices it hears, in order to project the self (or is it the city? the nation?) into the city. It is not merely that São Paulo is "like" London nor that the *paulistano* accent "sounds like" Italian. Rather, at issue is the fact that the poet psychotically perceives São Paulo as if it were London *and* simultaneously perceives it as a cheap plagiarism of London. At issue is the fact that English, French, Italian, Portuguese, and Tupi-Guarani all flow into and out of the "Eu lírico" polymorphously and perversely. "São Bobo" may be the name of a bum who passes by the poet, or it may be the poet himself as he projects his self into the city. Thus, the São Paulo of *Paulicéia desvairada* is not merely the space of the city, *but also* the harmonic-dissonant (yet silent, unvoiced) space in-between ("...") the self and the other, and between the self and the city now felt as a material presence. *And moreover*, São Paulo becomes the inability to reconcile either of the spaces just mentioned—the actual space of the city and the psychotic city hallucinated inside the poet's head, the double-space, a schizophrenic or double-headed non-conciliation—into a neatly contained unity.

Schizophrenic non-conciliation furthermore becomes a decidedly political problem in *Paulicéia desvairada*. In "O rebanho" ["The Flock"], for instance, the poet experiences a delusional hallucination in front of Congress. The congressmen, dressed in ridiculous high-hats, walk out of the Congress building with hand raised like zombies. They then form a parade line down Rua Marechal Deodoro (named after the general who rose up in revolt to end the reign Dom Pedro II), and the poet applauds this parade of "saviors" and "heroes of my beloved state" (PD 86). The "flock" of politicians stops on the lawn of the "Palácio do senhor presidente" ["the palace of Mr. President"], whereupon the congressmen all grow horns and beards, and transform into goats wearing wooden triangle bells in the place of neckties as they begin to graze on the presidential grass. We see, then, the subordination of the people's will, the subordination of the peoples' elected representatives, to a singular and increasingly dictatorial executive—"senhor presidente," the supreme "Eu"—who magically "shepherds" Congress to his lawn.

Yet we must still question the effectiveness of such political gestures. Returning to Jean-Luc Nancy for a moment, politics is *supposed* to occur in the face of intersubjective incommensurability. Once the subject sees past the tip of his or her own nose, the individual subject realizes that he or she is *finite*, has to face up to others who share existence, and thus has to deal with the fact that one's own narcissistic desires may need to be negotiated or foregone altogether. Politics in this way is rooted not in narcissism, but in subjective self-discovery—the discovery of one's own finite limits. Yet *Pauliceia desvairada* does not quite work this way. The political gestures of the volume *do* rest on the self-discovery of Mário's poetic "Eu." But this "Eu" does not really discover himself in and of himself, so much as he projects his own perverse desires and delusions voyeuristically onto others. He finds himself through others with whom he does *not* communicate, and who would probably not want anything to do with him even if he did. Such projections are purely subjective for the poetic "Eu"—aesthetic spectacles of the city and nation to which he alone is privy. Except...

Except that he has concretized his delusions in the form of a book.

Whatever we may think of the poetic "Eu," we have already seen multiple times how all matters of subjectivity—whether strictly personal/psychological or citizenship/collective identity—are structured by *typography*...the ellipses (...). Taken in this light, the poetic "Eu" *does* communicate with others who *read* his work. And as such, if intersubjective communication holds forth the possibility of politics, we must pay attention to the locus of that communication—the materiality of the book itself.

As I have already mentioned the "Prefácio interessantíssimo" is a very interesting piece, but the *really* interesting thing about it is that it is itself prefaced by another preface, in the form of a dedicatory letter "TO MÁRIO DE ANDRADE" (PD 58). This opening letter is written in such excessively ornate formal language that it cannot be read seriously. Nevertheless, the letter shows a clear command of educated Portuguese, and indeed, it establishes a clear sociocultural hierarchy of education between the letter-writer and his "dear master," Mário de Andrade. In fact, the letter-writer has learned *how to write* from his master, who "in the many brief hours in which you made me profit by thy side, thou spokest of thy confidence in free and sincere art.... Not from mine, but from thy experience did I the courage in my Truth and pride in my Ideal receive." At the end of the document, the letter-writer literally prostrates and humiliates himself at the feet of the master: "But I do not know, Master, if thou willst pardon the mediate distance between these poems and thy highest lesson.... I received in thy pardon the strength of being chosen by thee as thine only disciple; from he who in this moment of fearful martyrdom still calls out to thee as his Guide, his Master, his Lord" (PD 58). But here we should notice that the letter-writer is in effect sending his poems—that is, the poems to follow in *Paulicéia desvairada*—to Mário de Andrade. And this is precisely the case: the letter is a dedicatory epistle in which Mário de Andrade dedicates his own work "TO MÁRIO DE ANDRADE," *to himself*, and he punctuates the gesture by signing the missive, "Mário de Andrade / 14 de dezembro 1921 / S. Paulo." The very first text we read in the work therefore serves to establish the poetic "Eu"—by way of a parody of narcissism—as a fragmented subject, as someone who could subordinate his sycophantic self to his lordly self, and accordingly engage in epistolary dialogue with himself. The irony of this situation thus depends upon typography—the fact that one "MÁRIO DE ANDRADE" to whom the letter is addressed appears above another "Mário de Andrade" with which the letter is signed.

In this manner the dedicatory letter sets the *tenor* for the rest of the volume—the sense of ironic, parodic, subjective, and historical transition from "educated" traditional to "uncouth" *modernista* poetry that will be played out in the rest of the work. Or in terms more germane to harmonic verse we may think of *Pauliceia desvairada* as a kind of bibliographic arpeggio, in which the dedicatory missive serves as the tonic note for the three intervals to follow: the "Prefácio interessantíssimo," the 21 poems, and the libretto of "As enfibraturas do Ipiranga," which together do *not* form a narrative of the "new" Brazilian so much as they resonate against one another like an arpeggiated chord.

In other words, the book itself signifies—is itself a signifying practice—in addition to whatever the words within it signify. In light of the fact that the volume sets up Mário de Andrade as a kind of insane harlequin, it should thus be unsurprising that the *original*, first edition of *Pauliceia desvairada* (São Paulo: Casa Mayença, 1922) is itself two-headed, or multiheaded. It is quite likely that the title itself is not original, but cribbed from two other titles—the 1893 volume, *Les campagnes hallucinées*, and the 1895 *Les villes tentaculaires* by one of Mário's favorite authors, Émile Verhaeren.[39] From there we will notice that the first edition of *Pauliceia desvairada* has (at least) *two* covers.[40] The first (real) cap establishes the "harlequinal" motif of the work in a suit of diamonds (figure 2.1).

In addition to the harlequin reference, the motley arrangement of colors may also be taken as a visual instance of the print/social harmonics theorized and manifested in the work. The colors do not match or blend into one another, but stand in sharp juxtaposition such that they create a sort of optical vibration or dissonance. Yet this *first* image of *Pauliceia desvairada* is *not original*. As Telê Porto Ancona Lopes—the curator of Mário's papers at the Instituto de Estudos Brasileiros of the Universidade de São Paulo—has so carefully demonstrated, the first edition's front-cover not-so-subtly plagiarizes the design of another work she has found in Mário's library, a book of poems entitled *Arlecchino* by the Italian Futurist, Ardengo Soffici, published in 1918.[41] The first *Pauliceia desvairada* thus began as a translation, and a plagiarized translation at that, graphically so. Yet this plagiarized front-cover is also a double in another sense. In addition to the "harlequinate" front-cover, just after the "Prefácio interessantíssimo" and just before "Inspiração" and the lyrical poems, we encounter a title page that dates the work's production: "Pauliceia desvairada / dezembro de 1920 / a / dezembro de 1921." This is then followed by a kind of *faux* front-cover (figure 2.2).

This "drawing by Antônio Moya" evidently depicts the sun rising ("The Dawn of the New Day") over a statue in the Anhangabaú parks—and thus serves to link the "Prefácio interessantíssimo" to the

Figure 2.1 Front-cover of the first edition of *Paulicéia desvairada* (© The Family of Mário de Andrade, used by permission).

lyrical poem "Anhangabaú" and its depiction of classical statues, as well as to "As enfibraturas do Ipiranga" in which the heroic Juvenilidades Auriverdes have their feet buried in the soil of the park.

Harmony, then, is not just musical or poetic, but also social, political, historical, bibliographic, visual, tactile. Harmonics spread out

Figure 2.2 A drawing of Anhangabaú park that appears between the "Prefácio interessantíssimo" and lyrical poems in the first edition of *Pauliceia desvairada* (© The Family of Mário de Andrade, used by permission).

from the poet's delusional visions and into the world we inhabit, first in the form of two front-covers, one of which duplicates another front-cover, mirroring the harmonic dissonance theorized, enacted, and performed within those covers. The poetic/social structures governing the literary works within the book ring out to cover the visual structure of the covers containing those pages. Harmonic verse not only governs poetry, but also governs the material object in which that poetry appears, and from there presumably begins to govern the world around it. *Pauliceia desvairada* is, in this sense, not just a work about movement and translation, but itself *is* movement and

Figure 2.3 "The conclusion, therefore, is that there are two capital forces: love, which multiplies the species; and the nose, which subordinates it to the individual. Procreation, equilibrium."

translation. If the work plays with a schizophrenic "Eu" situated simultaneously in two São Paulos (one real, one parodic), the harmonic structure of the work *announces* to the reader an *other* vision of "order and progress," now understood as wrapped in the dissonant colors of a harlequinal suit of diamonds (figure 2.3).

Chapter 3

Verse Reverse Verse: Fake Autobiographies, Lost Translations, and New Originals of Vicente Huidobro's *Altazor*

Ideologies of American nationhood have historically arisen from what we could call the "lettered-creole" (*criollo-letrado* or *crioulo-letrado*) classes—American-born whites who were subservient to European-born lords, yet dominant over all other racial castes, during colonialism. We can say with some certainty that, except perhaps for the case of Haiti, lettered-creoles fomented independence movements and nation-building throughout the hemisphere in the nineteenth and twentieth centuries. The power of these classes derived from their command of writing and print media.[1] Thus, the literature of the lettered classes has been taken as a symbolic manifestation of their power, and therefore rigorously interrogated, deconstructed, and even (some might say, or desire) discarded over the past several decades. In this chapter, and all others of this book, I am essentially asking: Is there anything left in the tank of the lettered-creole?

Vicente Huidobro's status as both a canonical Chilean poet and a *criollo-letrado* has never been open to question. As the direct descendent of the García-Huidobro family of Santiago de Chile, Huidobro would have received the title of Marqués de la Casa Real had Chile not declared independence from Spain several generations prior to his birth in 1893. Huidobro pertained to the ruling class of oligarchs in charge of the continuing conquest of national territory at the turn of the century, including ongoing conflicts with the native Mapuche tribes in the south of Chile. Yet monarchical titles and conquest seemed to have mattered little to Huidobro, or at least mattered less than other aristocratic pursuits—chiefly women and poetry. Indeed, Huidobro fashioned himself publicly as a Chilean version of Don Juan Tenorio. In his semiautobiographical memoir, *Vientos contrarios* (written in 1926 at the ripe age of 34), the poet effectively begins the narrative with the story of how, at the age of 13 no less, he began an epistolary seduction of several prominent Parisian ladies from his bedroom in Santiago:

> At 13 years-old, while my classmates collected their stamps, I wiled away my time writing love letters to Lanthelme, then the queen of Paris, and at night I dreamt of the Countess de Noialles, whose portrait by De la Gándara had become my obsession.
> ....
> My loves with Lanthelme were more beautiful. To my burning letters she responded with a postcard and a photograph that I pegged to my heart with two thumbtacks.
> Later, in Paris, I learned from her sister that she used to say among her innumerable admirers:
> —The one who loves me most is *mon petit amoureux du Chili*. (VC 791–792)[2]

Huidobro did not associate his capacity for seduction as the product of his socioeconomic class, but rather of his own innate ability. At the end of the first part of *Vientos contrarios* he states bluntly, "A Don Juan is something absolutely distinct from a Tenorio. ... Don Juan does not need to move, nor run around desolate. Women rotate around him, while Tenorio rotates around women" (VC 800). The knave who relies solely on his family name ["Tenorio"] and class to gain access to women is, for lack of a better word, knavish; sexual prowess is not exclusive to the aristocracy, but only to the individual "Don Juan"—a kind of sexual meritocracy. As such, Huidobro claims that every generation is to have its own reincarnations of "Don Juan," beyond the mere reproduction of "Tenorios" of the socially dominant class. And here of course, Huidobro was to name *himself* as the next reincarnation:

> The lover is born, but is not made.
> In vain will the man who was not born with natural amorous abilities read the *Kama Sutra* and learn by heart the *Capelin d'Amour*, will never succeed in becoming the true love, the man who possesses *magnetic skin*, the conjurer, in a word, who attracts all women especially gifted as himself and more refined in perception than others of her kind.

He who was not born under the sign of Venus wastes his time in sexual studies and learnings. He will only succeed in representing a comedy without convincing his audience, and would do better to abstain and resign himself to being a man like the others, a common man in amorous struggles, before making himself into a buffoon. He will not be able to pass off his counterfeit coin to any woman *who understands*, and thus he should seek to join with a woman like any other, a woman as common as he is.

There are men (few, very few) who are true virtuosos in love, who make the body of a woman into an extraordinary, distinct musical instrument; like a pianist does to the piano, they know how to tease chords from her, and special and unique sounds. (VC 818; italics in original)

It is difficult to characterize Huidobro's extensive commentary on his own sexual prowess as anything other than boastful conceit. Even the wealthiest of aristocrats, claims the author, can be common men sexually speaking—and so they should resign themselves to the common woman. But Huidobro is the son of the goddess, a natural-born sexual lord.

But so what? What is the point of such patent arrogance? The matter—as I have perhaps too extensively laid it out here—would seem to have little or nothing to do with the literary-critical target of this book. As literary/cultural critics, we are trained to discount biography—and even more still, autobiography—as determinants of literary production. The New Critics and Structuralists taught us too well that the lives of authors and the lives of texts are fundamentally different quantities, that the truth of lived experience and the truth of the text do not necessarily intersect. So what does it matter that, immediately after naming himself a "son of Venus" peculiarly attuned to the elicitation of orgasmic music from women (*entendidas*) who *understand*, Huidobro provides one of the first public statements regarding the production of his major literary work, *Altazor*, one of the most canonical texts of Chilean literature?

> Here I am, in Silvana Plana, housed in the same room in which Nietzsche wrote the final pages of his *Zarathustra*.
> And so what? Nothing, absolutely nothing.
> Here I have written chapter V of my *Altazor*.
> And so what? Nothing, absolutely nothing. (VC 819)

In sum, in his autobiography Huidobro positions himself as the reincarnation of a literary figure (Don Juan) and perhaps the reincarnation of a philosophical great (Nietzsche); but here it is important to underscore that he is utilizing the *rhetoric* of autobiography to set himself up as the *new* embodiment of historical figures (Don Juan, Nietzsche, also later Napoleon) handed down to him through textual-rhetorical transmission. The author is creating (transcreating) himself into a rhetorical trope, calling up the dead in order to give his own face and name to them through the language of autobiography. ¿*Y qué?*

Huidobro is playing us. In *Vientos contrarios* he offers us some biographical clues as to the bibliographic production of *Altazor*, but in the same breath tells us that we should understand nothing of it. Indeed, Huidobro frames *understanding* itself as a kind of *nothingness* throughout his 1926 memoir; true *understanding* is something that cannot be spoken, or even thought, but rather it is a form of sexual (read: corporeal) magnetism, the province of the "magnetic skin" of those who understand. Understanding is therefore *not* an activity of the mind, is *not* something that can be conceptualized or learned, and especially *not* through books or reading. So what is the point of even reading *Altazor* or *Vientos contrarios* if reading does not produce understanding? Why the emphasis on the rhetoric of prosopopoeia, as suggested in the previous paragraph, if understanding is always left unspoken? I began this chapter by pulling evidence of Huidobro's *donjuanismo* from his autobiography in order to substantiate his stature as a *criollo-letrado*. To reiterate, following the thought of Angel Rama, it is now generally accepted that this class essentially "inscribed" the American landscape with "civilization" from the earliest moments of Iberian conquest, often through the production of "high" literature. As such, *letrado* literary production has been soundly criticized as the site of Eurocentric, *criollo* domination over the nation. Yet as a *letrado*, Huidobro has it all *backward*: understanding is never spiritual, incorporeal, or purely psychological; but understanding may be *psychic*, telekinetic, and for this reason, *unspoken* and *unwritten*—akin to Nietzsche's (via Zarathustra's) unspeakable (and unspeakably poetic) rejection of rational philosophy. This is the sense in which Huidobro may be trying to unravel the traditional creole project of territorializing the nation—by taking the rhetoric of *letradismo* and subjecting it to un-writing and un-speaking. In order to *understand* this, however, we will need to become "backward" readers ourselves, or at least we will need to "read backward" in order to unlearn our literary-critical training and "reconnect" autobiography, poetry, literary text, and nation to the physical body and lived experience. Of course, none of these elements may have ever been disconnected in the first place, which would in turn make the task of reconnection farcical. Which is, if you have not deduced it already, precisely the point of this chapter.

Qué bárbaro.

In Face of de Man: Huidobro and Autobiography

In preceding chapters, I sketched the construction of duplicitous nationalisms by poetic means. Works such as *Spring and All* or *Paulicéia desvairada* work to materialize contingent "*as if*" nations ("*as if* Brazil" or "*as if* United States"). These texts provide—through irony, plagiarism, or parody—constructions of the nation that tend to undermine dominant national ideologies of American nationhood. Yet how effective could any such duplicity be? We always understand that whatever construction of the nation that may emerge through these texts *is not* the actual nation, nor does it have the power of "reinscribing" the nation according to the text's own particular point of view. Such ineffectivity (especially if deliberate) has in fact long been held to be the hallmark of twentieth-century modernism, whether it be called "defamiliarization" or "estrangement" or just plain "difficulty." According to Peter Bürger's well-known formulation of modern aesthetic praxis the avant-garde work of art refuses to provide the receiver any coherent or effective meaning, and only through extreme semantic difficulty does the work purport to initiate a radical change in the recipient's life praxis.[3] Once normative rules of understanding are suspended, the reader may supposedly reorganize his or her entire worldview. Avant-garde "ineffectivity," according the Bürger's reading, would thus prove to be the most politically effective means of revolutionizing society. This is not a view that I share entirely, since I am inclined to think—perhaps tautologically—that ineffectivity is really only ever ineffective, unless we frame the issue of reception slightly differently. Modernist poetic texts *do not* in themselves change the world, nor does reading texts that one does not fully understand. The texts analyzed so far *do* present a world, present the nation, as a kind of contingency, as an *as if.* This aesthetic contingency, when realized to be contingent, does offer the possibility of a radical reorganization of national culture. However, it is still insufficient to leave the matter of radical change to the subjective response of the reader, since aesthetic reception seldom translates into direct political action. Instead, we must interrogate how the aesthetic textual object, beyond merely modeling a world through ironic doubling, begins to *infiltrate* the world it inhabits.

Recent historical circumstances have rendered it impossible to read *Altazor* without taking into consideration Huidobro's life and the world around his life. As we shall see, no valid or productive reading of *Altazor* can now proceed from strict divisions between the life of the text, the life of the author, and the world we inhabit. Yet these very divisions have proven decisive in the development of critical theory over the past century. Here I am not just paying homage to the New Critics, Russian Formalists, and French Structuralists, all of whom in their distinct ways isolated textual readings from biographical interferences of authorship; I am also referring to more contemporary critical movements. The historical foundations of deconstruction (if one can even speak of deconstruction having "foundations") lie precisely in the uneasy or untenable connection between life and text. To speak at the margins of philosophy, as Derrida did in the 1960s and 1970s, is precisely to develop strategies to break through barriers between the self-contained discourse of philosophy and the world axiomatically assumed to be exterior to it—an exteriority that philosophy may in fact construct. Whether or not such construction is really the case, the particular limit of critical theory and practice—recognized by Wittgenstein, Heidegger, Derrida, in short among great philosophical minds of the past century—is that language itself is a constituent part of the world, even though philosophy and theory employ discourse *as if* language could be considered beyond the "real" world and therefore capable of describing it.

This is nowhere more evident than in the rhetorical deconstruction of Paul de Man—a savage critic if there ever was one, and one whom we will negate in order to "return" to *Altazor*. We can safely say that everything de Man ever wrote relies on the confusion of text and life. The general argument of "The Rhetoric of Temporality," for instance, is that literature's modern capacity for self-criticism—that is, the historical passage from a normative, descriptive rhetoric to one that openly questions its own intentions—lies in shifts in the values of symbol, allegory, and irony (and the temporalities of these tropes) initiated during Romanticism. Self-critical literature appears to have become enabled in the ascension of irony as a dominant—in the kind of ironic doubling (*dédoublement*) that occurs in the moment, for instance, when one trips and falls, *and* simultaneously realizes that one is tripping and falling but is powerless to stop it. Likewise, irony operates in the simultaneous enunciation of language that is ridiculous, painful, or false, *and* the awareness that this language is ridiculous, painful, or false.

> The *dédoublement* thus designates the activity of a consciousness by which a man differentiates himself from the non-human world. The capacity for such duplication is rare, says Baudelaire, but belongs specifically to those who, like artists or philosophers, deal in language. His emphasis on a professional vocabulary, on *"se faire un métier,"* stresses the technicality of their action, the fact that language is their material, just as leather is the material of the cobbler or wood is that of the carpenter. In everyday, common existence, this is not how language usually operates; there it functions much more as does the cobbler's or the carpenter's hammer, not as the material itself, but as a tool by means of which the heterogeneous material of experience is more-or-less adequately made to fit. The reflective disjunction not only occurs *by means of* language as a privileged category, but it transfers the self out of the empirical world into a world constituted out of, and in, language—a language that it finds in the world like one entity among others, but that remains unique in being the only entity by means of which it can differentiate itself from the world. Language thus conceived divides the subject into an empirical self, immersed in the world, and a self that become like a sign in its attempt at differentiation and self-definition.[4]

Ironic doubling, if not the trope of irony itself, is the *means* by which two distinct worlds are differentiated: one the world of the "empirical self" (that of the physical body that trips and falls) and another the world "consciousness" (that of the man who sees himself falling, that of the human mind which expresses in language its knowledge of the world).

So effective is this "conscious" doubling in language that the subjective self (at once in the "nonhuman world" and differentiated from it) begins to resemble the differential relation of signifier-signified, the fundamental structure of language. The subjective self, made possible through irony, is evidently a kind of linguistic text; and so, reading literary texts would therefore offer the possibility of understanding the subject per se. Yet it is this subsumption of the subjective self into the world of language and rhetoric that causes so many problems in conceiving (of) the world in language and through language. In discussing one of Wordsworth's short (two-stanza) Lucy poems, for instance, de Man distinguishes two time-states of the lyric: the past, in stanza one, in which the poem's speaking subject is unaware that the girl (Lucy, "she") will die; and the present, in stanza two, in which this same speaking subject now realizes that "she" has become a lifeless thing.

> The difference [between past unawareness and present wisdom] has been spread out over a temporality which is exclusively that of the poem and in which the conditions of error and of wisdom have become successive. This is possible within the ideal, self-created temporality engendered by the language of the poem, but it is not possible within the actual temporality of experience. The "now" of the poem is not an actual now, but the ideal "now," the duration of an acquired wisdom. The actual now, which is that of the moment of death, lies hidden in the blank space between the two stanzas. The fundamental structure of allegory reappears here in the tendency of the language toward narrative, the spreading out along the axis of an imaginary time in order to give duration to what is, in fact, simultaneous within the subject.[5]

De Man effectively reads Wordsworth's poem as a form of consciousness in itself. Even in this very brief lyric of eight lines, the poem succeeds in allegorizing a subject's growth from an unknowing to a knowing state, here presented as a smooth narrative movement in "imaginary time" from past to present. Yet this consciousness is literally made possible by repressing an ulterior reality. The allegory of subjectivity succeeds by means of framing the moment of the girl's death as a nothingness, occurring in the blank space on the page between the two stanzas. One can only speak of subjectivity if it is transformed into rhetoric, poetics, and typography. If consciousness thus resides in its transformation into allegory, then irony would be the source of self-consciousness, the moment of surprise when one realizes that that which seemed to be a smooth narrative duration is actually just an instantaneous trick of rhetoric. Either way (self-)consciousness is only ever textual, lyrical, rhetorical. Awareness and wisdom come from allegory; self-awareness is ironic; but none is a "thing" as such in the empirical world.

As we proceed through de Man's work, the division between the world of experience and the world of language is to become increasingly disturbing. In "Autobiography as De-Facement," de Man analyzes the double movement between life and rhetoric, mind and body, or physical and conceptual, inherent in autobiography as a genre. All autobiography, claims de Man, rests upon the constitution of a specular subject (the "autobiographer") caught in the reflection between life and text, reality and rhetoric. This specular-autobiographical subject calls up his own voice (prosopopoeia) in order to present, metaphorically, his own face to the world, and thus to make his person known to others. "Autobiographer" is just a name, then, for a metaphorical subject suspended somewhere between the writer *of* an autobiography and the characterization of the writer *within* the autobiographical narrative. The authenticity, and hence the authority, of autobiography depends on the closed unity (the coherence or sameness) of these two sides of speculation ("writer of" vs. "writer within"). But such closure is impossible, since the very *difference* between the two is precisely what constitutes the autobiographical subject. Closure could only be the terminus, the negation, the death, of this subject:

> As soon as we understand the rhetorical function of prosopopoeia as positing voice or face by means of language, we also understand that what we are deprived of is not life, but the shape and sense of a world accessible only in the privative way of understanding. Death is a displaced name for a linguistic predicament, and the restoration of mortality by autobiography (the prosopopoeia of the voice and the name) deprives and disfigures to the precise extent that it restores. Autobiography veils a de-facement of the mind of which it itself is the cause.[6]

With these closing lines of his essay, de Man leads us into an allegory of autobiography, and therefore (perhaps) an allegory of life as we know it. The allegory may be schematized as a kind of syllogism: (1) Autobiography is a form of self-understanding, which de Man sees as a primarily ironic mode; (2) The self-understanding of autobiography occurs by means of the autobiographer calling his/her own voice and face into being metaphorically through prosopopoeia—through rhetoric, or really through a doubling of rhetorical tropes (i.e., metaphor via prosopopoeia); (3) Ergo, if looking at one's own face is how one understands oneself, and the autobiographer comes into existence only by calling up his/her own face to view, then the autobiographer must cut off his or her own face in order to look at it, to speculate on it. The title says it all: "Autobiography as De-Facement"—Autobiography *is* de-facement, at least as a rhetorical form or literary genre.

We can only speculate as to why de Man arrives at such grotesque conclusions. What can be stated directly is that he presents any connection between experience and language as an impossible juncture (con-fusion), one in which death (and with it, life) becomes merely "a displaced name for a linguistic predicament." In fact any truth to this statement would presuppose that language is a site for the displacement of a reality (death or life). Ultimately, de Man's argument rests on the unreality of language, literature, and rhetoric. The *specular* subject is just a reflection, and is by definition insubstantial, phenomenal, immaterial—and de Man therefore intends to shock us out of our belief that we are somehow otherwise. To this end, de Man may be correct, at least most of the time. The problem, however, is that he assumes autobiography to have a strictly mimetic function—to reflect a life that has already been lived—but never an ontological function. Any proper name (as, say, on the title page of *Blindness and Insight*) promotes ontology on some level, as if to say "I have been named Paul de Man, and thus will become Paul de Man." Autobiography, as de Man assumes it to be, is merely the literary or rhetorical representation (mimesis) of this becoming. What de Man therefore critiques is the veiled disjuncture between ontology (the authorial name "Paul de Man" on the title page) and mimetic representation (the authorial figure of "Paul de Man" in the pages subsequent to the front matter). Even if the autobiographical subject can be said to be constituted in the gap between ontology (life) and representation (de-facement), de Man's entire project requires a strict, even if oftentimes confusing, distinction between the two.

Yet this is not necessarily how autobiography functions in the case of Vicente Huidobro. As should be clear already what is nominally Huidobro's autobiography, *Vientos contrarios*, is an exercise in farce: written at a relatively early age, the autobiographer presents himself merely as the reiteration of other literary figures. The rhetorical world of nonfiction, in other words, can only be properly understood as fictional, and so, beyond telling the story of how he became "Vicente Huidobro," Huidobro is trying to become (again) Don Juan or Nietzsche or Napoleon. Yet this ridiculous autobiographical posture rings strangely true. We may characterize farce as a general tendency in Huidobro's life to create lived fictions. Along with Ezra Pound and Anita Malfatti, Huidobro may have been the first artist to bring avant-garde modernism to the Americas; in difference to these others, however, it is quite possible that Huidobro *invented* the aesthetic sensibility he was later to import to the Western Hemisphere. By his early twenties, Huidobro had managed to place himself squarely in the most significant literary and artistic circles of both France and Spain, really the first American to do so. In Paris, he was one of the founding contributors to the journal *Nord-Sud* along with Appolinaire, Aragon, Breton, Dermeé, Max Jacob, and Reverdy. Indeed, Huidobro invented—excuse me, *claimed* to have invented—the calligram, and thus instructed Appolinaire how to write modern visual poetry. In Madrid, Huidobro also helped found the *ultraísta* group with Gerardo Diego and Guillermo de Torre. Somewhat ironically, *ultraísmo* was to be carried to South America by the young Jorge Luis

Borges, such that the advent of *vanguardismo* in Latin America may not be one of unidirectional movement from Europe to America but rather one of circuitous return. Or not, since we have no way to conclude what Huidobro actually did in Madrid and Paris.

We can say for certain (more or less) that Huidobro did begin to formulate his central aesthetic philosophy, *creacionsimo*, between 1916 and 1918 at several talks at the Athenaeums of Madrid, Paris, and Buenos Aires, followed by numerous manifestoes. Depending on the relative historical importance one invests in Huidobro, Creationism either repeats or originates many avant-garde characteristics now assumed to be commonplace. In his manifestoes of the 1920s and 1930s, Huidobro wishes to inaugurate advanced forms of aesthetic creation in which artists would no longer be bound to mere mimicry or representation. Rather, poets must harness the internal laws of nature, abstracting them into an ideal system. From this subjective internalization of natural systems, the poet will use his technical expertise in order to return his art back out to the world as a *new* creation objectified by the poet in *new* forms.[7] Thus Creationism rejects imitative art subservient to the natural, and extols expressionistic creation in which the poet holds full dominion over the laws of the universe. In this way, the Creationist work of art would be nothing less than the creation of new worlds (or New Worlds?) in which the poet summons the power of a god, and his poetry the power of the *logos*. At certain points, in the manifesto entitled "La creación pura," such godlike power is framed as pagan, and indeed Native American: "This idea of the artist as absolute creator, of the Artist-God, was suggested to me by an old indigenous poet from South America (Aymara) who said: 'The poet is a god; do not sing to the rain, poet, make it rain.'"[8] In most cases, however, Creationism exhibits decidedly apocalyptic tendencies in the Judeo-Christian sense. In another manifesto, "La poesía," Huidobro posits Poetry (capital P) as a sort of messianic Alpha-and-Omega: "Poetry exists before the beginning of man, and after the end of man. It is the language of Paradise and the language of the Final Judgment, it milks the teats of eternity, it is intangible as the taboo of the sky. // Poetry is the language of Creation."[9] The intent of such allusions to Genesis and Revelations is unmistakably self-serving, for Huidobro is positioning *himself* both as the originator of the new art, *and* as a new artist who will herald the end of art and history as we know it. With Creationism, Man (capital M) has evolved fully, so that he may take control of the universe. As the first Creationist poet, Huidobro is evidently to be this first, fully evolved super-Man. For this to be the case, however, one final point of information must be provided. In "El creacionismo," Huidobro states: "The creationist poem is composed of created images, created situations, created concepts; it does not lessen any element of traditional poetry, save that within it such elements are integrally invented, without worrying about the reality or veracity anterior to the act of realization."[10] Huidobro does, of course, assign himself immense importance in the history of art and civilization. Yet he does so duplicitously, with full knowledge that he has paid no mind to "reality or veracity anterior to the act of realization." As a general word of caution, then, we must *always* assume that Huidobro acts duplicitously in *every* document attributed to him.

We could locate Huidobro, for instance, on the cusp of some speech-act theory. Creationist languages do not describe something exterior to it, but it is to be exactly what it says it will be; thus, Creationism rejects truth in favor of "the act of realization." By the same token this rejection of truth could just be the folly of a buffoon, as a good number of Huidobro's contemporaries certainly thought of him. That Huidobro's literary-historical significance is *not* widely recognized beyond Latin America has everything to do with his incredible arrogance, and his propensity for stretching the truth—if not completely obliterating it. It has been widely suggested that Huidobro falsified the publication dates of his works in order to present himself as a transformational figure of literary history. De Torre, for instance, famously accused Huidobro in 1925 of changing the date of an early poetic volume, *El espejo de agua*, from 1918 to 1916, evidently in order to position himself as a precursor to Iberian *vanguardismo*. (Editorial history has proven de Torre's accusations to be false; *El espejo de agua* was in fact printed in Buenos Aires in 1916, and received a second printing in Madrid in 1918.[11]) *Altazor* carries the date 1919 even though it was first published in 1931, partly in an effort to position the work at the beginning of the *entre-guerre* even though the work did not appear until the end of this period. As we have just seen, Huidobro fashioned himself as the first *avant-gardiste*, or as he was wont to say, "contemporary poetry begins in me." It is no small wonder, then, that Huidobro managed to alienate himself from every artistic movement that he associated with, including the Surrealists and a host of other groups in Europe and America. In fact, the only literary movement that did not expel Huidobro outright was *creacionsimo*, the one that he himself invented and to which he alone was the only real member. No other "-ism" would have him.

Apparently many of Huidobro's own friends would not have him either. While living in Paris in 1924, for instance, Huidobro disappeared from his home for three days. In the interim his first wife, Manolita, and his close friend, the Cubist painter Juan Gris, contacted the police and the diplomatic mission of Chile, and fended off journalists interested in the apparent scandal. After the three days, Huidobro reappeared rather nonchalantly at his home with his pajamas folded neatly under his arm. He claimed to have been chloroformed and kidnapped by a British secret society in retribution for a political tract, *Finis Britannia*, which he had written in support of Irish independence. The police, however, never confirmed his story, and an incensed Gris never spoke to Huidobro again.[12] The following year, while vacationing in Chile, Huidobro began a torrid affair with a teenager, Ximena Amunátegui, daughter of another aristocratic Santiago family. The ensuing scandal in Chilean high-society was such that Huidobro had to escape back to Paris, and once news of the scandal broke in Parisian society, then to New York City to let the air clear. In 1928, Huidobro returned "incognito" to Chile, and on one spring day, dressed with a low-brimmed hat, dark sunglasses, and a ridiculous fake moustache, he awaited outside a convent in a large black automobile for Ximena to run away from her boarding school. The two fled to Argentina, and from Buenos Aires on to France. Huidobro's arrival in Paris was greeted by another minor scandal caused, not only by Huidobro's imminent divorce from Manolita, but also the fact that Ximena's brothers had followed the couple back to Paris intending to exact murderous revenge upon the poet.[13] If it was not the British secret service or his own in-laws trying to kill him, then it was the Nazis. At the end of World War II, already in his late forties and having already run for the presidency of Chile twice (losing both times), Huidobro enlisted in the French army and joined the Allied assault on Germany. As a point of fact, he found himself in the Battle of Berlin, where he was to recover Hitler's telephone from the rubble of the Bunker. No one has ever verified whether Hitler even came near the phone, although Huidobro did display it prominently as such in his home. What is verifiable is that Huidobro suffered head trauma in the war from which he never fully recovered, leading to a violent stroke in late 1947 that was to prove fatal on January 2, 1948.

Whether any of these stories is actually true is irrelevant. Huidobro lived his life *as if* they were true. Huidobro treated his life *as if* it were no life at all, but rather an artifice to be created as he went along. His "life" was really his autobiography, a text whose ultimate "truth" depends not on verifiable references to some "content" but rather only on Huidobro's own willingness to spin a tale; the only reality in such a case is that the text of story exists, even if it is only the narration of a fiction. Critically speaking, life and the representation of life become unmanageable, to the extent that autobiography cannot represent a life if in fact that life was never lived. Rather, autobiography (the story Huidobro offered up to explain himself) is a pretext for creating an experience that must now be retold as real, even if we know it to be untrue. In this case there can be no specular difference between what we nominally call "life" and its "literary representation." Autobiography would be nothing less than an exercise in material practice, of taking the textual-rhetorical creation and making it real, and not vice versa. Of course, the level of duplicity required to achieve such an effect would strain matters of authenticity and the authority of lived-experience beyond what we are accustomed to. De Man's essays, for instance, are designed to attack one's false belief that one is an authentic subject; subjectivity is only discordant difference and not unified identity. At the very least, de Man attacks literary critics who believe they have the ability to read and speak of literary "unities" with any authority. The outcome of de Man's various attacks, however, is little more than nihilism. De Man constructs nothing from his deconstruction, but merely seems to relish his rhetorical acts of destruction. Yet this is really a *safe* kind of destruction precisely because de Man always operates within strict limitations. Literature and language are never quite real, and so destroying them (or using them to destroy something else) changes nothing in the world; if the autobiographical subject is only specular and never ontological, then the same must hold true for the de(con)struction of the autobiographical subject. In short, de Man never *actually* killed anyone—whatever part he played in the "death of the author."

In contrast, Huidobro's autobiographical life (or lived autobiography, take your pick) can only be considered an act of monumental bad faith and unmitigated buffoonery, and is for this reason *dangerous*. For if we can assume no separation between reality and representation, or between life and literature, then we will be led to unspeakable conclusions. Untruth becomes *everything* in Huidobro's life, such that it is pointless to debate what is true or not. As a type of text, Huidobro's life may be subject to what Benjamin called the "afterlife of the text"—a series of textual transmissions and translations that sustains the "original." And this afterlife may be revolutionary. We will get to the details soon, but for now suffice it to say that this lifestory does not *conclude* in 1948 with Huidobro's death, but will *include* motorcycle accidents, generous widows, blue and red pencils, and the Banco del Estado of Chile.

Itself Repeats History: A Narrative Synopsis of *Altazor*

If Huidobro's life was an exercise in literary practice, then what of his actual literary practice? In a way, Huidobro's afterlife begins at the end of *Altazor*, a moment that defies translation:

    Io ia

i i i o

Ai ai ai a i i i i o ia (A 111)

In the beginning of the work, we are introduced to a hero, named Altazor, who is falling to the earth in a parachute, though we never know when or where he has begun his descent, nor when or where it will end. With these final lines composed exclusively of vowels, then, we may be led to a representation of Altazor's screams as he falls through the sky. The vowels may be instantly transformed into pure onomatopoeia—a representation of the (nonlinguistic) sounds /a/, /i/, and /o/, conventionally symbolized by the graphemes *a*, *i*, and *o*, and with no semantic denotation beyond the enunciation of those sounds. Thus, the lines "defy translation" in that they may no longer pertain to the Spanish language in which *Altazor* was originally published, but rather to any and all languages that happen to employ the phonemes /a/-/i/-/o/ in phonetic-Latinate orthography. In such circumstances, there is no need to translate them since they are, in a sense, *already* translated into every phonetic-Latinate written language. Or perhaps, since onomatopoeia may be the most basic and "primitive" use of language,[14] the lines may stand prior to language as such—so that the need for translatability never arises in the first place. I would characterize a line such as "Ai ai ai a i i i i o ia," therefore, as an instance of "localized universality," motivated by a desire for a "pure and universal language." The final lines of *Altazor* denote sounds common to a great number of languages, yet we cannot ignore the fact that, on a material level, they appear in a script (i.e., phonetic-Latinate) that is specific to Western/European orthographies, or orthographies such as Vietnamese marked by the imposition of Western/European rule. The "universality" expressed in and by the lines can only be said to have been achieved in a limited or localized set of languages or written scripts. Therefore, the "task of the translator" moving between different phonetic-Latinate languages (e.g., Spanish-English, or Spanish-Polish, or Vietnamese-Swedish) is most likely a very easy task in this instance, since in effect the lines require no translation at all.[15]

But in what sense can we identify this localized universality as Chilean, Latin American, or American? The interpretation I have just provided is entirely shaped by the context of *Altazor* as much as the text of the poem. *Altazor* is composed of seven cantos of varying lengths, numbered by Roman numerals, and an introductory "Prefacio," all written in free verse. The Prefacio begins with a more or less understandable story line:

> Nací a los treinte y tres años, el día de la muerte de Cristo; nací en el Equinoccio, bajo las hortensias y los aeroplanos del calor. (A 9)
>
> [I was born at the age of 33 on the day Christ died; I was born at the Equinox, under the hydrangeas and the aeroplanes in the heat.]

Here we have a narrator, a "yo" who tells of the day of his birth; and we quickly learn that this narrator is named "Altazor" and that he is falling to his death through the sky in a parachute (though we never learn where he began his fall or when/where it will end): "Ah, ah, soy Altazor, el gran poeta, sin caballo que coma alpiste, ni caliente su garganta con claro de luna, sino con mi pequeño paracaídas como un quitasol sobre los planetas" (A 13). ["Oh yes I am Altazor, the great poet, without a horse that eats birdseed or warms its throat with moonbeams, with only my little parachute like a parasol over the planets."] If the narrative of *Altazor* (the work) or "Altazor" (the character) begins so straightforwardly, then, we must question how we get to the end of Canto VII—how we get from point A to point B:

> Semperiva
>   ivarisa tarirá
> Campanudio lalalí
>   Auriciento auronida
> Lalalí
>   Io ia
> i i i o
> Ai a i ai a i i i i o ia (A 111)
>
> [Livfrever
>   Lefdalafda dadeedah
> Campellationed lalalee
>   Auricental centauroral
> Lalalee
>   Eeoh eeah
> ee ee ee oh
> Ahee ah ee ahee ah ee ee ee ee oh eeah]

Obviously something has happened between *here* and *there*, something I would characterize as a regression, a "reverse" narrative beginning in communicable language and ending in phonemic nonsense. It is, in other words, a narrative sequence of formal disruptions that we will call a "reverse verse narrative."

The notion of a "verse narrative," let alone a "reverse verse narrative," by its very nature implies rather severe temporal complications. We usually think of "narrative" as a sequence of represented events, usually ordered by a logical progression, whether one of time or character development. If it is the nature of "narrative" to move forward, or at least to have some orderly arrangement of beginning, middle, and end, the nature of "verse" is quite the opposite—to move backward. As Roman Jakobson reminds us in "Grammatical Parallelism and Its Russian Facet," the etymology of the word "verse" implies a sense of "return":

> We have learned the suggestive etymology of the terms *prose* and *verse*—the former, *oratio prosa* < *prorsa* < *proversa* (speech turned straightforward), and the latter, *versus* (return). Hence we must consistently draw all inferences from the obvious fact that on every level of language the essence of poetic artifice consists in recurrent returns. Phonemic features and sequences, both morphologic and lexical, syntactic and phraseological units, when occurring in metrically or strophically corresponding positions, are necessarily subject to the conscious or subconscious questions of whether, how far, and in what respect the positionally corresponding entities are mutually similar.[16]

By the terms of Jakobson's etymologies, it almost seems natural to think of "narrative" only as "prose narrative," since prosaic "speech turned straightforward" may match the normative temporality of narrative representation. In the case of "verse narrative," however, a disjunction would seem to arise between what a narrative says or represents (a normatively unidirectional temporal sequence of represented events based on cause and effect) and poetic language itself (morphemes, lexemes, syntax, and phrases positioned around repetition and return). Ultimately, it is the *positions of language* that define "verse" and "poetry" for Jakobson—the ways in which linguistic signs may be positioned in relation to one another, and the ways in which the materiality of signs becomes accentuated in contrast to what is signified or represented. By characterizing *Altazor* as "*reverse* verse narrative," then, I am suggesting that the text operates, not just around material returns and regressions of the sign already implicit in "verse," but with a more advanced *double* regression of signic positions, a doubly regressive language, that produces a kind of temporal and material vertigo.

In *Altazor* we will not find much in the way of the precise phonemic, morphemic, or syntactic recurrences of which Jakobson speaks—rhyme and meter—although we will immediately recognize from the outset that its poetics is one of positional associations. For instance, we can return to the first line of the Prefacio:

> Nací a los treinte y tres años, el día de la muerte de Cristo; nací en el Equinoccio bajo las hortensias y los aeroplanos del calor. (A 9)
>
> [I was born at the age of 33 the day Christ died; I was born at the Equinox, under the hydrangeas and the aeroplanes in the heat.]

This line is constructed around sets of oppositional associational "vectors" within which the narrator is both located and suspended. The narrator is born as an adult, as a man-child who, born as a man, is the opposite of Christ, the divine man-child who was born as a child; and this anti-Christian stance of the narrator is accentuated by the fact that his birth is on the day of Christ's death. Furthermore, he is born on the Equinox, the Pagan precursor to Easter, the day that equalizes night and day; although we need to remember that on every Equinox there are in fact two Equinoxes, Vernal and Autumnal, such that we cannot tell on which Equinox the narrator was born on since we do not know whether he is located in the Northern or Southern Hemisphere. The narrator's birth also occurs *underneath* something, either under the feminized ground ("bajo *las* hortensias," *la tierra*) or from above, under the masculinized sky ("bajo *los* aeroplanos," *el cielo*). This single line thus captures an impressive number of *polar* opposites: birth/death, adult/child, day/night, north/south, Christ/anti-Christ, good/evil, Christian/Pagan, earth/sky, above/below, male/female, to which we could also add the *natural* flowers versus the *artificial* (man-made) aeroplanes, and the *ancient* world of myths versus the *modern* world of technology. These positional abstractions are important, since the Prefacio is positioned as a sort of biblical (or rather, an ironically anti-biblical) *allegory*. In one of the first scenes that he narrates, Altazor recounts a kind of "double Genesis," a double myth of origin, as he falls through the sky. At the start, Altazor tells of his first day:

> El primer día encontré un pájaro desconocido que me dijo: «Si yo fuese dromedario no tendría sed. ¿Qué hora es?»...(A 9–10)
>
> [On the first day I met an unknown bird who told me: "If I were a camel I'd know no thirst. What time is it?"...]

Although the utterance of "El primer día" echoes the language of the opening chapters of Genesis, the utterance only leads us to a talking animistic bird, who is unknown or "desconocido," whose words make little apparent sense, and who has no sense of time (let alone that this is the "first day"). All these attributes tend to ascribe to the bird a certain sacredness—an unknowable supernaturalness beyond human time and reason.

Immediately following the encounter, however, Altazor runs into a Judeo-Christian God who speaks of the Creation:

> Entonces oí hablar al Creador, sin nombre, que es un simple hueco en el vacío, hermoso como un ombligo.
> «Hice un gran ruido y este ruido formó el océano y las olas del océano.
> »Este ruido irá siempre pegado a las olas del mar y las olas del mar irán siempre pegadas a él, como los sellos en las tarjetas postales...
> (A 10)
>
> [Then I heard the voice of the Creator, who is nameless, who is a simple hollow in the void, lovely as a navel.
> "I made a great crashing sound and that sound formed the oceans and the ocean waves.
> "That noise will be stuck forever to the waves of the sea and the waves of the sea will be stuck forever to that sound, like stamps to a postcard....]

This section unmistakably alludes to the Genesis myth, an allusion so blatant that it seems more of a crude mimicry of allegory than a proper allegorical allusion. At the same time, however, the lines reinscribe the myth in a complex way. The Creator-God, rather than being the supreme substance, appears as the figure of emptiness; even more, he factors as a "double emptiness," a "hollow" within a "void" ["un hueco en el vacío"]. His *logos* is noise ["ruido"] evidently devoid of semantic sense. And while it is presumably prehistorical as the act of "original" universal creation, the *logos* here becomes quite modern. On the one hand, the noise of the *logos* seems pre-semantic, sound not yet formed into signification. Yet on the other hand, the power of *logos* engenders the mimetic translation, or really the metonymic identification, of the Creator's noise and the noise of the waves of the sea; noise in this sense *becomes* the sea, or *means* the sea. Here the attachment of noise to the waves seems to model an abstracted relation of sound to object, or to be more precise in this case, of sound to object-image.

In this abstract sense, the image seems to approach Saussurean analogies of signifier to signified—that is, similar to *modern* (structural linguistic) conceptions of sign. We find, for instance, the following account of language in the *Course in General Linguistics*:

> A language might also be compared to a sheet of paper. Thought is one side of the sheet and sound the reverse side. Just as it is impossible to take a pair of scissors and cut one side of the paper without at the same time cutting the other, so it is impossible in a language to isolate sound from thought, or thought from sound. To separate the two for theoretical purposes takes us into either pure psychology or pure phonetics, not linguistics.
>
> Linguistics, then, operates along this margin, where sound and thought meet. *The contact between them gives rise to a form, not a substance.*[17]

For Saussure, the linguistic sign (signifier/signified, sound/object-image) is analogous to two sides of the same leaf of paper; Huidobro also analogizes the sound-object relation to paper, the adhesion of a postal stamp to a postcard. Yet while the central image Huidobro presents is a primal moment of mythic creation, the point of reference for this image (in the Creator's own analogy, no less) is a modern thing, a product of the modern economy, contemporary consumerism, and tourism—the postcard, a *cheap* image that can be mailed and then discarded once it has been received.

Immediately following the passages just analyzed, Altazor's encounters with divine, quasi-biblical forces are again redoubled. Altazor soon meets "la Virgen" who seems to symbolize both erotic love ("Amame, hijo mío," she states, "Tengo tanta necesidad de ternura, besa mis cabellos..." (A 12). ["Love me, my child.../I have a need for tenderness, kiss my hair...."] As female, the Virgin also comes to symbolize difference ("Soy la Virgen, la Virgen sin mancha de tinta humana..." (A 12). ["I am the Virgin, the Virgin without human stain...."] In this sense, the apparition of the Virgin represents the last in a series of dialogic encounters marked by the maintenance of relational borders between interlocutors: animal/man, divine/human, mythic/historical, primordial/modern, and ultimately, male/female. Within these binary distinctions, however, it becomes difficult to tell which association pertains to each interlocutor. The Creator is clearly divine, for instance, but he finishes his creation with a mundane human activity: "Después bebí un poco de cognac (a causa de la hidrografía)" (A 10); he states ["Then I drank a little cognac (for hydrographic reasons)."] Likewise, the figure of the

Virgin, representing the "primal" desire of erotic coupling (copulation and copula), analogizes her own body to a modern invention:

> «Mira mis manos: son transparentes como las bombillas eléctricas. ¿Ves los filamentos de donde corre la sangre de mi luz intacta? (A 12)
>
> ["Look at my hands, they are transparent as light bulbs. Do you see the filaments where the blood of my pure light flows?]

As with the prior analogy between the *logos*, the sign, and postal stamps/postcards, the analogous point of reference of the Virgin's divine body is a disposable product of modernity and modern science: her hands are light bulbs, her veins are electrified filaments. The *modern* product, in other words, almost seems to stand prior to the eternal, divine body as some a priori object available for analogy. In the three encounters of the Prefacio, divinity is thus presented through a series of associational inversions: the animistic animal doubling to the anthropomorphic figure of the Creator, and then the anthropomorphic Creator doubled over by "gyno-morphic" figure of the Virgin.

These initial passages of Altazor's journey from birth to death, then, clearly establish allegorical modalities between the present text (*Altazor*) and an allegorical key (the Book of Genesis, Christian myths). Yet, far from endorsing the prior texts to which it alludes, the Prefacio positions itself *against* its allegorical key through the inscription of parodic *re*inscription. The very language of the Prefacio begins in a strikingly nonrealistic mode. We never really begin to understand the poem's language as a representation of the real, and in fact we may be inclined to understand the "real" purpose of words to be their propensity for abstraction—as I have done in isolating the "associational vectors" of the opening lines. Under such conditions, the potential of allegorical meaning becomes unhinged by the persistence of irony through a series of comic doublings of the origin: the moment of genesis splits between Christianity and a "primitive" animism; and then Christian myths are rather "cheapened" through their entrance into an economy of consumerism and tourism (light bulbs and postcards). The "doubling of origins" necessarily alters the position of history in the work since, although the allegorical "key" is quite old, the genesis actually spoken of in the Prefacio has now become "modern" or "modernized." "Origin" by definition precedes history as that event which allows history to progress, but here the origin "doubles over" as a modern event related in a modern text and is thus *re*positioned as the end of history. In distancing itself from the texts to which it alludes allegorically, in other words, the Prefacio exacerbates the temporal gap between its prehistoric origin (Genesis) and its own status as a modern thing, and thus allows for the ironization of their allegorical relationship. The Prefacio's reinscription of the origin establishes a kind of *battle royale* between irony and allegory as to which will become the dominant trope of the work; irony in the Prefacio enters into the poem's allegory as a disruptive force, as that which "trips up" the formality of the relationship between the present narrative and its allegorical key. And it is precisely such internecine rhetorical-tropological strife between the figure of irony and the figure of allegory that we will position as central to the overall narrative structure of the rest of the work.

If this account sounds familiar I should make clear that I am, in my way, characterizing *Altazor* as an allegorical manifestation of de Man's deconstruction of allegory and irony in "The Rhetoric of Temporality." To reiterate, de Man sets out to explain the literary-historical shift from eighteenth-century irony and allegory to a nineteenth-century preponderance of Romantic symbolism, in a way that sets the stage for an understanding of a twentieth-century (modernist) return to irony. To do this, de Man pinpoints sets of inherent differences that constitute the tropes:

> In the world of the symbol it would be possible for the image to coincide with the substance, since the substance and its representation do not differ in their being but only in their extension: they are part and whole of the same set of categories. Their relationship is one of simultaneity, which, in truth, is spatial in kind, and in which the intervention of time is merely a matter of contingency, whereas, in the world of allegory, time is the originary constitutive category. The relationship between the allegorical sign and its meaning (*signifié*) is not decreed by dogma; in the instances we have seen in Rousseau and Wordsworth, this is not at all the case. We have, instead, a relationship between signs in which the reference to their respective meanings has become of secondary importance. But this relationship between signs necessarily contains a constitutive temporal element; it remains necessary, if there is to be allegory, that the allegorical sign refer to another sign that precedes it. The meaning constituted by the allegorical sign can then consist only in the *repetition* (in the Kierkegaardian sense of the term) of a previous sign with which it can never coincide, since it is of the essence of this previous sign to be pure anteriority.[18]

In this sense, allegory must be viewed according to the interobjective (rather than "intersubjective") relationship between itself and some prior "allegorical key," and as a result allegory must remain *inauthentic*, a mere *repetition* of the object to which it alludes. The reader must recognize that the allegorical sign does not only have meaning in and by itself, but that the sign refers to a previously known, more true, and more authentic text, sign, or significance. Although allegory attempts to bring this "true meaning" to light, it only properly operates in the temporal estrangement from its origin. Paradoxically, then, the temporal displacement inherent in allegory must be mystified— not obliterated, but rather overlooked—in order for the "true" significance of the allegory to play itself out. Irony may thus enter into the picture as the trope of demystification or self-knowledge of allegorical inauthenticity. For de Man, irony carries us from an interobjective mode of understanding to an intersubjective one, since it requires *one to know* that something ironic is happening. Taking a cue from Baudelaire's thoughts on "the essence of laughter,"[19] de Man renders irony as the act of the subject's tripping and falling, and the subject's own self-knowledge, objectified in language, that s/he is about to fall down:

> In the idea of fall thus conceived, a progression of self-knowledge is certainly implicit: the man who has fallen is somewhat wiser than the fool who walks around oblivious of the crack in the pavement about to trip him up. And the fallen philosopher reflecting on the discrepancy between the two successive stages is wiser still, but this does not in the least prevent him from stumbling in his turn. It seems instead that his wisdom can be gained only at the cost of such a fall. The mere falling of others does not suffice; he has to go down himself. The ironic, twofold self that the writer or philosopher constitutes by his language seems able to come into being only at the expense of his empirical self, falling (or rising) from a stage of mystified adjustment into the knowledge of his mystification. The ironic language splits the subject into an empirical self that exists in a state of inauthenticity and a self that exists only in the form of a language that asserts the knowledge of this inauthenticity. This does not, however, make it into an authentic language, for to know inauthenticity is not the same as to be authentic.[20]

Curiously, "intersubjectivity" here occurs in the relationship between two "split personalities" of a single subject, in the movement between one self that is mystified and the same self capable of objectively recognizing its own mystification through language.

The rhetorical-deconstructive tendencies of *Altazor* have not been overlooked by Huidobro scholars. Indeed, I am in my way merely repeating gestures made by George Yúdice. In *Vicente Huidobro y la motivación del lenguaje*, Yúdice quotes directly from "The Rhetoric of Temporality" in order to situate *Altazor* within an intertextual tradition of "empty transcendence" [*"transcendencia vacua"*]. Yúdice finds Huidobro's work to be a continuation of the tropology of falling that is present in Milton, Goethe, Mallarmé, and, most significantly for Yúdice's reading, Baudelaire and Lautréamont. Especially in Lautréamont's *Les Chants de Maldoror*, the figure of the fallen angel emblematizes a demystification of Christian ideology, and therefore dramatizes an ironic, existentialist break with Western metaphysics that can also be found in the opening of *Altazor*. With these prior authors and texts, however, metaphysical rupture remains on the level of rhetorical figuration, and in such a context Yúdice situates Huidobro's innovation in the relocation of "empty transcendence" to a material network of normative linguistic codes rather than to the tropes of rhetoric. Metaphysical and ideological demystification in *Altazor* is performed by a definitive break with the "base" laws of language (grammar, phonology, morphology, syntax, and semantics) upon which rhetorical and poetic structures have been built. The purpose of this "structuralist" fall from language is therefore contradictory: demystification is made "real" by the "destructuring" of language *as printed on the page*, language as material; yet the destruction of language in *Altazor* merely sets the stage for *remystification*, for the creation of a "new" language capable of producing a "new" *mythos*:

> This attitude reveals a contradiction: languages are dead; to revive them they must be destroyed. There is, then, a destructive/constructive process parallel to the fall towards an unknown absolute. In *Altazor* the fall is not only demystification, but also an alternation between demystification/mystification. The process is analogous to the intention of "creating" a new and absolute language, the "authentic" language to which de Man refers, in the face of an inauthentic, mystified language.[21]

Altazor attempts to create a "new origin" for language and culture by *returning* to the linguistic matter upon which national cultural ideologies have been (and will be) constructed. Yet, granted that Yúdice's analysis was published over a quarter of a century ago, we need to confront the limitations of his thought (limitations Yúdice has clearly surpassed himself in the meantime). For Yúdice in 1978, the *originality* of Huidobro's Creationism resides in the material operation of language—in the non-referential disruption of linguistic structure. Yet the critic (in one of the earliest works of his long, distinguished career) does not push materialism to its fullest extent.

Yúdice's critique (just as de Man's before him) remains lodged in abstracted systems of linguistic form assumed to be common to all languages, but he does not consider language as physical matter printed in a book, nor the editorial history of how that book has come to be. Because language is posited as an abstract system, furthermore, Yúdice cannot consider the material context of culture in which *Altazor* appears. "Empty transcendence" pertains to a cultural nexus of intertextual relationships, yet the universality of linguistic relationships that Yúdice assumes as his critical base does not permit cultural specificity: the chain of relations from a Latin American text back to Lautréamont (the Uruguayan-born French writer), back to exemplars of French, German, and English literary traditions.

I am not so much interested in identifying the history of intertextual allusions in *Altazor*, as I am in analyzing how the materialist poetics of the work may serve to relocate the position of *Altazor* in history. Any formal logic of *Altazor*, whether immanent or transcendent, empty or full, should serve as a starting point from which to comprehend the cultural positions of the work. By ironizing Western/Christian modes of allegory, the Prefacio serves as a proposition for the work as a whole: it proposes the work as an allegory, but at the same time proposes an ironic disruption of allegory positioned against its allegorical key, employing nonrealistic language geared to the establishment of bipolar associational vectors. From these propositions, we will witness through the first three cantos of *Altazor* the steady dissolution of allegory, as well as any recognizable plot line. As Altazor (the character) falls he ceases to relate *events* and begins to reflect on his status as a poet, reflect on (modern) poetry in general, and self-reflect on his status as a poetic character made of words. As such, it becomes difficult to gauge whether Altazor is really speaking anymore, or whether we are instead receiving a direct communication from Vicente Huidobro. In any event, although a sense of story disappears from *Altazor* (the text), narrative does not cease to be; to the contrary, the more story and plot evaporate, the more *Altazor* becomes a "formal narrative"—a narrative that sequences distinct rhetorical, poetic, and ultimately linguistic forms together in temporal progression. The more the story of Altazor (the character) disintegrates, the more the story of *Altazor* (the work) materializes.

The first three cantos, for instance, are bound together, not by *content* necessarily, but by the various rhetorical postures or poses they take. Canto I is a dialogue between Altazor (the character) and

Vicente Huidobro (the author). The canto begins with a series of questions directed to Altazor:

> Altazor ¿por qué perdiste tu primera serenidad?
> ....
> Estás perdido Altazor
> Solo en medio del universo
> Solo como una nota que florece en las alturas del vacío
> No hay bien no hay mal ni verdad ni orden ni belleza
> ¿En dónde estás Altazor? (A 17)
>
> [Altazor, why did you ever lose your young serenity?
> ....
> You're lost Altazor
> Alone in the middle of the universe
> Alone like a note flowering in the heights of space
> There's no good no evil no truth no order no beauty
> Where are you Altazor?]

Altazor often responds to such questions with "Soy yo..." ["I am..."], a statement of his own subjectivity: for instance, "Soy yo Altazor el doble de mí mismo" (A 22) ["Altazor am I the double of my self"]. As the double of his own self, Altazor becomes a token of the ironic "split self" discussed by de Man. But more significantly, the doubling of self seems to obscure the distinction between "tú" and "yo" upon which the dialogue of the canto is based:

> Yo tú él nosotros vosotros ellos
> Ayer hoy mañana
> ....
> ...¿qué has hecho de mí Vicente Huidobro? (A 25)
>
> [I you he we they
> Yesterday today tomorrow
> ....
> ...what have you done to me Vicente Huidobro?]

The non-referential listing of grammatical subject-pronouns and temporal states leads directly to a shift in the dialogue: the author, who first appeared as a character addressing a character he has introduced as a poetic author, must now answer to a character who questions his author's intentions. Expressed in this way, we can no longer ascertain who the narrator of the narrative will be: Huidobro or Altazor?

This question is not resolved in Canto II, as any recognizable story line totally disappears. Instead, we are presented with an apostrophe to a woman, who may be the very figure of Beauty, but who nonetheless remains unidentifiable:

> Mi alegría es mirarte solitaria en el diván del mundo
> Como la mano de una princesa soñolienta
> Con tus ojos que evocan un piano de olores
> Una bebida de paroxismos
> Una flor que está dejando de perfumar
> Tus ojos hipnotizan la soledad
> Como la rueda que sigue girando después de la catástrofe...(A 50)
>
> [The joy of watching you alone on the couch of the world
> Like the hand of a drowsy princess
> With your eyes that evoke a piano of smells
> A sip of paroxysms
> A flower that has given up perfuming
> Your eyes hypnotize solitude
> Like the wheel that keeps turning after the crash...]

Canto II remains in a metaphorical mode, even though it breaks with typical modes of metaphor: the woman's eyes combine sound and smell ["un piano de olores"]; her eyes are then linked to taste ["bebida"] in a rather spasmodic image ["una bebida de paroxismos"]; and finally her eyes become the emblem of the aftermath of destruction. As an experiment in synesthesia, the metaphors offer little in the way of coherent sense. Yet merely by being incoherent, they do make us aware that they are metaphorical—a rather typical effect of avant-garde defamiliarization. This defamiliarized poetic self-reflexivity becomes more explicit in Canto III, which begins as a monologue on poetic creation:

> Todas las lenguas están muertas
> Muertas en manos del vecino trágico
> Hay que resucitar las lenguas
> Con sonoras risas
> Con vagones de carcajadas
> Con cortacircuitos en las frases
> Y cataclismo en la gramática...(A 58)
>
> [All languages are dead
> Dead in the hands of the tragic neighbor
> We must revive the languages
> With raucous laughter
> With wagons of cackles
> With circuit breakers in sentences
> And cataclysm in the grammar...]

From the Prefacio to Canto III, then, the "death of language" is represented by a series of rhetorical stances aligned in recognizable decline: the Prefacio is an allegorical dialogue between two texts, that is, intertextual movements between one text (the Bible) and another (*Altazor* itself); Canto I is a dialogue between two characters within the narrative; Canto II an apostrophe, a monologue spoken in "dialogue" to another figure who is absent from the conversation; and Canto III a monologue. As the narrative frustrates the meaningful possibilities of allegory (certainly, that is, the frustration of *Christian* allegory presented in the Prefacio), the more the work seems to also frustrate, rhetorically speaking, the circuit of speech communication as the notion of "conversation" and "dialogue" is reduced to "monologue."

By Canto III, moreover, it is not just rhetoric that breaks down, but also language itself. When Canto III enunciates in its opening line "Romper las ligaduras de las venas" (A 53) ["Break the loops (ligatures) of the veins"] we must understand this not merely as a ripping of the body, but more presciently as a ripping up of the textual *corpus* itself. This textualized carnage comes across most forcefully in a series of playful similes:

> Basta señora arpa de las bellas imágenes
> De los furtivos comos iluminados
> Otra cosa otra cosa buscamos
> Sabemos posar un beso como una mirada
> Plantar miradas como árboles
> Enjaular árboles como pájaros
> Regar pájaros como heliotropos
> Tocar un heliotropo como una música
> Vaciar una música como un saco
> Degollar un saco como un pingüino
> Cultivar pingüinos como viñedos
> . . . .
> Etc. etc. etc. (A 56–57)

> [Enough lady harp of beautiful images
> Of clandestine illuminated "likes"
> It's something else we're looking for something else
> We already know how to dart a kiss like a glance
> Plant glances like trees
> Cage trees like birds
> Water birds like heliotropes
> Play heliotropes like music
> Empty music like a sack

> Decapitate a sack like a penguin
> Cultivate penguins like vineyards
> ....
> Etc. etc. etc.]

The addition of "Etc. etc. etc." at the end of the strophe signals the establishment of a pattern carried forth without concern for the creation of meaningful or beautiful images. We have instead a braid of similes in which the immediate referent is thrown into a phrase to which it should not belong semantically. That is, the refer*ent* is not normatively associated semantically with the verb at the beginning of each simile; the verb, however, does pertain to the refer*and* at the end of each line, and the referand then becomes the disassociated referent of the next line. Thus, "miradas" has little semantic association with "plantar," though "plantar" is associated with "como árboles"; in the next line, "árboles" has little semantic association with "enjaular," though "enjaular" is associated with "como pájaros," and so on. The result is a long sequence of nonsensical similes that nevertheless appear as a surreal, automatic series of metaphorical images.

While this braid of similes disrupts semantic conventions of metaphor, the semantic function of the words themselves remains intact, such that we can be assured that "saco" means "sack" and "pingüinos" means "penguins." By Canto IV, however, the relational rules of language cannot be assumed to be guaranteed, since disruption and play on the level of structure becomes increasingly pronounced, producing a long series of syllabic and morphological displacements:

> Al horitaña de la montezonte
> La violondrina y el goloncelo
> Descolgada esta mañana de la lunala
> Se acerca a todo galope
> Ya viene viene la golondrina
> Ya viene viene la golonfina
> Ya viene la golontrina
> Ya viene la goloncima
> Viene la golonchina
> Viene la golonclima
> Ya viene la golonrima
> Ya viene la golonrisa
> La golonniña
> La golongira
> La golonlira
> La golonbrisa
> La golonchilla...(A 58)

> [At the horslope of the hillizon
> The violonswallow and the cellotail
> Slipped down this morning from a lunawing
> And hurries near
> Look here swoops the swooping swallow
> Here swoops the whooping wallow
> Here swoops the weeping wellow
> Look here swoops the sweeping shrillow
> Swoops the swamping shallow
> Swoops the sheeping woolow
> Swoops the slooping swellow
> Look here swoops the sloping spillow
> The scooping spellow
> The souping smellow
> The seeping swillow
> The sleeping shellow
> Look here swoops the swooping day...]

Though Eliot Weinberger does an admirable job of creating new sense in English, passages such as this become increasingly difficult to translate—since the poetic effect is peculiarly situated, at least for the moment, in the Spanish language. In this passage, words are split apart and recombined, such that "horizonte" and "montaña" become "horitaña" and "montezonte." Immediately following, the poem fractures the word "golondrina" ["swallow" (the bird)] into combinatory word-forms that are not themselves authentic words. Instead we have the repetition of the stem "golon-" combined with selections of other words seemingly produced because of their morphological or phonemic similarity: drina, fina, trina, cima, china, clima, and so on. Does the translator thus choose to carry forth these morphological-phonemic similarities into the target-language, or, as Weinberger does, create a new set of similarities suited to the target-language? Huidobro's original is a "transcreation" of the Spanish language, one that makes translation almost impossible.

The combination, recombination, and thus disintegration of language on the level of latent structure reach ludicrous heights in Canto V. The fifth canto consists almost exclusively of wordplays, building to the middle of the poem that announces:

> Jugamos fuera del tiempo
> Y juega con nosotros el molino de viento...(A 84)
>
> [We play outside of time
> And the windmill plays along...]

What follows from this chiasmic statement is perhaps the most famous section of *Altazor*, the "Molinos" [the "Mills"]: six-and-a-half to seven pages containing 190 iterations of the word "Molino" in prepositional phrases. As terrifyingly repetitive as it is, it also creates a stunning picture on the page (figure 3.1).

Indeed, the "Molinos" are a quite *graphic* representation, *avant la lettre*, of Roman Jakobson's "poetic function." As Jakobson states in 1958's "Linguistics and Poetics":

> What is the empirical linguistic criterion of the poetic function? In particular, what is the indispensable feature inherent in any piece of poetry? To answer this question we must recall the two basic modes of arrangement use in verbal behavior, *selection* and *combination*.... The selection is produced on the basis of equivalence, similarity and dissimilarity, synonymy and antonymy, while the combination, the build-up of the sequence, is based on contiguity. *The poetic function projects the principle of equivalence from the axis of selection into the axis of combination.*[22]

Each line may be read horizontally as the formulaic combination: ["Molino"] + [preposition (de, del, en, con, para, como, a, que, in that order)] + [verb nominalized by the addition of the suffix "-miento" or "-mento"]. The repetition of this formula, however, also produces a *vertical* reading—a vertical "falling" down the page in four typographic columns organized through syntactic selection: (A) "Molino" (one selection); (B) preposition (8 selections); (C) verb-form root (190 selections); and (D) suffix (2 selections, scattered): for example, "Molino (A)—de (B)—descubri (C)—miento (D)." The poetic effect of the section is thus produced by this vertical reading, as we notice (and combine semantically) the different selections of the roots of the prepositional object: for example, descubri-, escurri-, remordi-, redobla-, etc., all of which are displayed in a vertical column. In other words, the selection of these variegated *roots* drives the poetic combination of them; poetry is made "real," not only in the horizontal repetition of a syntactic formula but in the vertical combination of syntactic selections. In this sense, poetic selection and combination become *things* we can actually see and sense. If, as Jakobson posits, the poetic function accentuates the materiality of the sign (i.e., the material selection and combination of signs), the Molino section accentuates *Altazor's* materiality as printed matter. Typography itself instantiates the axes of selection and combination— factored as vertical and horizontal columns of typography—such

Molino de encabezamiento
Molino de encastillamiento
Molino de aparecimiento
Molino de despojamiento
Molino de atesoramiento
Molino de enloquecimiento
Molino de ensortijamiento
Molino de envenenamiento
Molino de acontecimiento
Molino de descuartizamiento
Molino del portento
Molino del lamento
Molino del momento
Molino del firmamento
Molino del sentimiento
Molino del juramento
Molino del ardimiento
Molino del crecimiento
Molino del nutrimiento
Molino del conocimiento
Molino del descendimiento
Molino del desollamiento
Molino del elevamiento
Molino del endiosamiento
Molino del alumbramiento
Molino del deliramiento
Molino del aburrimiento
Molino del engreimiento
Molino del escalamiento

Molino del descubrimiento
Molino del escurrimiento
Molino del remordimiento
Molino del redoblamiento
Molino del atronamiento
Molino del aturdimiento
Molino del despeñamiento
Molino del quebrantamiento
Molino del envejecimiento
Molino del aceleramiento
Molino del encarnizamiento
Molino del anonadamiento
Molino del arrepentimiento
Molino del encanecimiento
Molino del despedazamiento
Molino del descorazonamiento
Molino en fragmento
Molino en detrimento
Molino en giramiento
Molino en gruñimiento
Molino en sacramento
Molino en pensamiento
Molino en pulsamiento
Molino en pudrimiento
Molino en nacimiento
Molino en apiñamiento
Molino en apagamiento
Molino en decaimiento
Molino en derretimiento

Figure 3.1 The "Molinos" of the first edition of *Altazor* (reprinted under the authorization of the Fundación Vicente Huidobro).

that the words no longer *refer* to a "mill," but are *themselves* a mill, milling and spitting out combinations of linguistic roots *down the page*.

It is through this milling that we reach the end, and therefore the beginning, of the "reverse verse narrative." Canto VI presents increased tendencies to play with words that make less and less sense, because they are positioned in increasingly agrammatical constructions:

Bella tienda
Cristal nube
      muerte joya o en ceniza

Porque eterno porque eterna
                      lento lenta
Al azar del cristal ojos
Gracia tanta
            y entre mares
Miramares
Nombres daba
            por los ojos hojas mago
Alto alto
Y el clarín de la Babel
Pida nácar
            tenga muerte
Una dos y cuatro muerte...(A 103)

[The lovely shop
Cloud crystal
            death jewel or in ashes
For heternity for sheternity
            slowly slow
By chance the eyes crystal
Such grace
            between the seas
Sea views
Names given
            for the magician leaf eyes
High high
And the bugle of Babel
Beg for nacre
            have death
A two and four death...]

As indicated in this passage, the canto as a whole displays a startling lack of verbs. Moreover, the words may not have been selected for their semantic content, even though many of the words certainly carry mystical connotations. Rather, the placement of words tends to stress the formal categories by which language is classified. We have the repetition of word-forms in their masculine and feminine aspects ("Porque eterno porque eterna / lento lenta"); and these gendered divisions may be phonetically maintained in spite of semantic, etymological, or orthographic disparities (as with "ojos hojas"). Moreover, we cannot help but notice that the lines adhere to a more or less strict regimen of meter: words are ordered into tetrasyllabic lines, often combining into octasyllabics. Metrically, the canto returns us to a tradition of song-form verse in Hispanic literatures, capturing a resonance of magical incantation. In sum, we still have authentic words in this canto, but they are no longer arranged in any sort of meaningful grammar. The agrammaticality of the language nevertheless inspires grammatical classification and harkens a return to traditional modes of poetics. Significantly, this "harkening" is encoded into the limited semantic fabric of the poem: "Y el clarín de la Babel." This "clarion" apparently harkens a return to prior rhetorical modes of the work, as we have an *allegorical allusion* to the biblical myth of Babel.

In order to frame the nature of this return let me recapitulate the formal narrative I have laid out here, to emphasize its status as "reverse verse narrative." *Altazor* begins in allegory, which is to say that the reader may assume that the basic contract of communication is guaranteed according to preestablished norms of intertextual reference. Intertextual references begin to unhinge themselves, creating strife between irony and allegory in the form of a progressive descent of rhetorical postures in the early cantos. Rhetorical falling is then finalized by a self-reflexive disruption of the linguistic code. The "narrative of rhetoric" (or rhetorical disruption) becomes motivated and displaced by a "narrative of linguistic structure" (or structural disruption). That is, before allegorical or other "higher level" operations come into play, after Canto III the poem moves down a level to struggle with the *literal* meanings of words upon which any rhetorical meanings could be based. The more the work mills words down into smaller and more incomprehensible units, the more the basic materiality of the sign is accentuated, and the more the bibliographic condition of words as printed matter is accordingly accentuated. We are less and less concerned with the *meaning* of words, but rather how words appear as objects on the page—an increasingly extralinguistic concreteness.

This materialistic falling away from allegory, however, *ironically* returns us to an allegorical mode of reading starting from (or ending in?) "el clarín de la Babel." In Canto VII we finally return to a "primitive" state of language:

> Plegasuena
> Cantasorio ululaciente
> Oraneva yu yu yo
> Tempovío
> Infilero e infinauta zurrosía
> Jaurinario ururayú
> Montañendo oraranía
> Arorasía ululacente
> Semperiva
>   ivarisa tarirá
> Campanudio lalalí

                Auriciento auronida
Lalalí
        Io ia
i i i o
Ai a i ai a i i i i o ia (A 111)

Such lines contain fragments of syllables that could have some meaning, but on the whole these are just phonetic, or really phonemic, fragments. In other words, language has now regressed to a foundational, originary moment of language: the phonetic sound, yes, but more precisely the inscription of phonemes, to the point that we are left with only the most basic of phonemic components: vowels. But here we must be extremely careful in our usage of "primitive" and "originary" for we cannot ignore that the "primitive origin" nonetheless arrives at the *end* of the text. We have never really left the sense of "double origin" with which the Prefacio began, but only developed the double origin in certain directions. The "original language" is not immediate in *any* sense, for we only gain a sense of the "primitiveness of the origin" in which the text ends because it has been so thoroughly *mediated* by the uses and abuses of language narrativized by the work. Thus, the final canto may produce a *representation* of a return to linguistic origins, or a *realization* of a "modern origin" for a "new" language, or something that is paving the way for a new authentic or authentically pure language. Such ambivalence between representation and realization may further be conditioned by the "return" to the Babel myth in Canto VI, which begs us to consider the final canto allegorically. Are we thus to understand the end of *Altazor* as a pre-Babelian moment of pure language, one that has truly returned to a mythic site of linguistic origin? Is it a post-Babelian moment of the confusion of tongues, a "new language" that only adds to the contemporary diversity of language, and because of this diversity, contributes to the incommunicability between different tongues? Or in a sense more in tune with Huidobro's *creacionismo*, is *Altazor*'s end in fact a post-post-Babelian *re-instantiation* of a "new original" pure language, one that holds forth the renewed potential for universal communication?

Rather than providing answers to these questions, we will have to remain in a state of indecision in order to comprehend the notion of linguistic "originality" *as indecision. Altazor* presents us with a set of options between a "new" and an "original" language, and perhaps even a "new original" language; yet as mythic as these options may seem, they are nonetheless the product of history: the temporal context or situation established by the work's reverse narrative of forms, historically derived patterns of intertextuality, and the self-reflexive position of the work as a modern object. And now, returning to the purpose of this discussion, because this sense of "new original" seems so suggestively American, how does the formal narrative reversal of *Altazor* contribute to its status as Chilean, as Latin American, or as American in general?

Forward Regression: The Textual History of *Altazor*

If *Altazor* is such a self-reflexive text, how does its reflection on language also reflect on history and culture? Its self-reflexivity also includes a questioning of its own status as printed material, from the start of the book onward. Just as the narrative of *Altazor* plays around with a "doubling of origins," the book itself has double starting points. The title page of the first edition of *Altazor*, for instance, published by the Compañía Ibero Americana de Publicaciones in Madrid, clearly prints the date "1931" at the bottom of the page. This title page attributes a sketch of Huidobro, appearing on the page immediately preceding the title page, to Pablo Picasso. Just prior to Picasso's drawing, however, there is *another* title page. This first title page reads: "ALTAZOR / O EL VIAJE EN PARACAIDAS / Poema en VII cantos / (1919)." The book itself, then, has its own "double origin" in the form of double title pages, which in turn produce a literary historical schism. While the second title page clearly places the work in "1931," toward the end of *vanguardista* era, the first title page positions the work in "1919," precisely at the beginning of the period. Can it be any coincidence, then, that the number "1919" is itself a doubling of "19" and "19"?

This "double-dating" certainly implies historical duplication in some sense. Huidobro, however, has also been accused of deliberate duplicity, the deliberate falsification of publication dates in order to satisfy his own egotism. As David Bary has charged:

> By affirming that the text published in 1931 dates back to 1919, Huidobro attempts to acquire for himself priority with respect to his contemporaries, above all the Surrealists. The blind egotism of he who must be a precursor to everything is nothing more than one aspect of the idolatrized "I" upon which the metaphysical dilemma of the poem is based.
>
> To the falsification of the poem's date corresponds that of the solution Huidobro adopts for the literary-metaphysical problem of language.[23]

Unfortunately for Bary, textual historical evidence does not at all support the idea that "1919" represents a falsification. An early fragment of *Altazor* was published in the Parisian journal, *Transition* (edited by Eugene Jolas), in 1930 under the title "Fragment d'Altazor."[24] Those familiar with Jolas's journal may recall that the June, 1930 double-issue—one of *Transition*'s last—is particularly monumental, including contributions by William Carlos Williams, James Joyce (publishing parts of his then in-progress *Finnegan's Wake* for the first time), Alejo Carpentier, Joán Miró, Tristan Tzara, Samuel Beckett, Paul Bowles, Kay Boyle, Bob Brown, William Empson, Sergei Eisenstein, Carl Jung, and Pablo Picasso, among others. The "Fragment d'Altazor" published there also contains the date "1919." While the date would seem to confirm the historical origin of *Altazor*'s creation, the *Transition* fragment also complicates the notion of the poem's origin since this early version appears *in French*. The fragment is a version of the section previously encountered from Canto IV, the syllabic reversal of "horizonte" and "montaña" (here factored as "A l'horitagne de la montazon" with the deformations of "golondrina" presented as variations of "hirondelle"). This begs the question: Is the *Transition* fragment a *translation* from an original Spanish, or are we to understand the "final" published version as a translation from the French?

This is not an insignificant question if we go back to other previous printings of the poem. The first published appearance of any portion of *Altazor* ran in the Chilean newspaper *La nación* on Wednesday, April 29, 1925. This version would later be published as the opening section of the Prefacio, and it is written in Spanish. The *La nación* fragment thus opens up multiple layers of "originality" flowing through the work: the *first* publication of *Altazor* provides us the *first* section of the work, in which Altazor (the character) encounters the "double myth of Genesis" in the form of the animistic bird and the Judeo-Christian Creator-God. Upon closer inspection, however, one cannot help but notice that the *La nación* version appears, not as *Altazor*, but as "*Altazur* por Vicente Huidobro / Fragmento de 'Un Viaje en Paracaídas' *Traducción de Jean Emar*."[25] This "original" *Altazor*, therefore, is not *Altazor* at all, but rather some *Altazur*. And at this original moment of *Altazor*'s first publication, we learn that the version is not an "original" text, but rather a *translation* from some prior text evidently originally written in French. This "original" version, moreover, is not Huidobro's translation of his own work, but a translation by the Chilean poet Juan (aka Jean) Emar, who edited the "Notas del Arte" section for *La nación*.[26] Moving backward through textual history, through early versions of the text, does not appear to resolve questions of literary historical origin, but only raises more questions. Obviously, Huidobro began to write the text well before 1931, but the evidence we gather to support this fact only refers us back to some other original text that may or may not be the work written in Spanish that we have come to know as *Altazor*.

For most of the work's existence, scholars would have had to stop at the 1925 *La nación* fragment if they wished to recover the editorial origins of the work. By a strange accident of fate, however, the textual history of the work has been dramatically altered. In 1994, a notebook containing a manuscript—possibly the first manuscript—of *Altazor* was unexpectedly (re-)discovered. I myself have examined this notebook, now held with Huidobro's papers in the archives of the Fundación Vicente Huidobro in Santiago de Chile. At the time I visited the archives (1999), the secretary of the Fundación, Liliana Rosa, informed me anecdotally that at some point in the 1950s or 1960s Huidobro's son, Vladimir, was involved in a serious motorcycle accident in Chicago, and since he was bedridden for several months a married academic couple allowed Vladimir into their home to convalesce. As a gesture of gratitude Vladimir gave the couple a small, brown-paper notebook as a gift, and the couple held it unbeknownst to anyone until the husband's death in the early 1990s. This story seems highly implausible, as does the fact that a clean manuscript of such a major work should be lost for so long. Indeed, even though I have held the document in my own hands and taken copies of it, I had never been absolutely certain that it actually existed after I left Chile. Between 1999 and the time I am writing *Modern Poetics* I know of no scholarly article written on the (re-)discovery, and there seems to be little interest in what might be contained in the notebook.

By sheer coincidence, in early 2005 I made the acquaintance of Prof. Rosa Sarabia at the University of Toronto, who graciously lent me an exquisitely crafted facsimile edition of the manuscript notebook—one of only 1,000 copies produced under the auspices of the Fundación Vicente Huidobro in 1999. In his introduction to this edition, Andrés Morales confirms many of the incredible details of the manuscript's provenance—the "afterlife" of the manuscript from at least 1948 to the present:

> The happenstance history of the manuscript (found only a short while ago among old documents and objects of the poet) has cast doubt even as to its existence. Nothing or almost nothing was known of the original pages

Huidobro wrote in his own hand. The majority of studies on the texts note the absence of the manuscript without knowing of its exact whereabouts. Thus, the opportune and generous intervention of the Banco del Estado of Chile has permitted the conservation of the notebook in which the author wrote the greater part of what would be his great work, in the archives of the Fundación Vicente Huidobro in Santiago.[27]

In several footnotes to this statement, Morales proceeds to clarify:

A long process was necessary for the originals to arrive in the hands of the Fundación Vicente Huidobro. Their owner, Sra. Rina Uboldi de la Torre, mentioned the existence of the manuscript in 1994 to a counselor to the Fundación who, in turn, commented the fact to Vicente García Huidobro Santa Cruz (grandson of the poet and President of the Fundación Vicente Huidobro) who contacted Andrés Sanfuentes, President of the Banco del Estado and a great admirer of Huidobro's poetry and work, and it was he who promoted the petition for the acquisition of the original and its subsequent bequest to the Foundation in the role of caretaker.[28]

....

The required authentication of the manuscript has been realized by experts convened by the Banco del Estado and the Fundación Vicente Huidobro (the academics Adriana Valdés and Federico Schopf in conjunction with the physical bibliographic expert Paulina Cornejo).[29]

Despite this authentification, we should be cautious to claim the manuscript to be *the* original of *Altazor*, even if we have every reason to concur that it is *an* original of the work. The notebook is in itself rather underwhelming, being a plain, brown-paper notebook, inscribed mainly with graphite pencil, with occasional corrections in blue ink, blue pencil, and red pencil. Its physical appearance notwithstanding, the notebook nevertheless allows us to situate the literary-historical development of the work. Figure 3.2 reproduces the manuscript of the "Molino" section.

Earlier I spoke of the "Molino" section as a graphic instance of the axes of selection and combination in Jakobson's poetic function. Here, the reference to "axis" is yet more explicit: the selection of different nominatives align on the right into a column of lexical inscriptions, juxtaposed against the (non-)selection of "Molino de(l)" presented, not as lexemes, but through a series of ditto-marks that form a vertebral column just to the right of the notebook's spine. Moreover, the manuscript version of the "Molinos" lends credence to my characterization of the work as a "reverse narrative." The manuscript

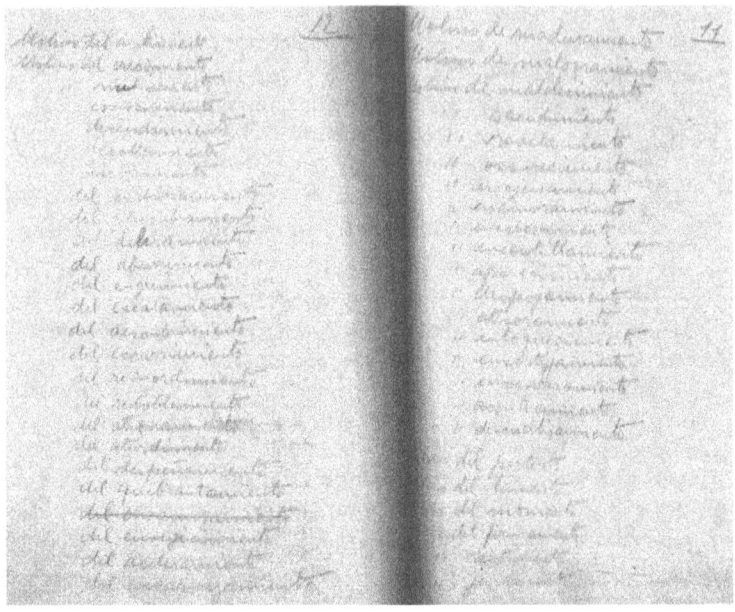

Figure 3.2 The "Molinos" of the manuscript of *Altazor*; pages appear in reverse order from the printed version, indicated by "12" coming before "11" (reprinted under the authorization of the Fundación Vicente Huidobro).

pages have been numbered *backward*, with page "12" on the verso appearing before page "11" on the recto. Indeed, the handwritten lines on this manuscript page 11 will appear, in the printed version, before the lines handwritten on page 12. The "Molinos" were therefore originally written by hand in one direction, and then subsequently published in the opposite direction. Seen in this way the formal "reversal" of *Altazor* is not just a figurative construct, but an historical fact. The final version of *Altazor* is *in fact* a reversal of its original.

Such reversal, furthermore, self-consciously positions the work within multiple national literary histories. In the middle of the notebook we encounter several pages of unpublished fragments that comment upon German Romanticism:

> El romanticismo alemán, esa neblina blanca llena de hadas luminosas
> Un mundo cruzado de fluídos misteriosos...[30]
>
> [German Romanticism, that white mist full of luminous fairies
> A world crossed by mysterious fluids...]

On the next page, we find a direct comment upon specific poets:

> El mundo se suicida en Kleist, enloquece en Hoelderlin, agoniza en Novalis, {y en su agonía descubre el hombre [illegible]} se desespera en [illegible], se sutiliza en Jean Paul, sueña en Brentano y canta en todos ellos el {más extraordinario} de sus cantos...
>
> [The world commits suicide in Kleist, goes crazy in Hoelderlin, agonizes in Novalis, {and in its agony man discovers [illegible]}, despairs in [illegible], grows subtle in Jean Paul, dreams in Brentano and sings in all of them the {most extraordinary} of its songs...]

As I implied earlier, part of Huidobro's *creacionismo* stands in relation to German Romantic aesthetics. In the manifesto "La creación pura," Huidobro seeks to extend (and deviate from) the historical aesthetics of Hegel and Schleiermacher; in the same piece, Huidobro also presents a Hegelian-dialectical scheme in which "Adaptive art" (defined as "Art in harmony with the medium/environment") will be superseded by "Creative art" (defined as "Art superior to its medium/environment"). Huidobro goes on to describe "Adaptive art" (the second in his tripartite historical scheme) as a high point in artistic development:

> The principal problems now have been resolved, and everything superfluous and unnecessary for the elaboration of the work has been carefully discarded. Sensibility then takes its place next to Intelligence and glazes the work with a certain heat that makes it less dry and gives it more life than in the first period. This second epoch marks the apogee of an art.[31]

This historical "apogee," however, will lead to a decadent stage of development ("Creative art") that, although decadent, will finalize "Man's" control over artistic media, his intelligence, and the world. In short, in the ultimate stage of "Creative art," the "Artist-God" will gain the power to create "new worlds." With the unpublished fragments provided earlier, the historical-aesthetic schematics of "La creación pura" gain in cultural specificity. Huidobro's tone in the fragments suggests that the ideal "harmony" of "Adaptive art" is to be found specifically in *German* Romantic poetry. In the "white mist" of German Romanticism, the world and poetry seem to be in perfect balance; the world "se sutiliza" and "sueña," such that the world "sings its most extraordinary songs" through the songs of Kleist, Hölderlin, Novalis, and others. But this is also the end of a world—one that "enloquece, agoniza, se suicida" in German.

Arguably, in this brief fragment Huidobro seeks to position *Altazor* as a teleological end of German literary history, a *telos* that will inaugurate a new age. Implicit in such characterizations, therefore, is the (re)location of Huidobro's own work within the German tradition: Huidobro is clearly thinking of his work as the ultimate manifestation of "Creative art," so that *Altazor* signals the *end* of German literary history, or at least the end of the German sense of *weltliteratur*.

Such a claim is only bolstered by the decidedly Nietzschean undercurrent throughout *Altazor*. As we have already seen, Huidobro claimed to have written parts of *Altazor* in Silvana Plana, in the same room where Nietzsche composed *Also sprach Zarathustra*. Yet the connection to the German philosopher is much stronger than that. The "doubling of origins" figuratively represented in *Altazor* does not merely parallel the Nietzschean critique of metaphysics (as most Huidobro scholars would concede); *Altazor*'s "doubling of origins" also represents an extension of Nietzsche's more substantive ideological critiques of German nationhood. It is patently clear that, in German Romantic philosophy (above all Hegel and Schleiermacher),[32] the origins of German culture were thought to be located to Germany's *south*, in ancient Greece, which in turn explains Germany's nineteenth-century fascination with Hellenic philology. As James Porter has argued, throughout his career Nietzsche consistently returned to German institutions of classical philology as "untimely," as critical practices that unwittingly forge *modern* ideologies of the German nation via the misrecognition of a foreign *past*:

> ...[P]hilology is an active agent in the construction of modern ideologies—which is to say, the constitutive illusions of modern cultural life. It is in these respects that classical study is quintessentially modern and that its ideology is closely bound up with the ideology of modernity. Modernity, in turn, actually requires the cultivation of antiquity for its own self-definition: only so can it misrecognize itself in its own image of the past, that of a so-called classical antiquity.... Standing in a critical relation to both the past and the present, the philologist of the future—foreshadowed in the first instance by Nietzsche himself—can begin to undertake the project of cultural criticism by underscoring philology's conditions of possibility. It can do this by foregrounding what it means to be untimely in the way that philology necessarily is, but also by exposing something of the *impossibility* of philology and its self-appointed tasks (this is its "antimony"). The program is a decidedly uncomfortable one to assume, for there seems to be no safe place for a practicing critic to stand: "These few [who are entitled to the critical distance afforded by philology] measure our present against antiquity,

as critics of the present, and they measure antiquity against their own [modern] ideals, and so are critics of antiquity."[33]

In this light, we can perceive *Altazor* as a yet more advanced "philology of the future" based upon (as seen in George Yúdice's interpretation) the rhetorical "doubling" of demystification/mystification. By enacting the apocalyptic destruction of language, *Altazor* tears language and culture away from its presupposed origins, localized in Hellenic and (in the case of the Prefacio) Semitic antiquity. Yet this is not an end in itself, as *Altazor* also seeks to create a "new origin" for language/culture—a "new" point of origin from which a "new etymology" may flow—to be located in modernity. Yet this "new and modern origin" is still indecisive, for the question remains: if the origin is no longer to be found in the ancient Greek south, where will the "new modern world" of the "new modern etymology" be (re)located?

Altazor's "new" point of origin is clearly *not* Germany. If anything, the manuscript notebook of the work suggests that the "modern origin" will emerge from the disruptive stratification of multiple languages and multiple national traditions. Figure 3.3 shows the original manuscript of the Prefacio, which is the first poetic writing found in the notebook. It is written *in French*: "Je suis me a trente trois ans le jour de la mort du Christ. Je suis me a l'equinoxe sans les hortenses et les aeroplanes de la chaleur."

Here quite clearly we have authenticated historical evidence that the authorized, published Prefacio is not an original precisely, but is in fact a Spanish *translation* from an *original* French. Thus, we are faced with a rather untenable situation: obviously, the text of *Altazor* may be identified in its final published versions, of which there have only been minor editorial variations since 1931; yet in identifying the poem with its published versions, we are also granting authenticity to these published versions, all of which are in fact merely translations of a second order from the original French text. This claim, however, would grant a certain level of historical primacy to the manuscript, situating Huidobro's handwriting as the final arbiter of what is original or unoriginal, authentic or inauthentic. But given that such manuscript notebooks are not usually meant for public display (they are normally private documents, not public or published), they should not really represent any sort of finality. By this I mean that we always understand that the text of the work will not be fixed in its final form by the manuscript, but that the text will ultimately be modified later. For this very reason, we utilize manuscripts as a register of history: manuscripts may be disorderly, fragments of the end of a work may be followed by fragments of the beginning of the work; but ultimately we are to understand that the first page of a manuscript provides us the first thing an author actually wrote, and each subsequent page of the manuscript follows chronologically in order until all pages of the notebook have been filled.

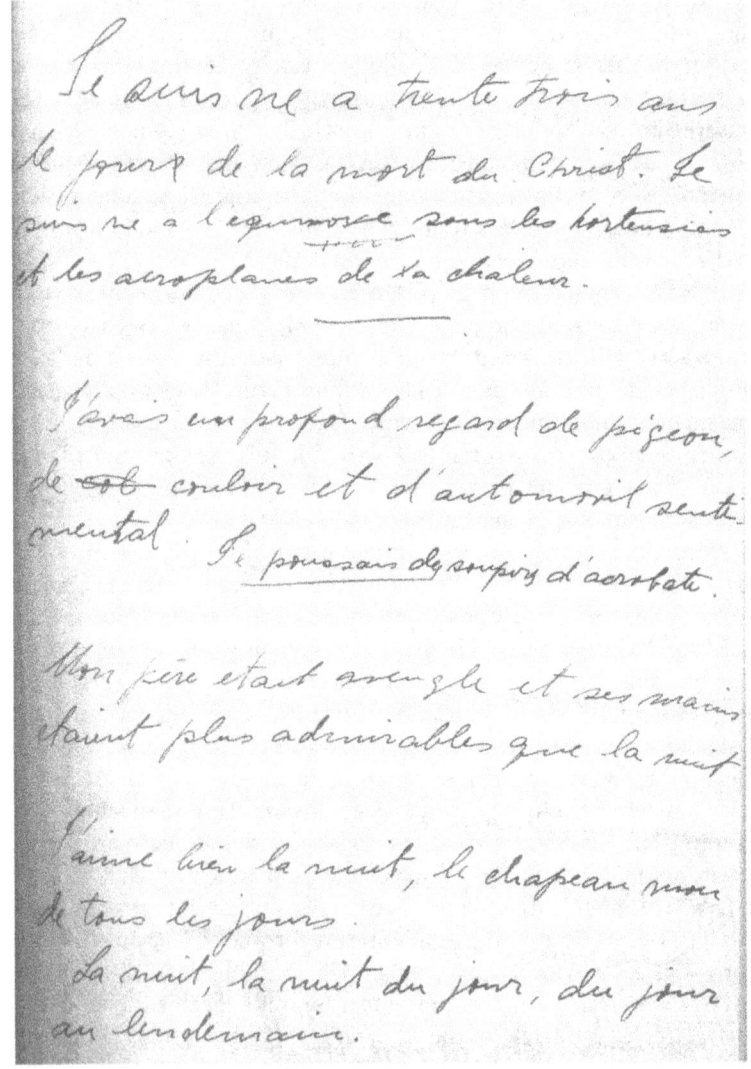

Figure 3.3 The first manuscript page of the "Prefacio" in French (reprinted under the authorization of the Fundación Vicente Huidobro).

This much should be so obvious that it need not be mentioned, except that the notebook of *Altazor* is quite odd among manuscripts in that it contains a stylized title page *prior* to the French text of the Prefacio (figure 3.4).

Figure 3.4 A title page of Huidobro's manuscript (reprinted under the authorization of the Fundación Vicente Huidobro).

This page is doubly odd in how it names things, for again we have to notice that it is written in French: "L'Habitant de su destin / ALTAZUR / le voyage en parachute—1919— / Vincent Huidobro"; with the secondary title "Altazor" inscribed in the upper-right corner. Here we can see a graphic displacement, then, between the enlarged script of "Altazur" across the center of the page and a smaller "Altazor" evidently added later in the top corner. Huidobro's originary, "Adamic" naming of the work appears as spatial and temporal displacement, with the later "Altazor" written "over" (i.e., "above") an earlier "Altazur." This graphic displacement of handwritten inscriptions allows us to visualize a phonemic displacement—that is, between "u" and "o"—in the original title of the work. In either case, we must conclude that both "Altazur" and "Altazor" are in fact written in French, given that all other elements of this title page are French. At the very least, we have a moment of linguistic uncertainty or duplicity: "Altazur" and "Altazor" may be inherently bilingual since the names remain consistent between French and Spanish. This is not to say, however, that names in general are untranslatable, since we see that the author—an author who will write himself into his poem as a character in Canto I—has in fact translated his own name into French, as "*Vincent* Huidobro" rather than "Vicente."

This translating of names encodes history into what appears to be a purely formal, neologistic invention. The name "Altazor" is loaded with manifold intertextual references. The name seems to echo that of "Maldoror" in *Les Chants de Maldoror* by the Uruguayan-born Lautréamont. It also deviates slightly from "Beltsasar," the Babylonian name given to Daniel by Nebuchadnezzar's eunuchs in the Old Testament Book of Daniel. (And here we may recall that Daniel/Beltsasar is the allegorical reader *par excellence*, as he reads Nebuchadnezzar's dreams to be divine prophecies of the Apocalypse.) In Huidobro scholarship, however, "Altazor" is most often read, not as an allusion, but as a neologism that combines the Spanish words "alto" and "azor" ["high" and "hawk"] which in turn figures Altazor (the character) as a bird flying on high. This specific interpretation in fact appears within the work itself in Canto IV: "Aquí yace Altazor, azor fulminado por la altura" (A 72). ["Here lies Altazor, hawk fulminated by height."] Read in its "original" French, however, "Altazur" opens the possibility of a *bilingual* combination of "Alto" [Spanish for "high"], and "azur" [French for "azure"]. If this were the case, then we would have a rather blatant reference to the poem "L'Azur" by Mallarmé.[34] In "L'Azur" Mallarmé's poetic persona imagines soaring into the blue sky on the wings of poetry, and therefore curses the sky for being so unattainable since the poet's body remains grounded on earth; in this way, Mallarmé ironically pays homage and mocks the poetic genius of Baudelaire, as "L'Azur" is composed of a series of overt references to *Les Fleurs du Mal*. In sum, the French title "Altazur" establishes an intertextual literary-historical circuit from South America to France and back again, regressing from *Vincent* Huidobro to Stephane Mallarmé to Charles Baudelaire to Lautréamont. Huidobro then stands not only at the apex of *French* poetic history, but has also produced a "higher" "L'Azur" than his predecessors could have written. Yet, when fed back into the loop of Huidobro's *creacionismo*, we should qualify that this height, this bilingual Alto Azur, must be registered as a *decadent* progression from the *perfection* of Symbolism.

Replete as it is with multiple doubles and doublings, this title page is itself a double of what precedes in the notebook. The third page in the notebook, for instance, contains an epigraph on the creative evolution of the poem:

> En realidad este poema fué empezado en 1918 a [illegible] raíz de la publicación de Ecuatorial (Madrid–Julio 1918) pero entonces solo escribí el Prefacio y el Primer Canto. Todo el resto fué escrito en Chile en 1919 y corregido en 1920. En octubre de 1919 Cansinos-Asséns habló de él en la "Correspondencia de España." Equivocadamente dió a todo el poema el título del prefacio "Altazor o El Viaje en Paracaídas."
>
> [In reality this poem was begun in 1918 just after the publication of Ecuatorial (Madrid–July 1918) but at that time I only wrote the Preface and the First Canto. All the rest was written in Chile in 1919 and corrected in 1920. In October of 1919 Cansinos-Asséns spoke of it in the "Correspondencia de España." Mistakenly, he gave to the whole poem the title of the preface, "Altazor or the Voyage in Parachute."]

Obviously, this statement must have been written *after* the manuscript, since it discusses the poem as if it were already a completed, published (at least partially) historical fact. For this reason, it is somewhat disturbing to find it positioned at the *beginning* of the notebook *before* we see any poetic manuscript. Furthermore, because this paragraph is addressed to an audience—some other reader—it appears as a note for posterity left for us to read. In this regard, the paragraph is significant not only in what it *does* but also in what it *says*. The paragraph seems to allude to the incorporation of Huidobro's text into the Peninsular Spanish literary tradition, mediated through the figure of Cansinos-Asséns, one of the foundational figures of Peninsular *vanguardismo* and *ultraísmo*. The entrance of the text into the tradition, moreover, marks the naming of the poem by Cansinos-Asséns, *and* simultaneously marks its deformative *mis-naming* at the hands of a Spaniard who mistakenly conferred the name of the preface upon the entire poem.

Given that the manuscript locates the work within German, French, and Spanish literary histories, can we not help but feel this act of *mis-naming* to be a curiously "American" phenomenon?

A Map of Indecision

In this chapter, I have attempted to characterize Huidobro's life and his work as a nexus of indecision. Critics have struggled to decide whether the author's poetry exhibits "Americanizing" or "Europeanizing," "localized" or "universalized," tendencies. But the farcical nature of Huidobro's biography does not permit us to make any absolute assertions in this regard. Within the terms of the text of *Altazor* itself, the "reverse verse narrative" structure of the work tends to confuse various temporalities, so that the more we move forward through the narrative of forms the more the poetry causes us to return. Thus, we become locked into a cycle of linguistic-cultural "demystification" and "remystification" so that the mythic "origin" (re)appears in the final canto as a moment of *re*inscription subsequent to the narrative. By moving to textual-historical evidence, I sought to show how *Altazor* does not delimit the *locations of culture*, but rather demarcates the *dislocations* and ultimately, the *relocations of culture*.

Yet we still have not gathered any direct evidence that would pinpoint where this "relocation" is to occur—indications as to where exactly culture will be relocated. In order to move in this direction, I would like to return or recapitulate my overall argument so far. I began my reading of *Altazor* by analyzing it as a sequence of various types of falling, which we might diagram as a vertical vector (figure 3.5).

The Prefacio first "knocks down" the myth of originary *logos* in Genesis by framing the Word as an act of falling between pairs of bipolar associations: birth/death, adult/child, day/night, north/south, earth/sky, above/below, male/female, natural/artificial, old/new, and so on. These polar vectors in turn propel a series of formalistic disruptions also marked by a sense of "falling down." Altazor (the character) falls from his birth to his death as he falls from the sky, and then falls out of the narrative entirely. The narrative structure of the work allegorically enacts a fall from the trope of allegory to the

Figure 3.5 An associational vector.

trope of irony, only to fall back into Babelian allegory. In this way, the work enacts a fall from rhetorical codes down to more primary linguistic codes upon which rhetoric must be based, down to bibliographic codes in which written language has been inscribed. The materiality of the linguistic sign is manifested bibliographically through orthographic, phonetic, phonemic, and morphemic displacements *down* an axis of selection, an axis itself made graphic in the physical act of vertical reading it produces. The end-result is a return to a *lower* "primitive" state of language, represented in the onomatopoetic "grunts" of the final canto, which seems to "double over" (in the de Man-ian sense) as an "inauthentically authentic" point of linguistic and cultural "modern origin."

The high degree of abstraction in this reading, furthermore, permits a kind of creative mapping of the "reverse verse narrative" structure of *Altazor* onto the material history of the work as inscripted matter, diagrammed in figure 3.6.

The indecisions of "backward reading" produced *within* the text tend to reflect *back* on the material circumstances of the text's production. The "doubling of origins" comes forth in the "double title pages" of the first edition, which ascribe two dates of origin to the work. From the editorial genealogy of printed versions of the text it remains unclear whether the text was originally written in Spanish or in French; at best these versions point to a duplicitous bilingual origin now lost in the "final" printed versions of the text. But *now*, because of a *contemporary* discovery we can *go back* to an original manuscript—which originally locates *Altazor/Altazur* as the terminal point of multiple linguistic and cultural traditions (Spanish, French,

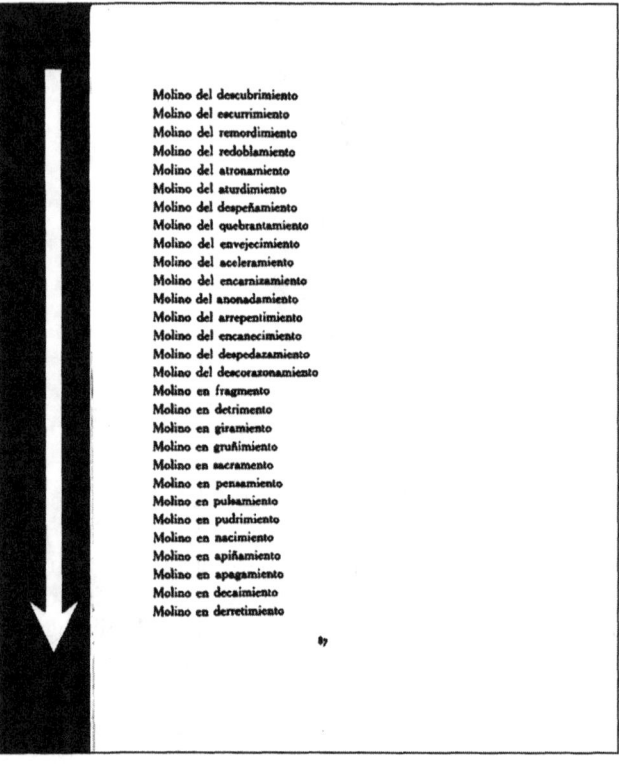

Figure 3.6 An associational mapping (reprinted under the authorization of the Fundación Vicente Huidobro).

German). The manuscript does *not* resolve these traditions into a unity. To the contrary, *Altazor* may be remarkable to the extent that none of its varied cultural positions/locations are ever reconciled into a unified whole. Such non-conciliation would not only represent a negative disruption of the European "universe," but also a radical construction of American "localism."

Indeed, the manuscript notebook provides us specific geographical coordinates in order to locate *Altazor* (or *Altazur*) in the Americas. When I stated earlier that the notebook was "doubly odd" because it had a French title page, I must admit that I was being rather duplicitous. In fact the manuscript notebook has *two* title pages (figure 3.7).

The French title page we saw before is in fact a *second* title page; and it is preceded by this first one written on the first page of the notebook, this (first) time written in *Spanish*: "Altazor / o / El Pasajero de

VERSE REVERSE VERSE 153

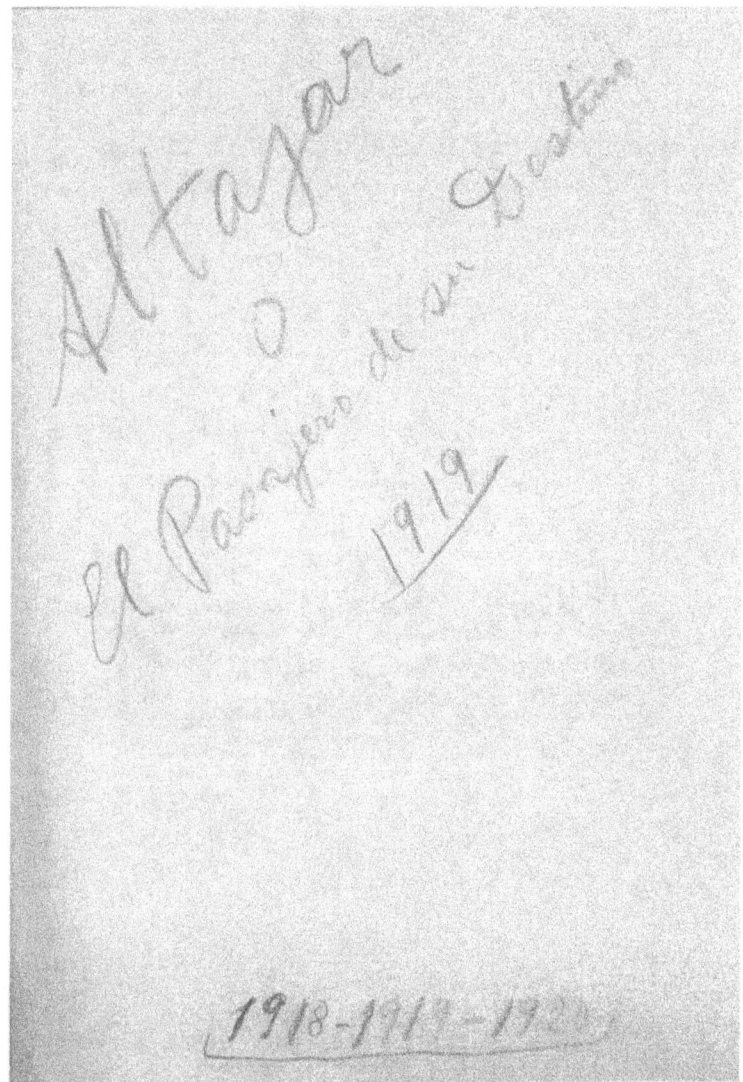

Figure 3.7 The *first* title page of Huidobro's manuscript (reprinted under the authorization of the Fundación Vicente Huidobro).

su Destino / 1919" with the dates at the bottom "1918–1919–1920." And it is plainly visible that this page is written in red pencil, with the exception of a marking in graphite pencil: the reinscription of the "o" in "Altazor" over the original "u" of "Altazur," a correction that is only partially visible in figure 3.7. Here we can actually see *Altazor*'s

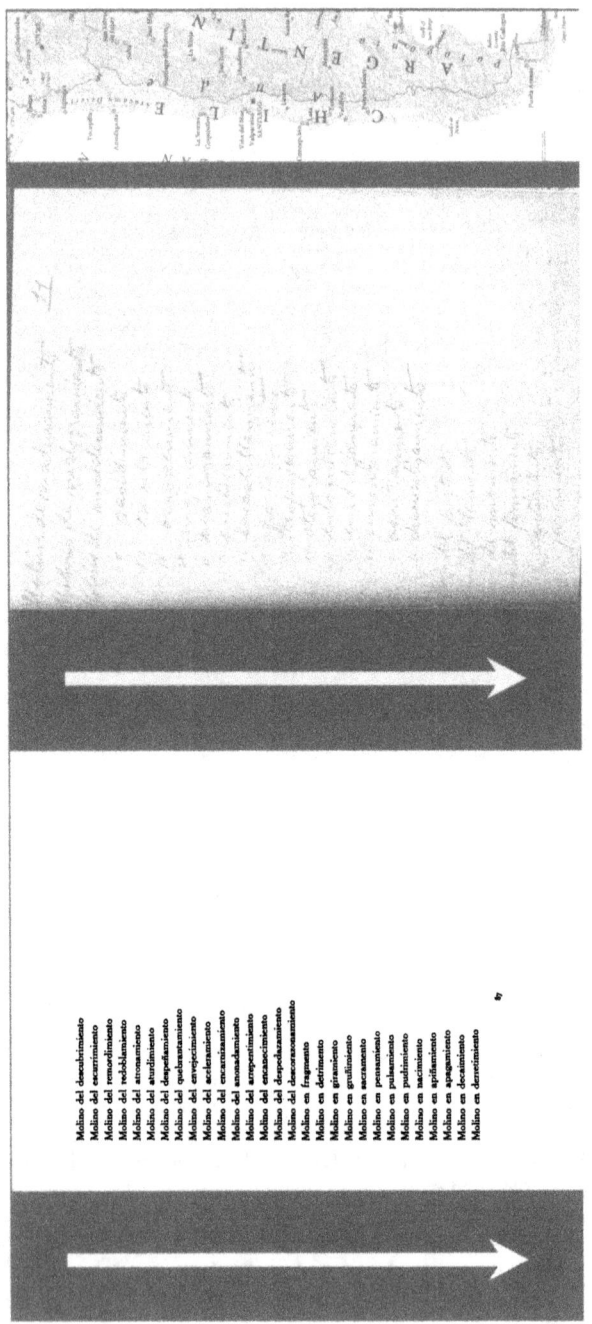

Figure 3.8 "Todo el resto fué escrito en Chile en 1919 y corregido en 1920" (reprinted under the authorization of the Fundación Vicente Huidobro).

"doubling of origins," since the first naming of the thing appears as a *reinscription* of "Altazor" over "Altazur," producing a visible historical stratification of orthographic displacement. The fact that this "Altazor/Altazur" must be understood *as originally Spanish* (rather than the French of the second title page) now opens new possibilities, as a combination of "Alta" and "zur," with "zur" being the phonetic equivalent of "sur" ["south"]. Thus, this Spanish "Altazur" enacts a geographic movement from the high-North to the low-South, and also a displacement between the *high* culture of the North to the *low* culture of the South, as the "zur" of the "South" is unmistakably misspelled in, of course, a self-consciously ironic manner.

In this way, we have just crossed a threshold between text and world. The *textual* logic internal to *Altazor* also operates to organize the cultural logic of *extratextual* materials: title pages, first editions, early printed versions, manuscripts, nonpublished fragments, authorial/authoritative naming. But the migrations between the textual and the extratextual need not stop with the book and its bibliographic provenance. If the poetic function of *Altazor* is editorial and bibliographic, the poetic function is also ontological: a synchronically presented series of orthographic, phonemic, and morphemic selections that can be projected into a series of suggestive associational combinations to produce dislocations of the European, oriented toward relocations of culture in the Americas.

This poetic function also happens to be a joke. As Julio Ramos once commented, there is a cruel pun in Spanish: that *enseñarle la lengua* also means *enseñarle la lengua*; that "teaching language" also means "sticking one's tongue out."[35] In the end, the punch line of *Altazor* and its ironic-allegorical *enseñarle la lengua* eventually comes across decisively as a non-conciliated map of indecision (figure 3.8).

Chapter 4

Alien Sedition: Anti-Semitism and Censorship in *The Cantos of Ezra Pound*

At the start of this book I axiomatically posited migration as the origin of America, and thus translation as the original language of the Americas. In preceding chapters, I have worked to demonstrate how modern poets concretized translation as a language in its own right. In doing so these poets framed not just multicultural encounter, but more powerfully framed the intercultural violence of migration as inherent to their sense of Americanism. This violence registers as rhetorical dislocation, typographical schism, and outright ethnic strife. Yet several questions still remain before I finish. The first question is a matter of subjectivity: How would intercultural violence, and the interlingual language of translation, be "internalized" as origins for American subject-formation? A second set of questions concern matters of *political* subjectivity: In what sense does intercultural violence demand a "politics of violence" in the Americas? How would American subjects born of violence factor into such politics? From where would a "politics of violence" derive authority over its subjects? In order to find out I would now like to confront one of the most difficult characters in American history, "Ezra Pound."

Treason

I have placed Pound's name in quotations, since it proves remarkably difficult to specify just who or what "Pound" is. The actual historical figure named Ezra Pound moved around quite a bit, especially in the first half of his life: Idaho, Indiana, Pennsylvania, London, and Paris. By the 1930s, Pound had settled in the Italian seaside village of

Rapallo with his two wives, Dorothy Shakespear and Olga Rudge, and his daughter, Maria. During the two decades or so (1925–1945) he spent in Rapallo he was to become an increasingly vocal supporter of Benito Mussolini, until his eventual arrest for treason by the United States Army at the end of the World War II. Throughout his stay in Italy, Pound also continued to produce his *Cantos*, parts of which justly offended a great deal of readers:

> Remarked Ben: better keep out the jews
> or yr/ grandchildren will curse you
> jews, real jews, chazims, and *neschek*
> also super neschek or the international racket
> specialité of the Stinkschuld
> bomb-proof under their house in Paris
> where they cd/ store aht voiks
> fat slug with three bodyguards
> soiling our sea front with a pot bellied yacht in the offing...(C 257)

These lines now appear on page 257 of *The Cantos of Ezra Pound*, the epic poem Pound spent some 60 years attempting to complete. I have, however, been somewhat deceitful in quoting them in the context of Pound's readership of the 1930s. Anti-Semitic passages are not entirely uncommon in *The Cantos*, and indeed Pound did write the aforementioned passage in 1937 or 1938. Yet, the fact is that few readers of Pound ever saw them as they appear here until a much later date. In fact, several of the aforementioned lines have been deliberately censored out of the work for most of its existence (see figure 4.3).

With the censorship of Canto 52, we have an instance of Pound's aesthetic creation coming into direct conflict with (what most would agree are) his entirely objectionable political views. Aesthetic expressions have been overwritten by certain ethical decisions regarding what expressions may be read or not. Such decisions necessarily impact definitions of the "American" that might emerge from the work, since *The Cantos of Ezra Pound* is a major work of the American poetic tradition that has evidently been censored for the decidedly un-American beliefs it expresses. There can be little doubt that this censorship has arisen as the result of social conflict over what ideas and beliefs should or should not constitute culture. Although the author clearly intended to say something about culture in the passage of Canto 52, other agents (editors? publishers? readers?) have come to find these intentions objectionable and have opted to block the transmission of the message altogether. Censorship emerges from stark disagreements of intention, that is, disagreement over who has the authority to speak (or refuse to speak) in the work of art.

We may thus think of Canto 52 as a space for sociocultural contentions to be represented, resolved, or left unresolved. In this sense, as much as it represents *conflict*, the censoring of Canto 52 also becomes significant as a point of *convergence* between several distinct forms of authority, several distinct value-systems, and indeed, several distinct modes of reading. As an aesthetic creation, *The Cantos* have been widely recognized as a great or major work of art; yet the work expresses ethical views widely to be considered outlandish, even criminal. This open divergence between aesthetic and ethical modes of evaluation converges into a singular act of censorship. Censorship, in turn, has become physically manifested on the page in the shape of black lines. These black lines in effect interrupt linguistic forms that constitute the poetic message. Just as aesthetics and ethics converge in this case, we also have an instance in which page layout clearly affects a formal understanding of the piece—so that reading *The Cantos* necessitates bibliographic interpretation, in addition to formal and sociocultural readings. I would argue, then, that it is precisely from these diverse meeting points (aesthetic-ethical, formal-bibliographic, all contained in a debate over culture) that we may define "American" as both a category of society and culture. Such convergences allow us to ask how we may classify certain aesthetic expressions as "American," in a way that challenges how the category "American" may be socially and ethically determined.

Although Pound is recognized as a distinguished U.S.-American poet, his own individual status as "American" became highly problematic during his lifetime. Pound lived most of his life in exile from the United States, and scarcely returned to the country of his birth from the time he left for Europe in 1908 until 1945. And he only made a handful of trips to the United States in the last years of his life (1958–1972). During World War II, Pound published two cantos written in Italian and published in Italy (Cantos 71 and 72), which praise the fascist war-effort, and which at one point honor a young Italian girl for leading a troop of Allied soldiers into a minefield. While few readers actually read these poems at the time they were published, Pound did find other means of voicing his opinions. In the latter years of the war, Pound made a series of propagandistic radio broadcasts from Rome on behalf of the fascist regime. These broadcasts proved to be sufficient evidence for the U.S. government to indict Pound for treason *in absentia* in 1944. Upon his arrest at war's end, he was convicted of treason and sentenced to death. By way of a compromise, government doctors deemed Pound mentally unfit to stand trial, and the government, in lieu of execution, imprisoned him in St. Elizabeths Hospital for the Criminally Insane in Washington for the next 13 years.[1] Thus Pound's only extended stay in the United States after the age of 20 occurred against his will, because he had been officially deemed "criminally insane" and "treasonous."

Even though texts such as *The Cantos of Ezra Pound* have gained recognition as central to the U.S.-American literary tradition, it is also doubtful that the author's works were originally intended to be "American." In writing *The Cantos* Pound intended both to record the history of his self-proclaimed "tribe" (i.e., Western Europeans and Anglo-Americans) and to instantiate an ideal society or earthly paradise for that tribe to inhabit. Although Pound drew upon U.S. history to delineate this ideal, his work was not necessarily geared toward the perfection of U.S. society, but rather toward the creation of an entirely new social order. Pound's desire for earthly paradise stemmed from a deep disgust with the geopolitical and economic climate in which he lived. In the passage with which this chapter began, for example, Pound protests an international system of finance and arms production (the "international racket") that he believed had only served to spread misery, war, and death. Private banks throughout European (and Euro-American) history had illicitly profited from charging usurious rates of interest—profits that were then poured into warfare and the manufacture of weapons. To Pound's mind, it became incumbent upon such "usurers" to encourage governments to go to war in order to provide a market for their machines of death. In response to this real or perceived predicament, Pound became enamored of fascism in the 1920s as providing a system of "social credit"[2] that could dismantle the "international racket," here personified as "Stinkschuld." In this sense, Canto 52 will instruct us of social programs (favored by fascists) directed to correct a prevalent "ignorance of [monetary] credit and circulation."

Yet Pound's support of fascism in this case seems to go beyond mere support of certain economic policies. For Pound banks were not just centers of usury, but were also the "specialité of the *Stinkschuld*"— Pound's shockingly crude epithet for the entire Jewish race. Here Pound explicitly indicts all Jews for the sins of "Stinkschuld," and thus calls for their wholesale elimination ("better get rid of the jews [*sic*] / or yr / grandchildren will curse you"). Even within the confines of this brief passage, Pound presents anti-Semitism as historically developed. The call to "get rid of the jews" is attributed to "Ben," a name that here refers to one of the founding fathers of the United States of America, Benjamin Franklin.[3] Pound thus promotes anti-Semitism as serving an absolute cultural "good," which deserves to be iterated and reiterated throughout history by great historical figures. Moreover, at a foundational moment of the United States a founding father of the nation has invoked the "necessity" of anti-Semitic ethnic cleansing, as if anti-Semitism were basic to the constitution of the "American" nation. This last point is of vital importance to poetic project of the work, since Canto 52 leads a sequence of poems entitled *Cantos LII–LXXI* (1940), which reconstruct an ethical history of the American Revolution. Pound thus brings together his anti-Semitic and his socioeconomic beliefs in social credit, because both are integral to a broader plan for the common national, cultural, and ethical "good" that Pound attempts to validate with his epic.

In this light, *The Cantos of Ezra Pound* must be considered in terms of regulation and censorship. Pound explicitly intends to regulate the constitution of society by means of regulating which texts and cultural artifacts deserve continued attention, by regulating how history should be written and received, and by regulating the ethnic composition of society itself. These regulatory endeavors are marked in *The Cantos* by efforts to block or "censor out" entire texts and histories—and even entire peoples such as the Jews. These types of censorship, furthermore, manifest themselves through a distinct poetics—that is, via complex patterns and structures of poetic signification that pretend to allow (or disallow) certain forms of society and culture to materialize. Pound therefore positions himself as *the* censor (in the true sense of that word) of cultural morals and ethics—as the official, imperial arbiter of good and bad, intelligence and ignorance.

Yet if we read *The Cantos of Ezra Pound* as a work of censorship, we also need to consider that the work itself has been regulated and censored by agents acting beyond the intentions of the author. This textual condition has led to some intractable problems for Pound critics. On the one hand the text contains its own clearly defined aesthetic, which cannot be read apart from the life and intentions of the author; on the other hand we cannot read the work apart from a social context that tends to diminish the value of the author and his work. Within the aesthetics of *The Cantos*, Pound positions himself as the arbiter of ethical right and wrong. Yet because of this "ethical" position Pound's editors have substantially altered his poetic *corpus*; and more presciently, in the aftermath of the war and the Holocaust, readers cannot interpret this aesthetic without recognizing that Pound has come down on the *wrong* side of history and ethics. A sort of critical bind thus emerges: within its own terms, *The Cantos of Ezra Pound* has immense aesthetic value, not the least of which is a poetry based on innovative formal-poetic structures that remain quite stunning even today, one capable of integrating the poet's own life into a global vision of world histories and cultural traditions. At the same time, this very poetry may be (indeed already has been) used as evidence to condemn the gross moral, ethical, and even criminal shortcomings of both poet and poem. Especially since 1980, a number of critics—most notably Robert Casillo, Reed Way Dasenbrock, and Tim Redman—have written articles and entire books tracing the deep seats of fascist ideology, anti-Semitism, and bald-faced hate manifest in Pound's great works.[4] Whatever Pound's aesthetic achievements for such critics, the goal of Pound's aesthetic may be to expound hatred and produce a totalitarian, culturally repressive society—and Pound's own texts serve as ample proof for this case. Set more clearly in terms of values, the ethical *depreciation* of the poet named Ezra Pound counteracts—even, perhaps, supersedes—any aesthetic *appreciation* of Pound's poetry.

The critical work of the scholars just named represents an important and necessary shift in Pound scholarship. As for myself, I judge the corpse named Ezra Pound to have been an insane, hate-filled fascist; but does this mean that his *corpus*—and by extension, all modernism—must be a reactionary, elitist aestheticization of authoritarian ideology? Perhaps it does, but rather than passively assuming it so, Casillo, Dasenbrock, and Redman began to provide detailed, critical investigations of the matter. Furthermore, such critics have had to confront an extant field of scholarship that had tended to side-step, excise, or ignore Pound's fascism and racism. In the immediate aftermath of the War, when Pound faced the real possibility of execution, concerted efforts were made to substantiate the aesthetic value of Pound's work. William Carlos Williams, E. E. Cummings, and Louis Zukofsky all issued public statements condemning Pound's politics, but praising his importance as a great American poet who did not deserve to die;[5] and the Chilean Nobel laureate Gabriela Mistral circulated a petition in 1952, signed by literary notables and presented to the president of the United States, to the same effect to have Pound released from St. Elizabeths.[6] After Pound's life was no longer at stake, however, Pound's family, friends, and critical scholars pushed efforts not to protect Pound's life, but to protect his *image* as a great U.S. poet. Pound's literary property trust worked to suppress Cantos

72 and 73, first published in the official journal of the fascist Italian navy, *Marina Repubblicana*.[7] And in critical readings from the 1950s and 1960s of Pound's work, scarcely any mention is made of Pound's sociocultural or political beliefs; instead favoring more formalist, New Critical close readings of his poetics. When Pound's politics were mentioned, even up to the final years of the twentieth century, creative maneuvers were often devised to downplay the extent of his extremism. In what is arguably the most important single work of Pound scholarship to date, for instance, Hugh Kenner states in *The Pound Era*:

> Of Germany and Italy in those years [the 1930s and 1940s] we have two main sorts of general knowledge. We know about their repression of opposition, including the German race-mystique and the miseries inflicted on Jews; and we know about their foreign policy, Hitler's obsession with expansion eastward, Mussolini's dreams of African empire. In his preoccupation with their economic recovery Pound was barely noticing these matters, so he and his critics talked past each other for decades.[8]

Here Kenner presents Pound's support of fascism as merely economic, or at least as ignorant of the genocidal impulses of fascist regimes. From the mid-1930s on, however, the systematic persecution of the Jews by the Nazi state was widely known throughout the world, and yet anti-Semitic statements continued to be littered throughout Pound's writings of the time. Kenner fully ignores all this in order to contextualize Pound's political beliefs as understandable and/or moderately justifiable.

In sum, a disjunction has developed in readings of *The Cantos of Ezra Pound* between ethical and aesthetic values. One vein of criticism diminishes or suspends any ethical judgment of the poet in order to substantiate his work as great American poetry. Another vein downplays the aesthetic value of the work, instead holding up the poet's texts and other documents the poet has left behind as evidence of his ethical lapses—lapses that gain importance because of the poet's presumed status as canonical, great, and American. Yet this disjunction, in whichever form of criticism it appears, seems highly problematic given that *The Cantos of Ezra Pound* is a work that strives to (re)unify aesthetic and ethical values, the practice of poetry with social praxis. It is the integration of poetic forms into sociocultural contexts (and vice versa) that remains understudied and misunderstood, both within Pound scholarship and literary/cultural criticism in general.

This problematic may most clearly be crystallized in the status of *The Cantos* as "American." At the time Pound entered into his most patently un-American phase—that is, at the point Pound's support of Italian fascism was becoming vocal enough to lead directly to his indictment (and conviction) for treason by the U.S. government—the principal subject-matter of Pound's *Cantos* turns sharply to U.S.-American history. While Pound continually deprecated his homeland throughout his career, the cantos of the late 1930s present U.S. history in a decidedly positive light. Indeed, the latter half of *Cantos LII–LXXI* is an unabashed glorification of John Adams, one of the key framers of ethical constitutional government and also the first president to overstep constitutional limits on presidential authority with his proto-dictatorial enforcement of the Alien and Sedition Act. But more than mere honorific, the explicit intention of Pound's representation of Adams is to infuse a European culture, which had fallen into a state of decadence, with the best that U.S. history had to offer. In many regards, the gestures made by Pound in these cantos reflect some form of patriotism, even if deviant.

How is it then that an author who was engaged in un-American activities—writing poems in support of an eventual enemy of the United States—could nonetheless produce an exemplary work of American literature? Or more precisely put, what about this text allows for its classification as an "American" work of art, even though the author of the text was to be officially deemed "un-American" by his own government?

Americanization: Orienting Brazil, Orienting Pound

Such questions are subjective, though perhaps not the same questions of subjectivity taken up in contemporary literary and cultural criticism. We are asking whether there can be a certain "subject-identity" of the *text* ("American") that goes beyond a subject-position of its author ("un-American"). Significantly, in questioning the status of *The Cantos of Ezra Pound* as an "American" work of art, we ourselves have already engaged a process of censorship, attempting to decide which subjects (and objects) should pertain to a certain culture and which should not. Indeed the etymological root of the word "censorship" goes back to the Latin *censor*—the title of the imperial Roman magistrate responsible for tax collection, population count (as in "census"), and the regulation of public morals. The *censor*, in other words, determined who and what was Roman or not Roman; any effort to decide the status of "American" (versus "un-American") should likewise be construed as censorious.

Censorship is not only an act of prevention or blockage, but also a process of regulation that allows or disallows certain forms of culture to materialize. We cannot, therefore, understand "censorship" in this way without aligning it closely with "form." That is, if we define "form" as the process by which content materializes—that which gives shape to matter or meaning—"censorship" is a necessary complement to this process, as that which selects and limits how and when certain forms will be expressed or left unexpressed.[9] Censorship may be defined both as an intrinsic property of expression, as well as an external imposition over expression. In producing *The Cantos*, for instance, Pound has selected to inscribe specific forms of poetic writing, necessarily excluding other possible avenues of expression—something we might term "self-censorship." On the other hand, whatever Pound's forms of writing in *The Cantos* express, these expressions come to constitute culture once they are printed and disseminated, whether as "American," "non-American," or "un-American" culture; and they are therefore open to censure by outside forces. Whether intrinsic or extrinsic, censorship is not merely the official castigation for cultural wrongdoings (or "un-American activities"); it is also part of the process by which we recognize the material conditions of American cultures in contradistinction to the negative or immaterial aspects of what "American" is not. Throughout preceding chapters, then, we have been tracing the development of various formal structures (political, economic, and literary-cultural) by which "American" may be defined or produced. I have therefore attempted to identify *non-conciliation* (or more precisely, *non-conciliatory transculturation*) as the productive form most adequate to the task of engaging the complex migratory processes central to any American culture. Since non-conciliation is *processual* (rather than teleological), it tends to avoid the trap of lapsing into chauvinistic nationalism based on culture purity, or even "bland" or "ideological" transculturation geared to the finality of multiculturalism or "pure *mestizaje*."

Even in its "bland" type, however, transculturation has the benefit of allowing multiple subject-identifications to form within a given geographic and cultural space, through the internal meeting, conflict, and miscegination of cultural groups—a process I would term "Americanization." As we will see in the discussion to follow, *The Cantos* have been structured to enact migratory shifts from precedent cultures, discarding wanton cultural forms (deculturation), in order to transculturate previous forms into a new social order (neoculturation) of earthly paradise.[10] Since this utopic position has been disrupted by nonauthorial authorities, however, we will also see how the very process by which the work has materialized follows a consistent pattern of transcultural conflict and integration, which has a direct bearing upon Pound's status as "un-American" and his reintegration into the "American." From this perspective, Pound's famous axiom to "make it new" cannot be read as a call for extreme novelty. To the contrary, it is the law of a continual historical process by which the "old" may be productively recontextualized in new ways. The "new" emigrates from the "old," re-forming the "old" in the process.

With this in mind, it is significant that *The Cantos of Ezra Pound* contains an Orientalist project in the translation and transmission of Chinese history and Confucian philosophy. Edward Said, of course, powerfully argued that Orientalist scholars have played a large role in *defining* the cultures they merely purport to describe. From at least the sixteenth century onward, argues Said, Western Orientalist scholars have succeeded in characterizing Eastern (and Southern) civilizations according to prescribed types (e.g., "heathen" or "degraded") that approach typologies of aesthetic stylization. Orientalist scholarship from the Occident has analyzed Asian cultures based on imposed stylistic codes that order European judgments of its East. These judgments, in turn, are "read back" onto Asia in the form of absolute truth—"truth" that is replicated not only by the administrators of colonial rule, but also by many "Orientals" living under that rule. The process by which "Asia" becomes the "Orient" in European eyes thus has a direct bearing upon all facets of East-West cultural interaction and colonial administration:

> For the Orient ("out there" towards the East) is corrected, even penalized, for lying outside the boundaries of European society, "our" world; the Orient is thus *Orientalized*, a process that not only marks the Orient as the province of the Orientalist but also forces the uninitiated Western reader to accept Orientalist codifications (like d'Herbelot's alphabetized *Bibliothèque*) as the *true* Orient. Truth, in short, becomes a function of learned judgment, not of the material itself, which in time seems to owe even its existence to the Orientalist.[11]

For Said, then, cultural formation becomes a matter of discursive authority. The discourse of European Orientalism has authorized Orientalist scholars to determine what "Oriental" is and what it is not. This further authorizes Europeans (non-Orientals) to permit certain expressions of culture in the colonized lands of Asia and censor other expressions out of existence, with the added effect of allowing Europeans to consolidate their own identity as "Occidentals." The concept of "Oriental" has little to do with the real, material contexts of Asian societies—until, that is, Asians become "Orientalized" at the feet of their Occidental judges. Does the incorporation of Chinese cultural artifacts into *The Cantos of Ezra Pound* have as its end, therefore, the Orientalization of Chinese culture? Or does Pound have some other purpose in mind?

In order to answer this question, we first need to address the location of Chinese language and Chinese texts within the overall form of the work. *The Cantos of Ezra Pound* does not contain much in the way of a linear narrative structure. Rather, the work consists primarily of textual fragments, which have been strategically placed in order to cohere into a utopic vision in the mind of the reader. We must therefore read *The Cantos* as a compendium of prior extant textual materials—a compendium, moreover, that not only anthologizes texts but also tells us how those texts have arrived to us over time. In Canto 1, for instance, Pound translates a section of Book XI of the *Odyssey* in which Odysseus performs animal sacrifices to call up and consult the ghosts of the dead. At the end of the canto, however, Pound's source-text for his translation erupts into the poem itself:

> And he strong with the blood, said then: "Odysseus
> "Shalt return through spiteful Neptune, over dark seas,
> "Lose all companions." And then Anticlea came.
> Lie quite Divus, I mean, that is Andreas Divus,
> In officina Wecheli, 1538, out of Homer.
> And he sailed, by Sirens and thence outward and away...(C 4-5)

At this point it becomes apparent that Pound has *not* been translating Homer's original Greek, but rather the sixteenth-century Medieval Latin version of the *Odyssey* translated by Andreas Divus of Justinopolis and published in the Parisian "office of Wechelus" in 1538. Thus, Pound not only narrates Odysseus's summoning of spirits, but also himself summons the spirit of the *Odyssey* as it has moved from ancient Greece to the obscure Renaissance translation Pound found in a Parisian bookshop, to Pound's own English translation of the translation. Throughout the rest of *The Cantos*, Pound recounts a global history (primarily Western European, though also Chinese and U.S. history) through an assemblage of outside texts he introduces into his own work: the letters of Sigismundo Malatesta, the writings of Thomas Jefferson, Dante's *Divine Comedy*, Provençal troubadour poetry, the Confucian *Analects* and *Odes*, and Remy de Gourmont's

Natural Philosophy of Love, to name but a few. Through these texts, Pound synthesizes or "subject-rhymes" a variety of ethical stances common to each of the texts he compiles: usury as a socially destructive force, methods of eliminating usury through economics based in "natural order" (e.g., "social credit"), the function of beauty and masculine sexuality in the maintenance of "natural" social order, public support of artists, and so forth.

To this end, both Chinese and U.S.-American histories become increasingly important to the ethical views expressed in *The Cantos of Ezra Pound*, especially in those parts written the 1930s. The China/Adams cantos, as *Cantos LII–LXXI* has come to be known informally, provide the most straightforward and linear narrative of history in the entire collected *Cantos*, and perhaps for this reason this section has remained understudied in Pound scholarship relative to other sections such as *A Draft of XXX Cantos* and the *Pisan Cantos*. Canto 53 begins a highly compressed rendering of Chinese history, starting with the Hia dynasty (in 2837 BCE) and ending in Canto 61 with the Manchu dynasty (ca. 1780). From there, the narrative abruptly shifts in Canto 62 to colonial Anglo America, whereupon Pound presents American Revolutionary history through the filtering lens of the life and times of John Adams, the second president of the United States. The link between the two histories is nothing more (or less) than tea, as the ideogram for *"tcha"* appears prominently on the first page of Canto 62. This is a perceptive observation on Pound's part, since the tea Britain began to extract from China in the eighteenth century (through trade in opium to which Britain addicted China for the next 150 years) was the same tea that would be heavily taxed by the crown in its American colonies, thus leading to the Boston Tea Party and the beginning of the American Revolution. Through *tcha* important historical cycles begin and end, as China's dynastic independence closes and America's republican independence begins.

But since Pound does not actually explain any of this in *The Cantos*, the appearance of *tcha* in the context of colonial America seems uncomfortably out of place, a cleavage that marks the distance between China and the United States. The sharp juxtaposition of the two is supposed to generate the primary ethical stance of the work, as if flooding into the gap between one history and the other: that there exists a "natural order," most clearly identified by Confucius, which served as the foundation of "right rule" in China throughout its various dynasties; and that the abrogation of this "natural order" by bad rulers only produced poverty, misery, and death for the country. Further, this same Confucian "natural order" can be found in the political ethics of John Adams, a system of ethics that Adams almost single-handedly infused into U.S.-American politics. When U.S.-American and European leaders strayed from Adams's way (as Pound believed they had done in the Great Depression) misery could only befall the entire "Western" world; when leaders such as Mussolini, however, established "right rule," they could be "rightly" praised.

Canto 52 serves as the prelude to this narrative, giving (among other things) Pound's condensed poetic synopsis of the Confucian *Li Ki*. The *Li Ki*, or *Book of Rites*, itself outlines the set of sacrifice rituals dynastic rulers must perform in order to rule properly. Pound's exploration of Chinese and American history therefore begins in the mythologized prehistory of Confucian ritualized codes of proper governance and comportment. This beginning, however, is not at all politically neutral, for, as witnessed earlier, the synopsis of the *Li Ki* is preceded in Canto 52 by Pound's own rant against Jews. Early on in 52 we read, "Stinkschuld's sin drawing vengeance, poor yitts paying for / Stinkschuld / paying for a few big jews' vendetta on goyim" (C 247). Pound appears to state here that *all* Jews as a race (named under the racist epithet "yitts") must "pay" for the transgressions and "bad rule" of certain wealthy Jews (here identified as "Stinkschuld").[12] As several of Pound critics have noted, by placing such anti-Semitic sentiments next to the sacrifice rituals of the *Li Ki*, Pound seems to be calling for the ritual sacrifice of the Jewish people in order to restore "natural order" to contemporary politics and economics.[13]

For better or worse, however, the transmission of all these messages is interrupted by the near-incomprehensibility of Pound's poetry. Part of the difficulty of these cantos is that almost all of Pound's words are mediated through other outside texts from which Pound has culled his historical information. Pound's rendering of the *Li Ki* in Canto 52, for instance, comes not from the original Chinese text, but from the French translation of Séraphin Couvreur, *Li Ki, ou mémoires sur Les Bienséances et les Cérémonies*, first published in 1913. The compressed Chinese history that follows in Cantos 53–61 finds its primary source-text in the *Histoire Générale de la Chine*, a 13-volume history written by the Parisian J. A. M. de Moyriac de Mailla in the late eighteenth century. Finally, Cantos 62–71 present revolutionary American history through the public writings, speeches, and private letters of John Adams, which Pound found collected in the three-volume *Works of John Adams* edited by Adams's grandson, Charles Francis Adams, in 1850.

Such textual mediations produce strange effects in the semantic field of the entire sequence of poems. First and foremost, bibliographic mediations prevent any sort of *im*mediate comprehension of Pound's language. We may understand individual words, phrases, and statements within the poems, yet intertextual references sufficiently fragment the narrative flow of the sequence such that the overall sense of the cantos will most often elude us without an annotated guide and/or a concerted study of textual history. The matter of semantic reference in the work is, in this way, not simply a matter of instantaneous correlation of signifier to signified, or of linguistic competence to meaning-production. To the contrary, language in *The Cantos* tends to expose its own transmission through time. In reading Pound's work, we are always to understand that Pound's words are *not solely his own*, that they have arrived to us through Pound *from other times and places*. While Pound's poems strive in their own fashion to present synchronic sense, they simultaneously attempt to display their own history in condensed form. Indeed, one of Pound's most startling contributions to U.S.-American poetics is this: what Pound termed his "ideogrammic method" whereby the sense of poetic language is not merely synchronic or merely diachronic, but always a hybrid of the two.

The term "ideogrammic method" refers primarily, of course, to Chinese written language in which graphic images stand for individual words or ideas. For Pound's work, however, Chinese ideograms are not merely interesting modes of writing; the ideogram structures the work as a whole. Pound's interest in the Chinese ideogram began with his introduction to the work of the U.S.-American Orientalist, Ernest Fenollosa.[14] In "The Chinese Written Character as a Medium for Poetry," Fenollosa addresses the problems of translating ideogrammic writing into Latinate script, work that Pound read as a sort of aesthetic revolution. Yet Fenollosa's aim in his Orientalist scholarship was not the domination or deprecation of Asian culture; to the contrary:

> It is unfortunate that England and America have so long ignored or mistaken the deeper problems of Oriental culture. We have misconceived the Chinese for materialistic people, for a debased and worn-out race. We have belittled the Japanese as a nation of copyists. We have stupidly assumed that Chinese history affords no glimpse of change in social evolution, no salient epoch of moral and spiritual crisis. We have denied the essential humanity of these peoples; and we have toyed with their ideas as if they were no better than comic songs in an "opera bouffe."
>
> The duty that faces us is not to batter down their forts or to exploit their markets, but to study and to come to sympathize with their

humanity and their generous aspirations.... We need their best ideals to supplement our own—ideals enshrined in their art, in their literature and in the tragedies of their lives.[15]

Although Fenollosa may sound overly simplistic and idealistic, his fundamental purpose in his writing is born out of respect for Asian cultures, to bring about a migration of Asian ideals westward for the betterment of U.S. and European cultures. Or rather, as much as Fenollosa may support the continued colonization of the "Orient" by "England and America," he finds the best means to do so through intellectual understanding rather than outright war and exploitation. Fenollosa's (and by extension Pound's) goal in translating the Chinese ideogram into new cultural contexts is not merely, therefore, the "Orientalization of the Orient," but rather its transcultural "Americanization"—where "Americanization" does not necessarily mean the destruction of Chinese culture through the imposition of the American, but also something like the "Chinafication of America."

Since "Americanize" is a somewhat suspect term with several possible connotations, we would be well served to model how Pound intends to "Americanize" the Chinese ideogram as a structure of poetry and culture in *The Cantos of Ezra Pound*. If we do not yet have such a model of "Americanization," we may in fact have to build upon a model of "Brazilianization" that has been constructed around Pound's ideogrammic method. Since 1950 Pound's poetry has been influential in avant-garde movements of Brazilian poetry, particularly *poesia concreta*. The initial group of concrete poets (Haroldo de Campos, his brother Augusto de Campos, and Décio Pignatari) that emerged from São Paulo in the 1950s named their first journal, *Noigandres*, after a passage in *The Cantos*,[16] and they deliberately positioned themselves as inheritors of a Poundian poetic tradition.[17] Yet one would be mistaken to view the Brazilian concrete poets as merely derivative of Pound, for they sought to mutate or "masticate" the Pound "tradition" in an act of cultural anthropophagy, cannibalism, ingestion. In critical essays such as Haroldo de Campos's "Ideograma, Diagrama, Anagrama," the Brazilian poet seeks not only to analyze, but to "Brazilianize," the poetics of Fenollosa and Pound.[18]

"Ideograma, Anagrama, Diagrama" is by no means a typical cultural critique. First published as the introduction to a collection of translated essays, which includes a Portuguese version of "The Chinese Ideogram as a Medium for Poetry," Campos's essay is in fact a formal-structural close reading of the Fenollosa/Pound ideogram. Not surprisingly for a concrete poet, Campos sets out to explore the visual aspects of written language that Fenollosa brings to the fore. For Fenollosa, notes Campos, ideograms can be composed of other sub-ideograms embedded within them, as in one of Fenollosa's most famous examples, "The sun rises in the east" (figure 4.1).

Reading from left to right, the simple ideogram for "sun" appears as part of the compound ideogram for "to rise," in which the "sun" appears above other sub-ideograms for "horizon" and "tree." The "sun" also reappears in "east," this time caught within the sub-ideogram "tree."[19] Writing therefore graphically represents the action in nature that it describes—the sun rising behind trees as it emerges from the eastern horizon. As such, written figures iconically manifest their own etymology, for Fenollosa (and thus Pound) quite clearly *saw* the derivation of the characters meaning "to rise" and "east" from the ideogram meaning "sun." Moreover, for both Fenollosa and Pound, this vision inexorably drew them back to a mythical, prehistoric moment when the "primitive" inventor of written language saw the sun rising in the east and encoded this action into ideograms. Linguistic history is thus compressed, yet still readily available, in each synchronic instance of the Chinese written figure; the ideogram both *compresses* and *stratifies* its own history.

Campos, however, is not so much interested in substantiating this mythical etymology as truth, as much as he is in exploring the production in ideogrammic writing of false etymologies, or as he puts it "suggestive pseudo-etymologies." In looking at Chinese ideograms, especially those composed of embedded sub-ideograms, one cannot help but draw suggestive meanings out of them, even if those meanings are not actually part of the true semantic function of the word. As one example, Campos considers the ideogram meaning "ocean." The left portion of the ideogram is a semantic classifier for "liquid"

Figure 4.1 "The sun rises in the east."

(radical no. 85 for "water"); the right portion in itself means "sheep" or "ram," yet as a sub-ideogram it is merely a phonetic graph for the pronunciation of *yang*$_2$ and actually has nothing to do with the meaning of the ideogram as a whole. Campos, however, cannot help but *see* both "water" and "sheep" in the ideogram, as illustrated by his diagrams at either side, *as if* the ocean were etymologically figured as a flock of sheep: "The Portuguese verb 'encarneirar' (designating the rippling of the sea in tiny foaming tides *as if like* a flock of sheep) and the French verb *moutonner* help us to explain the metaphoric process intuited (or constructed?) in this way *a posteriori*."[20] Thus, Campos reads ideograms in two distinct ways, which he terms (following Pound) a "double motivation" of the ideogram: an internal motivation in the ideogram's iconic representation of sound and sense; and an external motivation in the chain of "false" signifieds created (or constructed?) by the reader after the fact. And Campos views both of these motivations as equally viable, if not valid, modes of interpretation.

For Campos, suggestive pseudo-etymologies go to the very heart of all poetry. In *adding* to the possible meanings already denoted by the graphic sign, pseudo-etymology allows one to *create* causal or intentional associations among a broad selection of meanings, where no such associations previously existed; the ideogram, that is, *compresses* a long and variegated line of lexical selections—even those selected by the creative reader *a posteriori*—into a singular visual instant. On the one hand, this view of the ideogram mirrors Roman Jakobson's definition of the "poetic function," in that the ideogram projects a series of possible *selections* of words and meanings into an actualized associative *combination* of those words and meanings. On the other hand, Campos's view is determinedly deconstructive, in that the Chinese ideogram allows for the free play of signifieds within a single icon or signifier, a play that further serves to dislocate European logocentrism:

> [A]s an "intensified" model of the exercise of Jakobson's "poetic function" (whose intervention, though non-exclusive and non-excluding, becomes particularly relevant in the poetic usage of language and, thus, in the poetry of any age or school), this limit-case of the aesthetic dislocation of the "logocentric closure" of the Occident also proposes an instant synchronic model, immediately perceptible, *ostensible* (and for this even more "scandalous"), of that cunning "universal characteristic" (the projection of the paradigm onto the syntagm) traceable diachronically in all poetry, this rebel discourse, inflated by an *other logic*.[21]

In this way, Campos's "suggestive pseudo-etymology" suggests a critical "pseudo-history" of poetic theory. In elaborating Fenollosa/Pound ideogrammic poetics, Campos synchronizes a variety of contemporary scholarship on related areas: not only Jakobson and Derrida, but also the iconic symbolism of Charles Peirce, Sergei Eisenstein's theories of filmic montage, contemporary Asian linguistics, Sapir-Whorf semantics, Saussure's posthumously published work on anagrams, and so forth. Campos's purpose in this exercise is to create a total picture—a snapshot—of an entire critical tradition from the United States and Europe on the visuality of the sign and poetic interpretation/translation. In this, Campos does not necessarily seek to establish actual historical lines of influence amongst the theoreticians he cites, but rather to create *a posteriori* causal (or "pseudo-causal") links between far-flung scholars whom Campos sees as speaking to the same poetic problems. Campos strives to represent a synchronic-historical dialogue between intellectuals who in all probability had no contact with one another during their lifetimes. Not coincidentally, Campos represents this dialogue in a highly verbose style that borders on parataxis:

> It would be worthwhile to distinguish here, as has already been done in other moments of this work, between "external motivation" and "internal motivation." How, still, in a second surge, poetry "naturalizes" (thingifies) the sign, by the force of its "auto-reflexive" function, in the emphasis on the materiality of the message (Jakobson; *le mot-chose* of Sartre), the genetic *parti-pris*, accentuated by the "magic realism" of Fenollosa, loses importance, in favor of the formal (intrinsic) importance of the description. In this point, the Peircean notion of "diagram" permits the transcription ("translation"), to the realm of phonetic-alphabetic languages (or the poetics of these languages, where the palpable side of the sign assumes the primary plane), the Fenollosian (or Poundian) conception of the *ideogram* or the *ideogrammic method of composition* (relational syntax, parallelistic, paratactic), having Saussure (the Saussure of the "anagrams" as the "assyndetic succession" of paradigms) and Jakobson (especially that of the "poetry of grammar") as privileged mediators.[22]

Here Campos matches "internal motivations" of theoretical discourse itself (that which analyzes the intrinsic ability of poetry to materialize the sign as a thing) with his own "externally motivated" linkage of Jakobson, Saussure, Peirce, Fenollosa, and Pound within a common theoretical tradition. Jakobson and Saussure, of course, did not actually mediate the transition from Peirce's diagram to the

Fenollosa/Pound ideogrammic method in this regard. Yet, by equalizing all these sides *in a single sentence*, Campos creates the impression that all are vitally linked. Just as the ideogram functions iconically in the sharp juxtaposition of disparate visual images, Campos motivates a pseudo-historical development in poetic thought by juxtaposing four distinct modes of linguistic theory. His use of types of run-on sentences (parataxis) to do so is not only grammatically imperfect, but also emphasizes the process by which he fuses disparate concepts together.

Campos's emphasis on *pseudo*-history (itself based on *pseudo*-etymology) no doubt mocks the perceived status of the "American" as an imperfect or derivative copy that lacks value. Since the "true" or "original" etymological significance of the sign does not matter as much as the process by which variegated meanings are suggested, Campos moves us away from the concept of originality as the only viable mode of interpretation. Likewise, in translating Fenollosa/Pound thought into Portuguese, Campos carries entire formalist critical traditions into a new cultural context. Translation in this light becomes both an act of cultural transgression and an act of "originary" (if not "original") creation. Indeed, one of Campos's achievements in "Ideograma, Anagrama, Diagrama" is that he moves formal analysis into the realm of cultural critique, without abandoning the prospect of a truly formalist reading. For ultimately, Campos's own self-interest in Fenollosa and Pound becomes apparent:

> As a movement (or *tropism*) within Occidental discourse in the sense of breaking the structures of Aristotelian logic and alphabetic digitality-linearity, the concrete poetry of the 1950s (above all that of the so-called "heroic phase," or rather, that corresponding to the theoretical pieces synthesized in the *Plano Piloto* of 1958) seems to have forced this rupture to its maximum.... Starting significantly from the ideogram *via* Fenollosa/Pound (in an age when no one knew of the anagrammic adventures of Saussure), concrete poetry, in proposing itself as a phenomenon of "metacommunication" (or rather, as a poetic practice that used the phonetic system—*digits*—and an analogic syntax to create a *verbivocovisual* linguistic realm, able to participate simultaneously in the verbal and the non-verbal,—cf. *Plano Piloto*), was demarcating premonitorially an instance of convergence—a site or strategic *textual topos*—where, to Fenollosian "paragraphia" was added the Saussurean "paraphonia," through a commitment to generalized diagramming ("The poet is a *designer* of language"—D. Pignatari), that consolidated [*solidarizava*] the phonic plane to the graphic, magnetizing them both semantically.[23]

Campos thus synthesizes an entire theoretical-poetic history in order to locate Brazilian concrete poetry at the apex of that history. His interest therefore lies in the synthesis of a distinctly "Brazilian" poetics, and not just a universal poetics in general, with additional theoretical maneuvers that valorize his own *a posteriori* (or "pseudo-causal") introduction of foreign materials into Brazilian culture. In this manner, Campos enacts a transcultural migration of foreign literary theory to Brazil in order to reinscribe the set of values associated with "Brazilian." If *poesia concreta* represents a "premonitory convergence" of Fenollosian and Saussurean thought, it only becomes a "premonition" after Campos has successfully "Brazilianized"—in effect, "cannibalized"—both Fenollosa and Saussure. Indeed, this kind of "savage cannibalism" (through Oswald de Andrade's *antropofagismo*) is central to Campos's theories of American nationalism, as evidenced in his essay "Da razão antropofágica":

> Oswald's "Anthropophagy"—as I have written elsewhere—is a theory proposing the critical devouring of universal cultural heritage, formulated not from the submissive and reconciled perspective of the "noble savage" (idealized following the model of European virtues in the "nativist" vein of Brazilian romanticism by authors such as Gonçalves Dias and José de Alencar, for example), but from the disabused point of view of the "bad savage," devourer of whites, the cannibal. This last view does not involve submission (conversion) but, rather, transculturation, or, even better, "transvalorization": a critical view of history as a negative function (in Nietzsche's sense), capable of appropriation and of expropriation, of dehierarchization, of deconstruction. Any past which is an "other" for us deserves to be negated. We could even say, it deserves to be eaten, devoured, with the following clarifying proviso: The cannibal was a "polemicist" (from the Greek *polemos*, meaning "struggle, combat"), but he was also an "anthologist"—he devoured only the enemies he considered courageous, taking their marrow and protein to fortify and renew his own natural energies.[24]

We may therefore utilize Campos's "pseudo-history" as a premonitory model for the ideogrammic cultural formations represented in *The Cantos*. In the case of the China/Adams cantos, Pound uses the ideogram as a structural icon for the entire sequence by compressing whole volumes of history into his cantos—historical volumes that themselves have gleaned information from other prior texts. In this sense, *The Cantos* may be read as the end-result of Pound's own cannibalization or ingestion of foreign texts, with the bibliographic citations of his anthropophagy left overtly available to the reader. At the end of Canto 56, for instance, Pound's English words move seamlessly into a block of text taken not from Chinese texts, but from Moyriac de Mailla's *Histoire Gènèrale*:

> In '84 died General Li-ouen, in '85 Su Ta
> in 1386 peace
> HONG VOU declined a treatise on Immortality
>   offered by Taozers, Et
> En l'an trentunième de son Empire
>   l'an soixante de son eage
> HONG VOU voyant se forces affoiblir
>   dict: Que la vertu t'inspire, Tchu-ouen....(C 310)

Here the canto relates the dying words of the Sung Emperor Hung Vu, but does so by providing these words in the French translation of Moyriac de Mailla. Yet Moyriac de Mailla's words do not appear in quotation marks; rather the French has been incorporated into the body of the poem. Whether in French or English, we may receive the message that "Hong Vou" anointed "Tchu-ouen" as his successor; yet we may also glean the several bibliographic layers through which Pound has traveled in order to present this message. Pound's historical narrative does not just present a movement through time, but also represents the expansive strata of historical documentation and representations through which history is received; and these layers of texts are left stratified for the reader. Yet Pound simultaneously compresses the textual strata he elaborates, in order to produce highly condensed poems. Pound configures each of these poems in temporal succession from one canto to the next, in order to orchestrate a narrative that covers thousands of years. Yet this temporal and spatial configuration of history is designed to be condensed into a simultaneous harmonization of the "moral/ethical" themes and motifs present throughout the sequence.

In this way, we might conceptualize the entire China/Adams sequence as a sort of ideogram composed of three separate subideograms, brought together as a kind of extended parataxis: (1) Canto 52, which introduces the sequence; (2) the Chinese Cantos, 53–61; and (3) the Adams Cantos, 62–71. These three subsections of the sequence are placed together with little direct transition or connection, such that themes and motifs contained within each may vibrate or resonate with the others (akin to Mário de Andrade's harmonic verse), to make Confucian philosophy and John Adams's political philosophy "cohere." *Cantos LII–LXXI* thus attempts to motivate a transcultural migration of Chinese philosophy and history into an American context through the deployment of paratactic juxtapositions of cantos. This transcultural shift serves to synthesize a deliberate pseudo-history of American traditions. Confucius *becomes* "Americanized," so that John Adams may essentially *become* a good Confucian king—and thus an exemplar for modern world leaders—even though the actual historical connections between Confucianism and Adams are for all intents and purposes nonexistent.

If we read this transcultural shift as an aesthetic representation, however, we must recognize that it is an ethical representation, as well. Patterns of temporal stratification and compression—that is, ideogrammic patterns—are so consistently elaborated in China/Adams and elsewhere in *The Cantos of Ezra Pound* that we may rightly call them the primary formal structure of the entire work. This structure, however, must also be understood as *a structure of censorship*. Ideogrammic poetics as found in *The Cantos* require some authorizing agent (*censor*) who receives and mediates specific textual histories; who selects what historical information must be translated, paraphrased or elided; and who determines the point at which historical information can no longer be compressed further. One text is layered over prior texts by this agent so that the need for direct access to prior texts is no longer necessary; each canto overlays itself onto the external texts to which it refers so that the reader need only read *The Cantos* in order to recover an entire genealogy of textual transmission. The authorizing agent in this case, who is of course no less than Pound himself, must have sole power to regulate how textual histories are configured in the work, and to regulate how those textual histories may be received by a certain society of readers, in order for the ideogrammic method to function properly in the way the agent sees fit.

In this sense the ideogrammic poetics of China/Adams seem to become "despotic" structures, which require a single censor who mediates, regulates, and authorizes what the poetry may say, quite apart from simply authoring the poetry. Given this structural despotism, in turn, we see in passage after passage in China/Adams how poetic structures within the work correspond to broader political structures of the work's social context. Throughout Pound's Chinese history, for instance, we witness repeated instances when "bad rulers" fall prey to Taoists and Buddhists, and other instances when "good rulers" expel them. At these times, Pound uses epithets such as "bhuds," "shave-heads," and "hochangs" to describe Buddhists, in order to diminish the validity of Buddhism in general:

> The Prince of Ouei put out hochangs
> put out the shamen and Taotssé
> a.d. 444, putt 'em OUT
> > in the time of OUEN TI
> > "Let artisans teach their sons crafts"
> Found great store of arms in a temple
> The To-pa-tao went after the shave-heads, the hochang
> And the censor finally printed his placet
> > against extortionate judgements and greed of
> > the High Judge Yupingtchi...(C 283)

The expulsion of "extortionate greedy" Buddhists in this passage begins to subject-rhyme with Pound's call for the ritual sacrifice of Jews earlier in Canto 52; certainly the use of epithets such as "shave-heads," "hochang", and "yitts" places both Buddhist and Jew in an inferior category of men. Pound thus states that if good Confucian kings eliminated ("And the censor finally printed his placet") whole cultures in the past to reestablish a "natural" political order, then "naturally" good Confucian-fascist rulers of today must do the same. Here Pound is not merely reflecting on what has happened in history, but is employing history, and a history of textual transmission, in order to call into being new social configurations based on cultural purification, or rather, extermination. The censorship of bibliographic transmission at the heart of Pound's poetics thus attempts to govern a more general censorship of society and culture at large. As such, we begin to see that Pound has aligned his formal poetics with his fascist political beliefs in order to present those beliefs as "natural." Ideogrammic structures therefore are the crucial poetic forms that allow fascist and racist associations to be forged and presented as "inevitable" or "naturalized."[25]

Text and Extratext: Author and Authority

I am at war with myself, however, as to whether my interpretation of ideogrammic structure as "despotic" is entirely correct or incorrect. As a method of signification, ideogrammic poetics cannot signify without a consideration of the temporal transmission of language, which in *The Cantos* appears as the bibliographic transmission of history. Yet, the scope of such temporal investigations cannot stop at the limits imposed by Pound. In order for *The Cantos* to make sense, the text mandates that we pay attention to the textual transmission of *The Cantos of Ezra Pound* itself, in addition to that of other texts to which cantos may refer. Indeed, by looking at the sequence's editorial history, it becomes difficult to tell where exactly the text's structures of censorship end: whether these structures are contained solely within the poetic text per se, or whether they extend over extratextual elements as well.

Given that *The Cantos* were written in piecemeal fashion between 1915 and 1970, one must recognize that *The Cantos of Ezra Pound* as it is now published, distributed, and sold, is in fact an *anthology* of previously published books. Pound wrote his cantos in "blocks" and published these "blocks" as separate books, which were published simultaneously by two different editorial houses: Faber & Faber in London and New Directions in New York. The China/Adams cantos, for instance, were first published in a 1940 book entitled *Cantos LII–LXXI*. *Cantos LII–LXXI*, in turn, did not appear in a collected volume of cantos until 1956. And the "complete" *Cantos* did not appear until 1970, shortly before Pound's death in 1972. Just as the work must be read as a compendium of textual fragments, which Pound has collected into a "unified" epic, the book now entitled *The Cantos of Ezra Pound* must also be recognized as a compendium of previously published fragments of itself.

Figure 4.2 shows the first page of Canto 52 much as I received it when I began reading *The Cantos of Ezra Pound* in the early 1990s.

To reiterate, at the bottom of the page Pound locates the "international racket" of "jews, real jews" as:

>...specialité of the Stinkschuld
>   bomb-proof under their house in Paris
>   where they cd/ store aht voiks
>   fat slug with three body-guards
>   soiling our sea front with a pot bellied yacht in the offing,...(C 257)

Had I begun to read *The Cantos* even 10 years earlier, however, the reading of these lines would have been radically different. In figure 4.3, we see the same page from the New Directions first "complete" printing of *The Cantos* of 1970.

In this edition the last five lines of the page appear as straight black lines; furthermore, the first two mentions of "Stinkschuld," which in the 1991 printing appear as "Stinkschuld's sin drawing vengeance, poor yitts paying for / Stinkschuld," have been similarly altered.

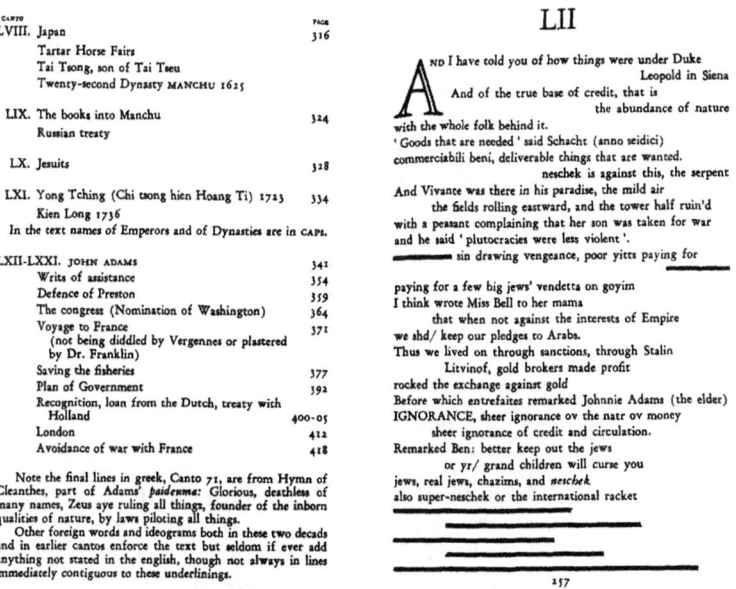

Figure 4.2 *The Cantos of Ezra Pound* (Fifth paperbound printing, 2007?), pp. 256–257 (reprinted with the permission of New Directions Publishing Corporation).

Figure 4.3 *The Cantos of Ezra Pound* (First clothbound printing of *Cantos 1–117* in one volume, 1970), pp. 256–257 (reprinted with the permission of New Directions Publishing Corporation).

"Stinkschuld" is in fact a replacement for the name "Rothschild." Pound's original 1938 typescript names the Rothschild family directly, "Rothschild's sin deawing [*sic*] vengeance, poor yitts paying for Rothschild"; and later, "...specialité of the Rothschild."²⁶ In the typescript Pound sent to the printers at Faber & Faber in 1939, Pound has crossed out the three instances of the name "Rothschild" with his pen, and included notes to the typesetter such as ".../ leave equivalent / space here for / word Rothschild." The galley proofs sent back to Pound from Faber contain ellipses dots for the name ("..........") though the rest of the writing remains intact; over these ellipses, however, Pound has handwritten the name "Stinkschuld." Although the exact documents showing when the black censorship lines were added are not to be found in the archives of Pound's papers at Yale's Beinecke Library, we can assume that they were added after these galley proofs.

All of these alterations came after rather extended negotiations over several months in 1939 between Pound and his editor at Faber, T. S. Eliot. Eliot quite explicitly feared potential reprisal from the Rothschild family when he read Pound's new work. In a letter dated July 15, 1939 (written on Faber letterhead) Eliot states,

> ...I am to write and tell you that they [Eliot's partners at Faber] have come round to the examination of the remarks which I made following you yourself pointing out certain passage in the first canto: I don't find anything libellious [*sic*] about Chinese emperors that isnt [*sic*] made safe by lapse of time, similarly about the Adams's, but they now agree with me that if you remain keen on jew-baiting, that is your affair, but that name of Rothschild should be omitted.

Pound responds to this by writing, "I fail; blast you, to t he [*sic*] use in spelling leprosy and syphils [*sic*] 'chicken pox'/ If the Pubrs / wish to be responsible, let 'em us a blank; i.E. [*sic*] a line of TEN dots." Pound then tells them to use the name "STINKSCHULD." In a letter dated "14 September 1939" Eliot writes back:

> I quite agree with you that the dots are bad, bugger up the metric completely, all the worse so near the beginning of the book. But the question aint [*sic*] so simple. We agree here that Stinkschuld won't do—too obvious a pointer. Also, what is just possible in ordinary times isn't desirable now. I think that the lines from "jews, real jews..." to "poppinjays" will have to come out, at any rate from this edition, because the reference to specific family is identifiable. Or probably it would do to leave out from "specialité of the..." to "poppinjays"

(why you spell popinjay with two pp I don't know). That's six lines, andalso [*sic*], of course, to leave out the line
    .... sin drawing vengeance, poor yitts paying for
                                         ....
That's the only way out I see.

The alterations Eliot mandated for the British Faber edition had a direct impact on the subsequent U.S.-American edition. The original New Directions *Cantos LII–LXXI* directly followed the settings of the Faber edition (printed earlier in 1940). In fact, Pound's American editor, J. Laughlin, had no idea of Pound's exact words in Canto 52 when he sent the volume to press, because they had already been censored. In a letter dated August 4, 1940 Laughlin states: "Cyantos [*sic*] is hon [*sic*] the press now. Wot [*sic*] was in them places where they put hin [*sic*] plack [*sic*] lines in Febrz [*sic*]? If you send me along those immortal voids by return hairpost [*sic*] we might manage to slip them in instead of nigsticks [*sic*]." Laughlin's comment points to the downright bizarre semantic disruptions caused by this form of censorship. For one, Laughlin's reference to the censored lines disparages African-Americans ("nigsticks"). Moreover, Laughlin immediately infers that there is something *underneath* these lines, that there exists *some prior text below which may be recovered later* ("Wot was in them places..."). To be sure, anti-Semitism and fascism *were* of great concern to both Eliot and Laughlin. In a letter from November 26, 1939 Laughlin tells Pound that "In most stores [booksellers] refuse to stock your books. Either they say they won't have them because you are a Fascist, or they say that youth has lost interest in you and they can't sell them."[27] Later, Laughlin would make repeated efforts to have Pound include a statement against anti-Semitic persecution at the start of *Cantos LII–LXXI*, only to be repeatedly frustrated. As for Eliot, in the aforementioned letter of September 14, 1939—coming as it does just weeks after the Nazi invasion of Poland—Eliot also concludes that anti-Semitism is not commercially viable. ("What is just possible in ordinary times isn't desirable now," a curiously phrased statement, at best.) Yet, by the same token, we must realize that Canto 52 was not censored merely because of Pound's fascism, anti-Semitism, or fanaticism, for all these elements are plainly accessible—and always have been—in other parts of the poem. Rather, Eliot was only concerned that certain of Pound's comments left Faber & Faber open to libel suits from the Rothschild family. Evidently, Laughlin came to share these concerns, and the lines remained blacked-out in both British and U.S. editions until 1986.

Nevertheless, censorship fueled speculation between 1940 and 1986 as to what was being withheld; readers obviously thought the black lines suppressed some fascistic, anti-Semitic content so much more horrible than the rest of the poem that it needed to be restrained.[28] Such a reaction should be thought of as an index to the *transformative* process of black-line censorship. Black lines are, after all, just black lines. But they tell us that words and phrases (and the meanings of those words and phrases) have been transformed into pure form—nothing but shape, color, and spatial arrangement, evacuated of semantic content. Further, they tell us that this transformation has occurred *over time*, that at some point in history someone has layered pure forms over an "original" language. While the black censorship lines are designed to block a certain semantic content, they still retain significant semantic functions. Black-line censorship informs readers of a *compression* of the poetic line into "nonsemantic" pure form, at the same time that it reveals the historical *stratification* of the lines' textual transmission. The black lines of censorship on page 257 of Canto 52 therefore conform to the same stratified-compressed ideogrammic structures of the rest of the poetic sequence; yet in this instance, they so conform because of external editorial and political concerns in opposition to the author's original intent.

There are other instances beyond Canto 52 in which structures of censorship operate both intra- *and* extratextually. The China/Adams sequence is the only book within the collected *Cantos* that retains its own, separate table of contents (figure 4.4).

Table

		PAGE
	Rays idiogram from Fenollosa collection	254
CANTO		
LII.	Li ki	257
LIII.	Great Emperors	262
	First dynasty HIA	
	Tching Tang of CHANG (second dynasty) b.c. 1766	
	Third dynasty TCHEOU b.c. 1122-255	
	Confucius (KUNG FU TSEU) 551-479	
LIV.	Fourth Dynasty TSIN, Burning of the Books 213	275
	Fifth Dynasty HAN b.c. 202	
	Eighth Dynasty SUNG a.d. 420	
	Thirteenth Dynasty TANG 618	
LV.	Tchun of TANG a.d. 805 Ngan's reforms	290
	Nineteenth Dynasty SUNG 960	
LVI.	Ghengis 1206	301
	Kublai 1260	
	Twentieth Dynasty YUEN (Mongol)	
	Lady Ouang Chi	
	HONG VOU died 1399	
	Twenty-first Dynasty MING 1368	
LVII.	Flight of Kien Ouen Ti	311

No one is going to be content with a transliteration of Chinese names. When not making a desperate effort at mnemonics or differentiating in vain hope of distinguishing one race from another, I mainly use the french form. Our European knowledge of China has come via latin and french and at any rate the french vowels as printed have some sort of uniform connotation.

Figure 4.4 Table of Contents for *Cantos LII–LXXI* (reprinted with the permission of New Directions Publishing Corporation).

While the primary contents-page at the beginning of the collected volume tells only of the names and dates of individual sections of the overall work, the subsequent table of contents for *Cantos LII–LXXI* tells us how to read the histories Pound will tell. The table provides a brief synopsis of the histories to be recounted, listing major events Pound will describe in the order he will describe them. It tells us that Chinese words should use French pronunciation, that the Chinese ideograms Pound uses come from Fenollosa's collection, but that in any event, foreign words only repeat what is said in English. All told, the table compresses the entire poetic sequence to its bare narrative minimum; at the same time it shows its own textual pedigree (from Fenollosa to Pound, Chinese to English via French) so that the reader may visualize the temporal arrangement of Pound's history. In material terms of book-production, the table literally rests on top of the poetic text that follows under it—a function that is also hermeneutic since the table attempts to direct certain interpretations, and even pronunciations, of the work at the possible expense of other modes of reading.

The table of contents is not the only instance of an external interpretative apparatus being attached to the text. Though Laughlin and Pound did not agree on an antidefamation clause to be added to the work, Laughlin did persuade Pound to allow the inclusion of introductory essays into the 1940 first edition of *Cantos LII–LXXI* in order to boost sales by clarifying certain difficulties in the text. Pound, however, did not want an actual introduction within the book; so Laughlin compromised by having a small, saddle-stitched booklet made for the introductory remarks, which was placed in an envelope pasted into the back cover of each copy of the book.[29] This booklet contains two short essays pseudonymously attributed to "H.H." and "S.D." respectively. One essay is a rather nice examination of Pound's metric, written (somewhat ironically as it turns out) by the Jewish-American poet, Delmore Schwartz, who signed it "S.D."[30] The other essay, "Notes on the Cantos," was written by J. Laughlin himself, who signed it "H.H." This second essay contains a reluctant appreciation of Hitler's economic policy. In placing *The Cantos* in aesthetic, political, and economic context, Laughlin writes, "In the past decade—the heyday of Marxism—it has been customary for liberal critics to sneer at Pound's economic ideas. Current events, with sinister irony, give them the lie—the success of Hitler's national inflation has proved that the idea of a socialized credit system is not ridiculous."[31] In retrospect these remarks (quoted here without the full context of Laughlin's essay) might be taken as inflammatory, so let me clarify. Laughlin was in no way a Nazi sympathizer, and in fact he loudly denounced Nazi-ism from its inception. Moreover, in the context of the Great Depression many intellectuals in the Americas and Europe struggled to consider various ideological alternatives—including many such as fascism and Stalinism—that turned out to be, not just dead-ends, but genocidal. Laughlin was thus placed in an untenable historical situation. The press he founded, New Directions, had championed modernist aesthetics—having already established itself by the late 1930s as the central distribution node of U.S. modernism. His essay, then, attempts to anticipate potential criticism of Pound's ideology in order to make *Cantos LII–LXXI* palatable to a book-buying public. Laughlin therefore strives to consider fascist economic policy in isolation from fascist cultural ideology, to present a "clean" view of social credit as tacitly distinct from "dirty" ideology of ethnic cleansing. The editor has attempted to balance his own competing aesthetic, cultural, and economic sensibilities; unfortunately it is now patently obvious that the aesthetic, cultural, and economic "sensibilities" of fascism were never separable.

Present-day readers of *The Cantos of Ezra Pound* would never know that these essays even existed, nor would they even know that Canto 52 had once been censored, if they only read the collected *Cantos* published after 1986. The copyright page of the most recent edition of the *Cantos* states unequivocally, "First clothbound *printing* of *Cantos 1–117* in one volume, 1970. First published paperbound as NDP824 in 1996" (emphasis added). This version, which I bought in 2008, also states that it is the "Fifth paperbound *printing*" (emphasis added). Rather innocuously, such statements intend to inform us how *the* book has been reprinted and reformatted over time. However, a careful reading of other information presented on the copyright page tells a slightly different story. The official statement of copyright ownership over the work reads as follows:

Copyright © 1934, 1937, 1940, 1948, 1950, 1956, 1959, 1962, 1963, 1965, 1966, 1968, 1970, 1971 by Ezra Pound
Copyright © 1969, 1972 by the Estate of Ezra Pound
Copyright © 1973, 1986, 1993 by the Trustees of the Ezra Pound Literary Property Trust
Copyright © 1942 by *Vice Versa*
Copyright © 1950 by Harcourt, Brace & World, Inc.

These statements of multiple copyright cover the variety of ways the *Cantos* were published and distributed since at least 1934, both in "complete" books after 1956 and in "incomplete" sections published as separate books. Legal ownership of the work, furthermore, is assigned to multiple entities over time: "Ezra Pound," "The Estate of Ezra Pound," "The Trustees of the Ezra Pound Literary Property Trust." This editorial variegation is left even more palpable—and yet at the same time, strangely censored—in other editions of the "complete" *Cantos*. When I began reading the work, for instance, the copyright page for my 1991 twelfth printing states:

> First printing of *Cantos 1–117* in one volume, 1970
> Second printing, 1971
> Third printing, 1972
> Fourth printing, 1973
> Fifth printing, 1975
> Sixth printing, 1977
> Seventh printing, 1979
> Eighth printing, 1981
> Ninth printing, 1983
> Tenth printing, 1986
> Eleventh printing, 1989
> Twelfth printing, 1991

Most readers familiar with *The Cantos* know, however, that these are not merely "printings," but rather that whole new *versions* of the work have appeared since 1970. Some editions of *The Cantos* have 120 cantos, some have 117; some do not contain the Italian Cantos 72–73, some place these cantos at the end, some place them in order, some add an English translation of 72; and, of course, some "printings" censor portions of Canto 52, and some do not. The statement on the copyright page thus (incorrectly) posits the existence of a singular *Cantos 1–117*, which appears merely to have been copied in subsequent "printings." In other words, an attempt has been made to censor the multiple extant versions of *The Cantos* through a de facto compression of the text into a singular edition named *Cantos 1–117*, at the same time that the historical transmission of the work is left quite visibly stratified, often with one "printing" resting on top of another since 1970.

We must therefore conceptualize the poetry of *The Cantos of Ezra Pound* as a material volume of textual matter, regardless of whether that matter may be considered strictly "poetic" or not. This is so because the ideogrammic structures of stratification and compression that govern the poetic text extend themselves over what bibliographic scholars normatively call "extratextual" elements. Moreover, such structures have continued to extend their reach well after the death of author as witnessed in the publication history of the work from 1970 to the present. The question therefore remains: if the ideogrammic structures of the total volume of text are indeed structures of censorship, then who is the agent who authorizes this censorship?

Chinafication

Earlier I stated that Pound served as a kind of despotic censor over *The Cantos of Ezra Pound*, which potentially allowed for a classification of the work as "fascist" and indeed "anti-Semitic." As such, the name, "Pound," serves as a signature that formalizes and authorizes censorship and that allows for certain aesthetic, cultural, political, and religious/ethical classifications *of the text*, as distinct from the text's author. *The Cantos of Ezra Pound*, however, represents a rare instance when the name of the author is contained in the title of a work penned by that author. We do not normally refer to *Moby Dick*, for instance, as the *"Moby Dick of Herman Melville* by Herman Melville," although we can (and do) refer to *"The Cantos of Ezra Pound* by Ezra Pound." Indeed the dust jacket of the volume, the spine of the volume, and the two title pages of the book all state unmistakably, *"The Cantos of Ezra Pound."* The name of the author is, in a concrete sense, embedded into the text attributed to the author.

In fact, the author's signature is an integral part of the poetic text itself. In addition to its appearance in the title, there are several instances throughout *The Cantos* where the author names himself, and two rather important instances occur in China/Adams specifically. In Canto 62, for instance, we read:

>...and as for Hamilton
> we may take it (my authority, ego scriptor cantilenae)
> that he was the Prime snot in ALL American history
> (11th Jan. 1938, from Rapallo)...(C 350)

Authority over the work is here explicitly invested in "ego scriptor cantilenae" ["I the writer of cantos"], further punctuated by the inclusion of a specific date and place to the signature. Any doubt that this "ego scriptor" is anyone but "Pound" can be dismissed later, in Canto 64:

> Upon which he offered me a retaining fee of one guinea
> which I accepted
>   (Re which things was Hutchinson undoubtedly scro-
>   fulous ego scriptor cantilenae
>   Ez. P)...(C 360)

In this instance, Pound moves from speaking in a poetic persona (John Adams states, "I accepted a retaining fee of one guinea") into speaking as Pound in the subsequent parenthetical aside, naming himself "Ez. P" in order to justify his particular interpretation of history.

In other words, Pound's signature assures the reader that Pound is able to speak and to produce viable poetic messages. The problem, however, is that this signature, "Pound," has become textualized. The signature has been transformed into textual matter to be regulated by the same formal-poetic structures as any other element in the text. Once the authorizing signature has been subsumed into the ideogrammic method of the text, it becomes subject to the same textual-historical compressions and stratifications that govern the total material volume of the text. We have already seen, in fact, that the temporal complexities of the ideogrammic method stem from the fact that Pound's words *are not solely his own*, that they have arrived to us through Pound *from other times and places*. The subject who speaks in *The Cantos* may be Pound himself, or it may be Moyriac de Mailla, or Confucius, or John Adams, all spoken through Pound. So while Pound may retain legal, copyrighted ownership over the work, we as readers are always to understand that textual-historical propriety over words and citations must be dispersed to multiple authors and translators over time. Pound takes "samples" from other authors and translators, and he has not had to ask their permission to do so since all of the texts he incorporates ("cannibalizes") are now in the public domain. All the same, even if we were to equate "authority" strictly with "copyright propriety," we would still have to confront the fact that the modernist poet named Ezra Pound *did not* retain legal, copyrighted ownership over the work even within his own lifetime. After World War II, to repeat, Pound was arrested by the U.S. Army for treason and committed to St. Elizabeths Hospital for the Criminally Insane in Washington, D.C. until 1959. Legal custodianship of Pound's literary property was then entrusted to an estate governed by Pound's family and friends. Yet even prior to this legal maneuvering we have already seen how print versions of the work(s) had already been substantially modified through negotiations—often legally binding negotiations designed to mitigate the possibility of litigation—between editors and the author in order to regulate the reception of the work by readers.

The textualized signature of "Pound"—which authorizes the structures of censorship that are at the poetic heart of the work—ceases to refer to a specific person. Rather, "Pound" may be best thought of as a *condensed* notation for a complex set of *stratified* social relations between authors, editors, family members, legal codes, external texts, historical figures, and readers. Any time we ascribe agency to "Pound"—as I have done throughout this chapter in phrases such as, "Pound writes...," "Pound states...," "Pound says..."—we pay reference, whether we like it or not, to this set of relations ideogrammically condensed into the name. In other words, authority over the work is not situated in one human being (one corpse), but has been dispersed into a set of relations (a textual *corpus*) between multiple social agents whose intentions may or may not be in accordance with one another. In the "Brazilianized" terms provided to us by Haroldo de Campos, the bibliographic transmission of the work—which has bound intra-textual poetic forms to extratextual censorship of those forms—compels us to create a "suggestive pseudo-etymology" of the sign, "Pound." In reading the "Pound Sign," we necessarily create causal "pseudo-historical" associations amongst a determined selection of players within a set of social relations, even though these relations may be obscured in normative usages of the sign. This "social construction of authority"—if not the "social construction of authorship" favored by contemporary textual scholars—can therefore be seen as a necessary interpretative base for the proper understanding of the work.

Indeed, by recognizing authority as socially constructed, we are now in a position to make productive ethical determinations about this text. *The Cantos of Ezra Pound* strives toward a kind of "reverse" mimesis—not the representation of reality, but rather the replication of the work's anti-Semitic vision into a wider social context. Yet the formal structures utilized to enact this reverse mimesis tend to decentralize or de-authorize the principal anti-Semite of its vision. While the *content* of *The Cantos of Ezra Pound* exhibits unquestionably anti-Semitic motives, there is no "natural" *formal* complement to this content with which to justify the supposed viability or inevitability of anti-Semitism. The social pressures exerted on the work on the level of form—social pressures that are admitted into the work *by the work's own formal structures*—are simply too variegated and contentious to sustain anti-Semitism as anything "natural." By shifting the locus of authority away from a singular author into a set of social relations we may now identify the prevalence of racist hatred in this text, to recognize the function of anti-Semitism within the aesthetic project of the text. At the same time, however, we may still effectively demarcate the involvement of this text (and its critical after-life) as an aesthetic representation of the drastic ideological conflicts and sociopolitical reconfigurations of the 1930s and 1940s, and indeed beyond. While Ezra Pound himself called for the elimination of Jews in support of fascist ideology, external authorities have made concerted efforts to suppress, condemn, or circumscribe anti-Semitism and fascism in ways that are visibly manifest on the page and therefore recoverable through poetic reading.

Our reading of *The Cantos of Ezra Pound* does not allow for cultural purification, or for that matter cultural purity. It does, however, encourage social and cultural mixing in its limited way. The ideogrammic structure of China/Adams permits a kind of miscegenation of Chinese and U.S.-American histories, with an eye toward new cultural formations (neoculturation.) This permission for miscegenation necessitates the identification of an authority who speaks—a speaking subject. Aesthetic form (ideogrammic structure) in effect becomes the medium through which the speaking subject ("Pound") expresses social and ethical relations, whether contentious or not. Thus, while the man named Ezra Pound may have been "un-American," and may have intended to express "un-American" beliefs in his work, the poetic forms in that work produce an *other* "Pound" who may be valued differently, both aesthetically and ethically. "Pound" becomes transculturated or cannibalized, a non-conciliated site where various social parties meet, conflict, or merge.

But when I say "transculturated," I do not mean "resolved" or "fixed," but rather something much more *indecisive*. The "Pound Sign" is marked by multiple levels of historical violence that disrupt any possibility of neat closure. At their root, *The Cantos* are driven by the need to do away with homicidal economic exploitation ("usury"), and to this end the work provides a historical primer for the emergence of globalization—an international intensification of exploitative capitalism Pound already saw in formation by the 1930s. Pound's "tribe" for which he intends his *Cantos* is therefore, appropriately, an "internationalized nation" with historical roots in Greece, Rome, China, Egypt, France, Italy, Britain, the United States, and more. However, Pound's ethical stance against exploitation is itself driven by genocidal impulses, particularly in the author's perceived need to kill off Jews and Buddhists. Significantly, genocide also plays into whatever transculturation the work purports to enact, especially with respect to Chinese culture. While as I mentioned, Fenollosa remained reverent toward China, *The Cantos*' use of Fenollosa's ideogrammic poetics is not really geared to the preservation of Chinese culture, except as a dead relic. By folding Confucianism into his Occidental "tribe," Pound effectively signals the disintegration (read: extermination) of the Chinese as a preface to the reintegration of the Occidental nation. It is therefore no accident that Chinese history ends in *The Cantos* in 1780, with the emergence of the tea/opium trade and Britain's colonial domination of China.

Pound's presentation of global history seems woefully limited now that China appears to have shed its colonial past and has begun to assert its power in the global market—that is, now that China has passed from a modern colonized nation to becoming a global colonizer. But such a judgment—identifying the incorrectness of Pound's historical views—is still a part of the process. The "censorious" forms—poetic structures—of *The Cantos* do indeed begin to structure the world around them ("reverse mimesis"), first by organizing the signifying practice of "extratextual" materials surrounding the poems, and then consequently by organizing the work's historical milieu (structuring the signifying practice of history). But as they do so, these structures also announce a curious "death of the author," in which the genocidal impulses of Ezra Pound are "decapitated" by the cannibalizations of the "Pound Sign." "Pound" is not one person, nor even a corpse now disintegrating in a cemetery in Venice next to the grave of Igor Stravinsky. "Pound" is a continual—one might say, vibrant—process of cultural movement, historical contention, negotiation—and translation. The "original" has been obliterated, but the violence of translation carries on.

What could be more *American*?

Epilogue

I would like to conclude, briefly, by retracing my steps:

Spring and All critically remaps subjectivity in relation to the American nation-state. Yet significantly, this possibility is raised on the level of the object (the text) and is not confined to subjectivity itself (i.e., the subject-position or heritage of the poetic "I" or the author). The politics of nation-formation in the America of *Spring and All* revolve around the objectification of others *against whom* a national people may likewise be objectified. Yet underneath the political ideology of objectification, we will find modes of dependency, privation, and migration—framed poetically—that may critically undermine the political project. To reiterate, migration and translation are not necessarily *subjective* processes in the case of *Spring and All*. Rather, they are best seen as material movements between prose and poetry, blackness and whiteness, typography and blankness, form and content, subject and object.

In subsequent readings of *Paulicéia desvairada* and *Altazor*, we encountered similar double-movements between the concretization of a national territory/national people and the material conditions of the poetic text. Poetic materialization in these cases does in fact "serve up" a modernized nation, but does so by way of parody and irony. Mário de Andrade's work must be read as an effort to cope with the clash of new cultures and societies within the city-space of São Paulo and the national territory of Brazil. The Brazil it produces, however, is at best a duplicitous parody of nationhood, and at worst a psychotic spectacularization of state incorporation. Thus, *Paulicéia desvairada* addresses a political problem brought forth by immigration and modernization (e.g., the entrance of new industrial classes from abroad); yet, the text also dislocates the nation from itself and in doing so allows new mappings of urban and national territory.

From the introduction onward, I have sought to characterize the "American" as a priori *deconstructed*—that which never really has an "origin," but which is always already preconditioned as a translated copy. Yet deconstruction may remain utterly safe—innocuous, ineffective—if it only remains on the level of literature and textuality. In my reading of *Altazor* I sought to demonstrate how such poetic remappings might extend outside the text. With *Altazor*, thus, deconstruction is something far more powerful. Huidobro's work self-consciously situates itself in translation—suspended in migratory movement. Within the world of the text, *Altazor* appeals to received literary and linguistic structures that it simultaneously deconstructs and obliterates. Yet given historical perspective, we can now begin to see how the "internal" migratory logic of the text exceeds the text itself. In effect, the text begins to organize (and *devour*) its historical transmission across time and space. The work itself works to revise its *own* history from manuscript to print. The end-result of this process of deconstruction, I believe, is the reassertion of the Latin American nation—now seen to be, just like Altazor and *Altazor*, as ironically suspended between North and South.

These readings give way to the remapping of *The Cantos of Ezra Pound*. The politics of the *Cantos* are truly horrendous—of that there can be little doubt. However, ethical judgments over the work have typically assumed it to be governed by an increasingly fascistic authoritarian author, just as the work seeks to justify a new world governed by a fascist dictator. In reality, it is not the subject who governs the object, but the other way around. Poetic structures *inherent* to the work in fact function *against* any singular subjective voice, and in so doing function to splay subjectivity into a variegated set of objective (and object-oriented) social relations. Above and beyond his aberrant beliefs, Ezra Pound is "American" to the extent that he remains subject to continual retranslations, remappings, across various sociohistorical *contexts*.

In this sense I have attempted to characterize poetic texts not merely as reflective of their political-economic milieu, but more powerfully as *productive forces*. Poetry produces social context, as much as it has been produced by that context. And what poetry produces flows from the cultural logic(s) of migration and translation. Whatever Hemispheric Inter-American studies will be will follow from the hemisphere's propensity for remapping itself. The difficulty presented by American cultures is that *there is no single map* of the Americas, and nothing like an *original* map from which the space of the hemisphere may be traced. Consequently, there is no way to situate American cultures firmly in time and space. Rather, there are only multiple *remappings* of the Americas, which therefore open historical-spatial dynamics between cultural remapping and political-economic production. There is no original map of the Americas, just a (textual) series of remappings purporting to translate originals that never existed in the first place.

The remapping of the Americas is not just a graphic representation of space. It is also a means to understand how space is produced, inclusive of the function(s) of subjectivity in space. At no point do I suggest that the subjects in question have ever reached some finality—no "pure product of America." Rather the American subject is formed in processual movement (migration) between self and other, now perceived as an *internal* logic of subjectivity. The American subject is bound *into* the "other" object. Moreover, at no point do I suggest that the objects in question in this book have ever been finalities either. I have taken pains not to accept the literary text as a *thing*; all the poems analyzed here have been presented as a process of "versioning" in which the work of art can only be construed as a series of different versions of itself. The actual text we read—the book we hold in our hands or the image splayed on our screens—is only ever a "re-version." The poem is process.

Under globalization, a map of the Americas may very well already be in formation, according to which the political-economic dominance of the powers that be may be assured. This map may take shape as a unified field of territory held together by U.S. and/or Anglo-American dominance; more likely it may take shape as a unified field (a free-trade zone), the stability of which is maintained by the collusion of multiple hegemonic forces—regional "mini-hegemons" in the form of national powers and multinational corporations. *However*, such remappings of the American hemisphere require poetic imagination. For globalization to exist in the first place, one needs to imagine hemispheric territory as both virtual and concrete—one imagines itself to be at once alive in a unique material place *and* in a place one imagines to be seamlessly connected to everywhere else in the hemisphere. This "poetic imagination," as I have worked to demonstrate, is at once object (poem, text) and subject (imagination, cognition). Remapping is nothing less than the poetic concretization of what a world could be, but in this case "poetic" emerges in the form of an inexorably intermeshed "subject:object" or "object:subject." This skews, mutates, the very notion of what an "imagination" is. If contemporary political and economic processes seek to map a colossal zone of free trade, the historical formation of American cultures as "American" must be understood as both an enabling and inhibiting force of the mapping process.

If globalization seeks an integrated map of the Americas, poetry responds by showing this to be a *remapping*. If globalization seeks a language to give this remapping meaning, poetry responds by speaking the language of *translation*. And who is the migrant who crosses (translates) this remapped, resignified map of the Americas? *In-between* the pages you now hold in your hand, the migrant is *you*.

Notes

Preface

1. Earl E. Fitz, Rediscovering the New World: Inter-American Literature in a Comparative Context (Iowa City: University of Iowa Press, 1991); Djelal Kadir, Columbus and the Ends of the Earth: Europe's Prophetic Rhetoric as Conquering Ideology (Berkeley: University of California Press, 1992); Vera Kutzinski, Against the American Grain: Myth and History in William Carlos Williams, Jay Wright, and Nicolás Guillén (Baltimore: The Johns Hopkins University Press, 1987).
2. Donald Pease, "National Identities, Postmodern Artifacts, and Postnational Narratives," boundary 2, 19.1 (1992): 1–13; Werner Sollors, ed., Multilingual America: Transnationalism, Ethnicity, and the Languages of American Literature (New York: New York University Press, 1998); Anna Brickhouse, Transamerican Literary Relations and the Nineteenth Century Public Sphere (Cambridge: Cambridge University Press, 2004).
3. Djelal Kadir, "Introduction: America and Its Studies," PMLA, 118.1 (January 2003): 9–24.
4. Roberto Fernández Retamar, Para una teoría de la literatura hispano-americana (México, DF: Editorial Nuestro Tiempo, 1981); and Calibán: Apuntes sobre la cultura en nuestra América (México, DF: Editorial Diógenes, 1971).
5. Jorge Schwartz, "¡Abajo Tordesillas!" Casa de las Américas, 33.191 (April–June 1993): 26–35.
6. Fitz, Rediscovering the New World; Richard Morse, New World Soundings (Baltimore: The Johns Hopkins University Press, 1989).
7. Luiz Madureira, Cannibal Modernities: Postcoloniality and the Avant-Garde in Caribbean and Brazilian Literature (Charlottesville, VA: University of Virginia Press, 2005); Fernando Rosenberg, The Avant-Garde and Geopolitics in Latin America (Pittsburgh: University of Pittsburgh Press, 2006).
8. Deborah N. Cohn, History and Memory in the Two Souths: Recent Southern and South American Fiction (Nashville: Vanderbilt University Press, 1999); Debra A. Castillo, Redreaming America: Toward

a Bilingual American Culture (Albany, NY: State University of New York Press, 2005).
9. Brickhouse, Transamerican Literary Relations and the Nineteenth Century Public Sphere; Gretchen Murphy, Hemispheric Imaginings: The Monroe Doctrine and Narratives of U.S. Empire (Durham, NC: Duke University Press, 2005); Caroline F. Levander and Robert S. Levine, eds., Hemispheric American Studies (Camden, NJ: Rutgers University Press, 2007).
10. Gloria Anzaldúa, Borderlands/La Frontera (San Francisco: Aunt Lute Books, 1999, 2nd ed.); José David Saldívar, Border Matters: Remapping American Cultural Studies (Berkeley: University of California Press, 1997); Néstor García Canclini, Culturas híbridas: Estrategias para entrar y salir de la modernidad (Buenos Aires: Editorial Sudamericana, 1992); Walter Mignolo, Local Histories/Global Designs: Coloniality, Subaltern Knowledges, and Border Thinking (Princeton, NJ: Princeton University Press, 2000).
11. Let me be clear that the economic recovery of which I speak was not at all equally distributed among Latin American populations. I merely mean that Latin American national economies stabilized and expanded, in tandem with national political stability (the definitive end of military dictatorships, the lurching end of armed insurrections (e.g., the Peruvian Sendero Luminoso), nominally democratic processes, etc.). But in fact, disturbingly vast populations continue to live in dire poverty. And it very well may be the case (as in Chile for example) that macroeconomic recovery served to depress income among the lower middle- and working classes so as to "prepare" the national economy for globalized investment, thereby offering a large and cheap workforce.
12. Fitz, Rediscovering the New World, 1.
13. Walter C. Bronson, A Short History of American Literatura (Boston: D.C. Heath & Co., 1919), 3.
14. John Macy, The Spirit of American Literature (Garden City, NY: Doubleday, Page, & Co., 1913), 3.
15. Robert E. Spiller, "The Cycle and the Roots: National Identity in American Literature," Toward a New American Literary History, ed. Louis J. Budd, Edwin H. Cody, and Carl L. Anderson (Durham, NC: Duke University Press, 1980), 4.
16. See, Michael Bérubé, "American Studies without Exceptions," PMLA, 118.1 (January 2003): 103–113.
17. Hortense J. Spillers, "Who Cuts the Borders? Some Readings on 'America,'" Comparative American Identities: Race, Sex, and Nationality in the Modern Text, ed. Hortense J. Spillers (New York: Routledge, 1991), 4–5.
18. César Vallejo, "Contra el secreto profesional," Las vanguardias literarias en Hispanoamérica, ed. Hugo J. Verani (México, DF: Fondo de Cultura Económica, 1986), 192. My translation.

19. Rubén Darío, Poesía, ed. Ernesto Mejía Sánchez (Caracas: Biblioteca Ayacucho, 1977), 179. My translation.
20. Antonio Candido, Formação da literatura brasileira (São Paulo: Livraria Martins Editora, 1959), 8. My translation.
21. Emir Rodríguez Monegal, The Borzoi Anthology of Latin American Literature, ed. Emir Rodríguez Monegal with Thomas Colchie (New York: Alfred A. Knopf, 1992), xiii.
22. See Pedro Henríquez Ureña, "El descontento y la promesa," Seis ensayos en busca de nuestra expresión (1928), in Obra Crítica, ed. Emma Susana Speratti Piñero (México, DF: Fondo de Cultura Económica, 1960), 241–253; and Andrés Bello, "Autonomía cultural de América" (1848), Conciencia intelectual de América, ed. Carlos Ripoll (New York: Las Americas Publishing Company, 1966).
23. Fernando Ortiz, Contrapunteo del tabaco y el azúcar (1940) (Barcelona: Editorial Ariel, 1963); Angel Rama, Transculturación narrativa en América Latina (México, DF: Siglo Veintiuno Editores, 1982); Antonio Cornejo Polar, Escribir en el aire: Ensayo sobre la heterogeneidad socio-cultural en las literaturas andinas (Lima: Editorial Horizonte, 1994); Walter Mignolo, The Darker Side of the Renaissance: Literacy, Territoriality, and Colonization (Ann Arbor, MI: University of Michigan Press, 1995).
24. Alberto Moreiras, The Exhaustion of Difference: The Politics of Latin American Cultural Studies (Durham, NC: Duke University Press, 2001); Haroldo de Campos, "Anthropophagous Reason: Dialogue and Difference in Brazilian Culture," trans. Odile Cisneros, Novas: Selected Writings, ed. Odile Cisneros and A. Sérgio Bessa (Evanston, IL: Northwestern University Press, 2007), 157–177; Oswald de Andrade, "Manifesto Antropófago," A utopia antropofágica (São Paulo: Editora Globo, 1990), 47–52.
25. Silviano Santiago, "Latin American Discourse: The Space In-Between," trans. Ana Lúcia Gazzola and Gareth Williams, The Space In-Between: Essays on Latin American Culture (Durham, NC: Duke University Press, 2001), 25–37.
26. Justin Read, "Manners of Mistranslation: The Antropofagismo of Elizabeth Bishop's Prose and Poetry," CR: New Centennial Review, 3.3 (2003): 297–327.
27. Mignolo, Local Histories/Global Designs; Aníbal Quijano and Immanuel Wallerstein, "Americanity as a Concept, or the Americas in the Modern World-System," International Journal Of Social Sciences (UNESCO), No. 134 (November 1992): 549–557.
28. A note on literary-historical concepts: I would like to define "modern" as a concept, equally valid across the Americas, that describes a literary period beginning in 1850 and ending roughly in 1960 or 1970. This definition would be broad enough to encompass various turns to modernization across the hemisphere, not only in literature, but also politics, economics, transportation, communication, urbanization, etc.

However, I also recognize that this is not a widely held definition of "modern." Unfortunately, conceptual schemes are not the same in the Americas: the period I focus on in this book pertains to "modernism" in Anglo America, "vanguardismo" in Spanish America (where "modernismo" occurred just prior, 1880–1920), and "modernismo" in Brazil. For the sake of convenience I hold all three concepts, all of which are more similar than different, under the singular rubric of "modern," foregoing any attachment to a particular "-ism."

1 Enter the Cannibal: Dependency, Migration, and Textuality in William Carlos Williams's *Spring and All*

1. This is the central thrust of Alberto Moreiras's concept of "dyssemetrical gaze" in his biting critique of subaltern studies, *The Exhaustion of Difference: The Politics of Latin American Cultural Studies* (Durham, NC: Duke University Press, 2001).
2. Benedict Anderson, *Imagined Communities: Reflections on the Origin and Spread of Nationalism* (London: Verso, 1991).
3. José David Saldívar, *The Dialectics of Our America: Genealogy, Cultural Critique, and Literary History* (Durham, NC: Duke University Press, 1991), 4.
4. José Martí, "Our America" (1891), trans. John D. Blanco, in Julio Ramos, *Divergent Modernities: Culture and Politics in 19th Century Latin America* (Durham, NC: Duke University Press, 2001).
5. Roberto Fernández Retamar, *Calibán: Apuntes sobre la cultura en nuestra América* (México, DF: Editorial Diógenes, 1971); and *Para una teoría de la literatura hispanoamericana* (México, DF: Editorial Nuestro Tiempo, 1981).
6. See John Guillory, *Cultural Capital: The Problem of Literary Canon Formation* (Chicago: University of Chicago Press, 1993).
7. Gayatri Chakravorty Spivak, "Can the Subaltern Speak?" *The Post-Colonial Studies Reader*, ed. Bill Ashcroft, Gareth Griffiths, and Helen Tiffin (London: Routledge, 1995).
8. Retamar, *Calibán*, 60.
9. Reed Whittemore, *William Carlos Williams, Poet from New Jersey* (Boston: Houghton Mifflin Company, 1975), 13–17.
10. Even Marzán admits,

    Williams, who habitually covers his sources..., of course, nowhere explicitly attests to his performing this translation. And one can argue that "The Red Wheelbarrow" came to Williams not derived directly from "Brilliant Sad Sun" but by the original experience that remained with him so vividly that over time it inspired separate poems with the same imagery. But that argument would leave the poem hollow of important semantic

possibilities, flattening the dimension of the "red wheelbarrow" while disregarding parallel instances of the imaginary translation that produced that image. (Julio Marzán, *The Spanish-American Roots of William Carlos Williams* [Austin, TX: University of Texas Press, 1994], 162) Marzán is incorrect on two counts: First, as we shall shortly see, the biographical genesis of "The Red Wheelbarrow" has already been well established, and it is not what Marzán claims it to be. As a result, second, semantic possibilities of the poem cannot be hollowed out if they were not there to begin with; through circular logic, Marzán claims that readers who do not agree with his faulty logic are depriving the poem of meanings that he has placed into the poem based on faulty logic.
11. Marzán, *The Spanish-American Roots of William Carlos Williams*, 163.
12. Góngora's presence is palpable, e.g., in the *modernista* poetry of the Nicaraguan Rubén Darío, and in the *vanguardista* work of the Spanish-Cuban poet Dámaso Alonso.
13. Robert Lowell, "William Carlos Williams," *Collected Prose* (New York: Farrar, Straus, Giroux, 1987), 42. Lowell's "essay" in the *Collected Prose* is in fact a collection of three separate pieces: Lowell's 1946 review of *Paterson, Book One*; his 1948 review of *Paterson, Book Two*; and a short piece entitled simply "Dr. Williams" from 1962. The citation provided here comes from the last of these three.
14. Ibid., 42.
15. Pound wrote his Master's thesis on Lope de Vega, and his *Cantos* are littered with formal and structural nods to the Spanish Baroque.
16. Richard A. Morse, *New World Soundings* (Baltimore: The Johns Hopkins University Press, 1989), 62.
17. Ibid., 63.
18. Oswald de Andrade, "Manifesto Antropófago" (1928), *A utopia antropofágica* (São Paulo: Editora Globo, 1990b), 47–52.
19. I am aware that this statement appears to differ sharply from the conclusions of Sarah Castro-Klarén in her reading of the "Manifesto Antropófago." In "A Genealogy for the 'Manifesto Antropófago,'" Castro-Klarén begins with the common notion that Oswald's manifesto must be read in light of the consolidation of the Brazilian nation: "'The nation' stands for that entity capable of integrating the fragments, oppositions, and contradictions inherited from the dislocations of peoples, cultures, and languages that the regime of coloniality brought about" (Sarah Castro-Klarén, "A Genealogy for the 'Manifesto Antropófago,'" *Nepantla*, 1.2 [2000]: 297). After an exhaustive genealogy of the indigenous references in the manifesto, and the ultimate path of Oswald's thought through his 1950 thesis "A crise da filosofia messiânica," Castro-Klarén *correctly* concludes, "Anthropophagy does not construct integrated subjects.

Rather it is an endless voyage toward an infinite and indeterminate alterity" (312). Indeed, this is one of the central conclusions of this chapter and this book, as well; save that I hold the "indeterminate alterity" of which Castro-Klarén speaks to be wrapped up in the processes of American nationhood, not necessarily opposed to the nation.

20. Luiz Madureira, *Cannibal Modernities: Postcoloniality and the Avant-Garde in Caribbean and Brazilian Literature* (Charlottesville, VA: University of Virginia Press, 2005), 51.
21. Ibid., 50.
22. Haroldo de Campos, "Anthropophagous Reason: Dialogue and Difference in Brazilian Culture," trans. Odile Cisneros, *Novas: Selected Writings*, ed. Odile Cisneros and A. Sérgio Bessa (Evanston, IL: Northwestern University Press, 2007), 160.
23. Morse, *New World Soundings*, 66.
24. Ibid., 68.
25. Ibid., 69.
26. Ibid., 22.
27. Ibid., 23.
28. Thus, whereas dialects in Spain, Portugal, and England vary from town to town, kilometer by kilometer, in the Americas distinct dialect-communities tend to extend over huge expanses of space.
29. Ibid., 198–199.
30. It does not seem coincidental that Europe's "rebirth" of culture (Renaissance) corresponds exactly to the initial stages of colonizing the rest of the world.
31. Walter Mignolo, *Local Histories/Global Designs: Coloniality, Subaltern Knowledges, and Border Thinking* (Princeton, NJ: Princeton University Press, 2000), 305.
32. Ibid., 338.
33. Ibid., 54.
34. Fernando Henrique Cardoso and Enzo Faletto, *Dependency and Development in Latin America*, trans. Marjory Mattingly Urquidi (Berkeley: University of California Press, 1979), 28.
35. See two essays by Cardoso, "The Consumption of Dependency Theory" (1977) and "Globalization and International Relations" (1996), in the volume, *Charting a New Course: The Politics of Globalization and Social Transformation* (Lanham, MD: Rowman & Littlefield Publishers, Inc., 2001).
36. *Webster's New World Dictionary*, Third College Edition (New York: Prentice Hall, 1994), 430.
37. Circumstances will force us to retreat from this reading somewhat, as is explained in the next section of this chapter.
38. What did Montaigne say "Of the Cannibals"? "Not at all bad, that.—Ah! But they wear no breeches!"

39. Quoted in Bill Mohr, "The Wheelbarrow in Question: Ideology and the Radical Pellucidity of William Carlos Williams' Images," *William Carlos Williams Review*, 24.2 (Fall 2004): 29. Mohr retrieves the quote from William Rose Benét, ed., *Fifty Poets: An American Auto-Anthology* (New York: Duffield and Green, 1933), 60.
40. William Carlos Williams, *In the American Grain* (New York: New Directions, 1956), 211.
41. James Breslin, *William Carlos Williams, an American Artist* (New York: Oxford, 1970), 78.
42. Ibid., 78.
43. William Carlos Williams, *I Wanted to Write a Poem: The Autobiography of the Works of a Poet*, ed. Edith Heal (Boston: Beacon Press, 1958), 36.
44. A. Walton Litz and Christopher MacGowan, "Appendix A: A Note on the Text," *The Collected Poems of William Carlos Williams, Vol. 1*, ed. A. Walton Litz and Christopher MacGowan (New York: New Directions, 1986), 467.
45. The Greg-Bowers "method," also known as "conservative," derives from two groundbreaking methodological studies: "The Rationale of the Copy-Text" by W. W. Greg (1950–) and "Some Principles for Scholarly Editions of Nineteenth-Century American Authors" by Fredson Bowers (1975 [1964]). Although still broadly utilized in English Departments, the Greg-Bowers school has largely been modified or discarded entirely by contemporary social-historicist methods of editorial theory. We should also mention that the Greg-Bowers method is not generally utilized outside of English Departments, especially in Latin America where French genetic methods are far more prevalent. For more detailed analyses and critiques of these matters, consult G. Thomas Tanselle's *Textual Criticism since Greg: A Chronicle, 1950–1985* (Charlottesville, VA: University of Virginia Press, 1987) and Jerome J. McGann's *A Critique of Modern Textual Criticism* (Charlottesville, VA: University of Virginia Press, 1983).
46. And this is precisely the question analyzed with such skill by Burton Hatlen in "Openness and Closure in Williams' *Spring and All*," *William Carlos Williams Review*, 20.2 (Fall 1994): 15–29.
47. Donald Wesling, "Emotion Deriving from Sequence in William Carlos Williams's *Spring and All*," *William Carlos Williams Review*, 24.2 (Fall 2004): 41–47.
48. Ibid., 46.
49. Siegfried Kracauer, *The Mass Ornament: Weimar Essays* (1927), trans. Thomas Y. Levin (Cambridge, MA: Harvard University Press, 1995).
50. Walter Benjamin, "The Work of Art in the Age of Mechanical Reproduction," *Illuminations*, ed. Hannah Arendt (New York: Schocken Books, 1969), 242. "Communism responds by politicizing art."

2 The Reversible World: America as Dissonance in Mário de Andrade's *Paulicéia desvairada*

1. Jean-Luc Nancy, *The Inoperative Community* (Minneapolis: University of Minnesota Press, 1991), xxxvii–xxxviii.
2. Joaquim Machado de Assis, *The Posthumous Memories of Brás Cubas* (1881), trans. Gregory Rabassa (Oxford: Oxford University Press, 1997), 82–83.
3. After the Napoleonic invasions of Iberia, the Portuguese crown relocated to Rio de Janeiro in 1807. When Dom João VI returned to Lisbon in 1821, he left his son Pedro in Brazil as regent of the colony. After substantial discontent among Brazil's landed oligarchs, Pedro decreed Brazil's independence in 1822—becoming Dom Pedro I.
4. See Marisa Lajolo and Regina Zilberman, *A formação da leitura no Brasil* (São Paulo: Editora Ática, 1996), 122–145.
5. Instituto Brasileiro de Geografia e Estatísticas, *Sinopse estatística do Brasil, Ano IV* (Rio de Janeiro, 1938), 21–22 and 96–98.
6. For a comprehensive history of radio before and during the Vargas years, see Bryan McCann's *Hello, Hello Brazil: Popular Music and the Making of Modern Brazil* (Durham, NC: Duke University Press, 2004).
7. See Randal Johnson, "The Institutionalization of Brazilian Modernism," *Brasil/Brazil: Revista de Literatura Brasileira/Journal of Brazilian Literature*, 3.4 (1990): 5–23.
8. Tulio Halperín Donghi, *The Contemporary History of Latin America* (1967), trans. John Charles Chasteen (Durham, NC: Duke University Press, 1993), 233.
9. Prefeitura de São Paulo, "Programa de desenvolvimento da Zona Leste," http://ww1.prefeitura.sp.gov.br/portal/a_cidade/urbanismo/zona_leste/index.php?p=372&more=1&c=1&tb=1&pb=1, 2004 (accessed March 2006).
10. Richard A. Morse, *From Community to Metropolis: A Biography of São Paulo, Brazil* (Gainesville, FL: University of Florida Press, 1958), 167–181.
11. Ibid., 279.
12. Ibid., 12.
13. Ibid., 174–175.
14. Nicolau Sevcenko, *Orfeu extático na metrópole* (São Paulo: Companhia de Letras, 1992), 31. My translation.
15. The neologism "Paulicéia" can be taken two ways: First, as a proper noun to name the city of São Paulo; and second, as a verb—a conjugation of a nonexistent verb "pauliceiar," in which case "Paulicéia desvairada" would either translate as "It paulicinates delusioned," or as a command, "Paulicinate delusioned!"
16. Menotti del Picchia, Plínio Salgado, Alfredo Élis, Cassiano Ricardo, and Cândido Mota Filho, "Nhengaçu Verde Amarelo" (1929), *Las*

vanguardias latinoamericanas: Textos programáticos y críticos, ed. Jorge Schwartz (Madrid: Cátedra, 1991), 153.

17. I have deliberately chosen to use my own English translations of *Paulicéia desvairada* for this chapter, foregoing the only English translation of *Paulicéia desvairada* yet published: *Hallucinated City*, trans. Jack E. Tomlins four decades ago (1968). The Tomlins translation is quite good, and moreover has proved historically significant as the only extensive translation of Mário's work into the English language. However, perhaps owing to the date of its publication, many of the sexual and psychosexual connotations of the volume—meanings that are crucial to the critique rendered in this chapter—do not come across immediately to the contemporary reader, as perhaps they would have in the 1960s.

18. Significantly, the word "ode" also suggests "odéio" or "hate."

19. Mário de Andrade, *Introdução à estética musical*, ed. Flávia Camargo Toni (São Paulo: Editora HUCITEC, 1973), xi–xii. Biographical information is provided in Toni's introduction to the volume.

20. Racial/racist categorizations in Brazil are notoriously difficult, and certainly far more complex than many other places in the world. A preponderance, if not outright majority, of Brazilians have African and European and Indigenous heritage. In Mário's case, it is most likely that he self-identified as "white" and did not self-identify as "mulatto" and certainly not as "black." Nevertheless, Mário's contemporaries and scholars have always known that he was, to one degree or another, mulatto. Race does not necessarily enter into Mário's works—he never wrote literature in order to represent mulatto culture, for instance. Yet we may still speculate as to whether he was perceived as such and therefore (at least initially) perceived as coming from a socially subordinate class, even if such perceptions were (and are) totally erroneous.

21. Benedito Nunes, "Mário de Andrade: As enfibraturas do modernismo," *Revista Iberoamericana*, No. 126 (January–March 1984): 64. My translation.

22. Mikhail Bakhtin, "Discourse in the Novel" (1935), *The Dialogic Imagination*, ed. Michael Holquist (Austin, TX: University of Texas Press, 1981), 276. Obviously Bakhtin wrote his essay some 13–14 years after Mário published *Pauliceia desvairada*. As for Saussure, it is highly doubtful that the *Cours de Linguistique Générale* had reached Brazil by 1921.

23. João Luiz Lafetá, *Figuração da intimidade: Imagens na poesia de Mário de Andrade* (São Paulo: Martins Fontes, 1986), 8. My translation.

24. Gilberto Freyre, *Casa-grande e senzala: Formação da família brasileira sob o regime de economia patriarcal*, Vol. 1 (1933) (Rio de Janeiro: Livraria José Olympio, 1969), 65. My translation.

25. Vicky Unruh, *Latin American Vanguards: The Art of Contentious Encounter* (Berkeley: University of California Press, 1994), 42–43.

26. These two tendencies (site-specificity and historical rupture) are manifest in the title itself. "Ipiranga" is the original Tupi-Guaraní name for the area of São Paulo, and also the name of a river in the city upon whose banks Dom Pedro I declared Brazil's independence from Portugal; the Avenida Ipiranga is one of São Paulo's major streets, crossing the Centro Novo several blocks from where the action of "As enfibraturas do Ipiranga" is to take place. The historical-nationalistic-native name stands in stark contrast to the Latinate neologism, *enfibraturas* (or in English "enfibratures"), such that the title juxtaposes the old and the new in a way that would appear to promote a "new" historical creation, the new Brazil.
27. As Antonio Candido has written of *modernismo* in relation to Vargas's "revolution" of 1930 in his essay "A revolução de 1930 e a cultura":

    Until 1930 the predominant and most accepted literature adjusted itself to an ideology of permanence, represented above all by grammatical purity, which tended at its limit to crystallize language and adopt Portuguese literature as its model. This corresponded to the official expectations of a culture of façade, made to be seen by foreigners, as was in part the Old Republic. It found its propagandist in the Barão do Rio Branco, its model in the style of Rui Barbosa, and its symbolic institution in the Academia Brasileira de Letras, still powerful in the 1920s despite the attacks of the modernists (these seeming at the time a transitory eccentricity.) Yet from 1930, the Academia started to become what it is now: a club of intellectuals and the like, without major repercussion or influence in the life of literary movement. ("A revolução de 1930 e a cultura," *A educação pela noite & outros ensaios* [São Paulo: Editora Ática, 1989], 186; my translation)

28. Nunes, "Mário de Andrade," 70. My translation.
29. Charles A. Perrone, "Presentation and Representation of Self and City in *Paulicéia Desvairada*," *Chasqui: Revista de literatura latinoamericana*, 31.1 (May 2002): 21. Strictly speaking, the suffix *-cidade* does not in fact exist, for the actual suffix morpheme is *-idade*. Yet "*-cidade*" happens to be used commonly in Portuguese, and in the context of this poem-for-performance the reiterated c+suffix provides a convenient and multitoned echo of the urban(e) and combinatory scene being played out.
30. Ibid., 22.
31. The Trianon park still exists—across the street from the Museu de Arte de São Paulo—although the mansions of the Avenida Paulista have almost entirely been replaced with skyscrapers, as the area is now the center of São Paulo's financial services sector.
32. Of course, *Paulicéia desvairada* was written well before Oswald de Andrade's "Manifesto Antropófago." Nevertheless, "Os cortejos" does suggest the consumption of human flesh.

33. Iracema is the name of a fictional native princess created by the Romantic author, José de Alencar, as a figure for Brazil's natural potential, similar to Longfellow's Hiawatha in the United States. Iracema is also an anagram of "America."
34. Roberto Schwarz, "The Cart, the Tram, and the Modernist Poet," *Misplaced Ideas: Essays on Brazilian Culture* (London: Verso, 1992), 112.
35. Perrone, "Presentation and Representation of Self and City in *Paulicéia desvairada*," 20.
36. Ibid., 22.
37. David William Foster, "Mário de Andrade: On Being São Paulo-Wise in *Paulicéia desvairada*," *Iberoamericana. América Latina—España—Portugal*, 5.19 (2005): 28.
38. Ibid., 33.
39. Thus, the title of *Paulicéia desvairada* is not just a multilingual doubling, but the doubling of a double trans-Atlantic reference:

    In his indispensable retrospective essay "O movimento modernista" (1942), Mário wrote that he had imagined his poetical São Paulo adventure via *Les Villes tentaculaires* (1895) by the Belgian poet Émile Verhaeren. Nearly every discussant of *Paulicéia desvairada* alludes to that source, but precious few—notably Lafetá and Lopez—appear to have actually read the collection in question. It followed Verhaeren's *Le campagnes hallucinées* (1893), raising the possibility that Mário's title resulted from fusion of the two French titles, as Lafetá also speculates. (Perrone, "Presentation and Representation of Self and City in *Paulicéia desvairada*," 20)

40. These covers are reproduced in *Poesias completas*, ed. Diléa Zanotto Manfio. They also appear in the facsimile of the first edition prepared by Jorge Schwartz for the *Caixa Modernista*.
41. Telê Porto Ancona Lopes, *Mariodeandradiando* (São Paulo: Editora HUCITEC, 1996), xv.

3 Verse Reverse Verse: Fake Autobiographies, Lost Translations, and New Originals of Vicente Huidobro's *Altazor*

1. See Angel Rama, *The Lettered City*, trans. John Charles Chasteen (Durham, NC: Duke University Press, 1996); and Benedict Anderson, *Imagined Communities: Reflections on the Origin and Spread of Nationalism* (London: Verso, 1991).
2. All English translation of *Vientos contrarios* are my own.
3. Peter Bürger, *Theory of the Avant-Garde* (Minneapolis: University of Minnesota Press, 1984)
4. Paul de Man, "The Rhetoric of Temporality," *Blindness and Insight: Essays in the Rhetoric of Contemporary Criticism* (Minneapolis: University of Minnesota Press, 1983), 213.

5. Ibid., 225.
6. Paul de Man, "Autobiography as De-Facement," *The Rhetoric of Romanticism* (New York: Columbia University Press, 1984), 81–82.
7. Vicente Huidobro, "La creación pura," *Obras completas* (Santiago de Chile: Editorial Andrés Bello, 1976), 718–722.
8. Ibid., 719. My translation. Juan Larrea (*Torres de Dios* [Madrid: Editora Nacional/Libros de Poesía, 1982]) has suggested that this statement attributed to an Aymara shaman may be an act of deliberate plagiarism. Larrea cites the quotation in the work of the French art-historian, Maurice Raynal, attributed to a Hindu poet. Since Larrea identifies Raynal as one of the historians who has excluded Huidobro from the *Nord-Sud* group, Larrea questions whether Raynal has changed the poet-figure from Aymara to Hindu in order to discredit Huidobro, or whether Raynal has in fact shown Huidobro to be an outright liar.
9. Vicente Huidobro, "La poesía," *Obras completas*, 716–717. My translation.
10. Vicente Huidobro, "El creacionismo," *Obras completas*, 733. My translation.
11. See Braulio Arenas, "Vicente Huidobro y el creacionismo," *Obras completas de Vicente Huidobro* (Santiago de Chile: Editorial Andrés Bello, 1976), 23.
12. Larrea, *Torres de Dios*, 103–105.
13. Ibid., 131–135.
14. To clarify, I myself am not invested in the notion that onomatopoeia is "primitive." Rather that in the imitation of "natural" sounds, onomatopoeia has been traditionally framed as emanating prior to the formation of arbitrary semantic sign-systems. The objection to such a view is, of course, that written forms of onomatopoeia such as the quotation just cited still appear in a written notation that is just as arbitrary as any other use of language, thus calling into question the "primitiveness" of the trope. Nevertheless, moving past the issue of the "primitive," we have such a direct correlation between the word-form and its (non-)sense in a line such as "Io ia," that the line's translatability between different languages using the same orthographic tokens is, in a sense, guaranteed even prior to its enunciation.
15. Eliot Weinberger, who has produced the most widely disseminated English translations of *Altazor*, does in fact translate these lines, "Ahee ahee ahee a ee ee ee ee oh eeah," evidently in order to preserve the *phonetic* sense of the original. However, it strikes me that the original *typographical* sense does not necessarily render the verses un-understandable to the English-language reader.
16. Roman Jakobson, "Grammatical Parallelism and Its Russian Facet," trans. Krystyna Pomorska and Stephen Rudy, *Language and Literature* (Cambridge, MA: Belknap Press, 1987), 145–146.

17. Ferdinand de Saussure, *Course in General Linguistics*, trans. Roy Harris (La Salle, IL: Open Court, 1986), 111. Italics in the original. With this quotation I do not at all mean to imply that the image from *Altazor* is a *direct* allusion to Saussure, or that Huidobro necessarily had any interest in or knowledge of Saussure. I merely suggest that when taken together, a felicitous concurrence arises between Huidobro and Saussure in terms of their figuration of the sound/object-image relation, a figuration I hold here to be decidedly "modern."
18. De Man, "The Rhetoric of Temporality," 207.
19. De Man bases his reading of irony from Baudelaire's essay, "De l'essence du rire" (in *Curiosités esthétiques: L'Art romantique et autres Oeuvres critiques*, ed. H. Lemaître [Paris: Garnier, 1962]).
20. De Man, "The Rhetoric of Temporality," 214.
21. George Yúdice, *Vicente Huidobro y la motivación del lenguaje* (Buenos Aires: Editorial Galerna, 1978), 165.
22. Roman Jakobson, "Linguistics and Poetics," trans. Krystyna Pomorska and Stephen Rudy, *Language and Literature*, 71. Italics in the original.
23. David Bary, *Huidobro, o la vocación poética* (Granada: Universidad de Granada, Consejo Superior de Investigaciones Científicas, 1963), 114.
24. Vicente Huidobro, "Fragment d'Altazor," *transition*, Nos. 19–20 (June 1930): 194–195. The fragment is reproduced in the critical edition, *Altazor/Temblor de cielo*, ed. René de Costa (Madrid: Cátedra, 1981), 189–190.
25. Vicente Huidobro, "Altazur: Fragmento de 'Un viaje en paracaídas,' traducción de Jean Emar," *Notas de arte, no. 42*, in *La nación* Vol. 30 (Miércoles, April 29, 1925), A7. Emphasis added.
26. Emar's family happened to own *La nación*. The translation of this "Altazur" appeared in a section of the newspaper given to Emar ("Notas del arte") in which Emar used to promote modern, *vanguardista* aesthetics.
27. Andrés Morales, "Un manuscrito que abre mil puertas," in Vicente Huidobro, *Altazor de puño y letra* (Santiago de Chile: Banco del Estado de Chile, 1999), 10. My translation.
28. Ibid., 10n3.
29. Ibid., 10n5.
30. All quotations from the manuscript notebook for *Altazor* have been taken from the facsimile edition in Vol. 1 of *Altazor de puño y letra* (Santiago de Chile: Banco del Estado de Chile, 1999). Since this facsimile does not have page numbers, none can be provided for my citations. Quotations from the notebook are followed by my English translations.
31. Huidobro, "La creacion pura," *Obras completas*, 718. My translation.
32. In Hegel's *Philosophy of History*, e.g., "Spirit" first emerges (in incomplete form) in Greek antiquity; the motivation of history is thus to be

found in the finalized materialization of "Spirit" in modern Germany.
33. James I. Porter, *Nietzsche and the Philology of the Future* (Stanford, CA: Stanford University Press, 2000), 6–7. Porter quotes Nietzsche from the essay "We Philologists."
34. Stéphane Mallarmé, "L'Azur," *Selected Poetry and Prose*, trans. Hubert Creekmore (New York: New Directions, 1982), 14–15.
35. Julio Ramos, "El don de la lengua," *Paradojas de la letra* (Caracas: Ediciones eXcultura, 1996), 3–21.

4 Alien sedition: Anti-Semitism and censorship in *The cantos of ezra pound*

1. Consult Humphrey Carpenter's *A Serious Character: The Life of Ezra Pound* (New York: Delta, 1988), 489–850, for an exhaustive account of Pound's life during this period.
2. Following the theories of Major C. H. Douglas, Pound believed in the state nationalization of banking in order to facilitate the redistribution of purchasing power (wealth) to the people at large. Both Pound and Douglas believed that in the current economic system, corporate profit derived from inequality between workers' purchasing power (wages, salaries) and production costs; in order to make up the difference banks had to extend credit for which they charged usurious rates of interest. Douglas therefore claimed that nationalized banks should extend "social credit" for free—equalizing the disparity between purchasing power and production, i.e., reflecting the "true" cost of labor that had "naturally" been placed into each product. Of course, this system would work best if the state commanded both banking and industry—thus Pound's support of fascism.
3. Pound found the remarks on a document attributed to Franklin later proven to be a forgery after the publication of Canto 52. One might also suspect that "Ben" plays off of Mussolini's name, "Benito." Such a reading would imply an associational connection between the early American history and the fascist Italian state, which is wholly in line with the sequence of poems in which Canto 52 appears. Further, in Pound's postwar poetry, Pound also refers to Mussolini as "Ben," most famously at the start of the Pisan Cantos: "Thus Ben and la Claro *a Milano*/by the heels at Milano" (C 439).
4. See Robert Casillo, *The Genealogy of Demons* (Evanston, IL: Northwestern University Press, 1988); Reedway Dasenbrock, "Jefferson and/or Adams: A Shifting Mirror for Mussolini in the Middle Cantos," *ELH*, 55.2 (Summer 1988): 505–526; and Tim Redman, *Ezra Pound and Italian Fascism* (New York: Cambridge University Press, 1991).

5. These statements can be found in *The Case of Ezra Pound*, ed. Charles Norman (New York: The Bodley Press, 1948).
6. Comité International en Faveur d'Ezra Pound, "Letter of Appeal for Signatures on a Petition to the President of the United States for the Release of Ezra Pound from Confinement in St. Elizabeth's Hospital, Washington, DC" (1948).
7. These two cantos did not appear in the collected *Cantos* until 1985. One of the first and best accounts of their editorial trajectory may be found in Barbara C. Eastman's article, "The Gap in *The Cantos*: 72 and 73" (*Paideuma*, 8.3 [Winter 1979]: 415–427). A vociferous denunciation of their content has been provided by Robert Casillo in his "Fascists of the Final Hour: Pound's Italian Cantos," *Fascism, Aesthetics, and Culture*, ed. Richard J. Golsan (Hanover, NH: University Press of New England, 1992). A much more sympathetic account of the background of Cantos 72 and 73 appears at the end of Massimo Bacigalupo's English translation of the poems, "Ezra Pound's Cantos 72 and 73: An Annotated Translation," *Paideuma*, 20.1 and 2 (Spring and Fall 1991): 9–29.
8. Hugh Kenner, *The Pound Era* (Berkeley, CA: University of California Press, 1971), 410.
9. In this way the "form-censorship" dichotomy I have described here approaches a similar conception in the work of Pierre Bourdieu, especially "Censorship and the Imposition of Form." As he states regarding the discourses of specialized fields of academic knowledge:

> The specialized languages that schools of specialists produce and reproduce through the systematic alteration of the common language are, as with all discourses, the product of a *compromise* between an *expressive interest* and a *censorship* constituted by the very structure of the field in which discourse is produced and circulates.... The metaphor of censorship should not mislead: it is the structure of the field itself which governs expression by governing both access to expression and the form of expression, and not some legal proceeding which has been specially adapted to designate and repress the transgression of a kind of linguistic code. ("Censorship and the Imposition of Form," *Language and Symbolic Power*, trans. Gino Raymond and Matthew Adamson [Cambridge, MA: Harvard University Press, 1991], 137–138)

Bourdieu then adds: "By imposing form, the censorship exercised by the structure of the field determines the form—which all formalist analyses attempt to detach from social determinisms—and, necessarily, the content, which is inseparable from its appropriate expression and therefore literally unthinkable outside of the known forms and recognized norms" (139). Of course, in this chapter I am attempting to engage a kind of formalist analysis that would connect form directly with social determinisms.

10. See Fernando Ortiz, *Contrapunteo del tabaco y el azúcar* (1940) (Barcelona: Editorial Ariel, 1963).
11. Edward W. Said, *Orientalism* (New York: Vintage Books, 1978), 67.
12. Such sentiments are quite explicitly echoed in many of Pound's letters from the period. In one letter from February 1940, Pound responds to J. Laughlin's (Pound's editor at New Directions) request for an antidefamation clause in Pound's contract:
    I dont [*sic*] mind affirming in contract, so long as I am not expected to alter text. You can putt [*sic*] it this way. The author affirms that in no passage shd/ the text be interpreted to mean that he condems [*sic*] any innocent man or woman for another's guilt, and that no degree of relationship, familial or racial shall be taken to imply such condemnation. But no group national or ethical can expect immunity not accorded to other groups. / Damn the word artistic. This poem is HISTORY. Certainly the crime by whomever committed, and membership ina [*sic*] race, (whatever race) does not free the members of same from censure. (Ezra Pound and James Laughlin, *Selected Letters*, ed. David M. Gordon [New York: W.W. Norton & Co., 1994], 114)
13. Casillo, *The Genealogy of Demons*, 253–264.
14. Though Pound and Fenollosa never met, Fenollosa's widow bequeathed her husband's papers to Pound after Fenollosa's death in 1908. Pound quickly recognized Fenollosa's thought as resonating with Pound's own Imagist aesthetic, and began to publish Fenollosa's works as an *Ars poetica*.
15. Ernest Fenollosa, "The Chinese Written Character as a Medium for Poetry" (1920), *Instigations*, ed. Ezra Pound (Freeport, NY: Books for Libraries Press, Inc., 1967), 358.
16. "Noigandres" is a word of unknown origin and meaning that appears in the poetry of Daniel Arnaut, and in Canto 20: "And he said: Noigandres! NOIgandres! / 'You know for seex mon's of my life / 'Effery night when I go to bett, I say to myself: / Noigandres, eh, *noi*gandres, / 'Now what the DEFFIL can that mean!'" (C 89–90). The Brazilian concretists thus took "Noigandres" as emblematic of poetic freedom. See Charles A. Perrone, *Seven Faces: Brazilian Poetry since Modernism* (Durham, NC: Duke University Press, 1996), 25–66, for further discussion of the formation of Brazilian concretism.
17. As Augusto de Campos has stated referring to the origin of Brazilian concretism: "The artists clarify well, I think, my poems and also those of Haroldo, and the aesthetic-strategic position of the entire Noigandres 'group'...[as] an objective observation (examination + comparison) of the historical evolution of poetry. MALLARMÉ (Un Coup de Dés) — POUND — JOYCE — CUMMINGS" (*Poesia, Antipoesia, Antropofagia* [São Paulo: Editora Cortez & Moraes Ltd., 1978], 59; my translation).

18. Haroldo de Campos, "Ideograma, Anagrama, Diagrama" (1977), *Ideograma: Lógica, poesia, linguagem*, org. Haroldo de Campos (São Paulo: EDUSP, 1994), 23–107. Since this essay has not been translated into English in its entirety, all citations are my translation.
19. Fenollosa, "The Chinese Written Character as a Medium for Poetry," 387–388.
20. H. de Campos, "Ideograma, Anagram, Diagrama," 51.
21. Ibid., 104.
22. Ibid., 81–82.
23. Ibid., 102–103.
24. Haroldo de Campos, "Anthropophagous Reason: Dialogue and Difference in Brazilian Culture," trans. Odile Cisneros, *Novas: Selected Writings*, ed. Antonio Sérgio Bessa and Odile Cisneros (Evanston, IL: Northwestern University Press, 2007), 159–160.
25. See Ronald Bush's "Excavating the Ideological Faultlines of Modernism" (*Representing Modernist Texts*, ed. George Bornstein [Ann Arbor, MI: University of Michigan Press, 1991], 67–98) for a more extensive discussion of this process of ideological "naturalization" throughout the entire course of *The Cantos*. Though Bush argues for the radical ideological openness of *The Cantos*, he also admits that certain of Pound's writings reveal:
    …a view of the world in which politics can be justified as inevitable and natural. If, after all, poetry is the unmediated expression of an enduring human nature, there must also be a political arrangement that is its natural complement. This would in the 1930s become the justification for Pound's fascist advocacy of the Confucian tradition, in which man as political animal stands to earth as what the *Cantos* call "two halves of the tally"—that is, two halves of a broken tally stick, which when rejoined make a perfect fit. (69)
26. All original typescripts, galleys, and letters mentioned from here on forward, unless otherwise noted directly, are held in the Ezra Pound Papers, Yale Collection of American Literature, Beinecke Rare Book and Manuscript Library. The typo "deawing" is corrected by Pound's pen in the typescript by placing an "r" above the "e."
27. Pound and Laughlin, *Selected Letters*, 107–108.
28. Robert Casillo, e.g., has called these lines an instance of an "unprintable fury" on the part of Pound (Casillo, *The Genealogy of Demons*, 260).
29. This negotiation between Pound and Laughlin can be found in their letters from 1940, now held in the Ezra Pound Papers of the Yale Collection of American Literature at the Beinecke Rare Book and Manuscript Library.
30. S. D. (Delmore Schwartz), "Notes on the Versification of the Cantos," saddle-stitched pamphlet insert to Ezra Pound, *Cantos LII–LXXI* (New York: New Directions, 1940).
31. H. H. (James Laughlin), "Notes on the Cantos," saddle-stitched pamphlet insert to *Cantos LII–LXXI*, 9.

Bibliography

Anderson, Benedict. *Imagined Communities: Reflections on the Origin and Spread of Nationalism*. London: Verso, 1991.
Andrade, Mário de. *Hallucinated City*, trans. Jack E. Tomlins. Nashville: Vanderbilt University Press, 1968.
———. *Introdução à estética musical*, ed. Flávia Camargo Toni. São Paulo: Editora de Humanismo, Ciência e Tecnologia (HUCITEC), 1973.
———. *Poesias completas*, ed. Diléa Zanotto Manfio. Belo Horizonte: Villa Rica, 1993.
Andrade, Oswald de. *Pau-Brasil*. São Paulo: Editora Globo, 1990a. Orig. pub. 1925.
———. *A utopia antropofágica*. São Paulo: Editora Globo, 1990b.
Anzaldúa, Gloria. *Borderlands/La Frontera*. 2nd ed. San Francisco: Aunt Lute Books, 1999.
Arenas, Braulio. "Vicente Huidobro y el creacionismo." In: *Obras completas de Vicente Huidobro*. Santiago de Chile: Editorial Andrés Bello, 1976.
Bacigalupo Massimo. "Ezra Pound's Cantos 72 and 73: An Annotated Translation." *Paideuma* 20, 1 & 2 (Spring and Fall 1991): 9–29.
Bakhtin, Mikhail. *The Dialogic Imagination*, ed. Michael Holquist. Austin, TX: University of Texas Press, 1981.
Bary, David. *Huidobro, o la vocación poética*. Granada: Universidad de Granada, Consejo Superior de Investigaciones Científicas, 1963.
Bello, Andrés. "Autonomía cultural de América." *Conciencia intelectual de América*, ed. Carlos Ripoll. New York: Las Americas Publishing Company, 1966. Orig. pub. 1848.
Benjamin, Walter. *Illuminations*, ed. Hannah Arendt. New York: Schocken Books, 1969.
Bérubé, Michael. "American Studies without Exceptions." *PMLA*, 118.1 (January 2003): 103–113.
Bourdieu, Pierre. "Censorship and the Imposition of Form." *Language and Symbolic Power*, trans. Gino Raymond and Matthew Adamson. Cambridge, MA: Harvard University Press, 1991. 137–159.
Bowers, Fredson. *Essay in Bibliography, Text, and Editing*. Charlottesville, VA: University of Virginia Press, 1975.

Breslin, James. *William Carlos Williams, an American Artist.* New York: Oxford, 1970.
Brickhouse, Anna. *Transamerican Literary Relations and the Nineteenth Century Public Sphere.* Cambridge: Cambridge University Press, 2004.
Bronson, Walter C. *A Short History of American Literature.* Boston: D.C. Heath & Co., 1919.
Bürger, Peter. *Theory of the Avant-Garde.* Minneapolis: University of Minnesota Press, 1984.
Bush, Ronald. "Excavating the Ideological Faultlines of Modernism: Editing Ezra Pound's *Cantos.*" *Representing Modernist Texts*, ed. George Bornstein. Ann Arbor, MI: University of Michigan Press, 1991. 67–98.
Campos, Augusto de. *Poesia, antipoesia, antropofagia.* São Paulo: Editora Cortez & Moraes Ltd., 1978.
Campos, Haroldo de. "Ideograma, Anagrama, Diagrama." *Ideograma: Lógica, poesia, linguagem*, org. Haroldo de Campos. São Paulo: Editora da Universidade de São Paulo, 1994. 23–107.
———. *Novas: Selected Writings*, ed. Odile Cisneros and A. Sérgio Bessa. Evanston, IL: Northwestern University Press, 2007.
Candido, Antonio. *A educação pela pedra e outros ensaios.* São Paulo: Editora Ática, 1989.
———. *Formação da Literatura Brasileira*, 2 vols. São Paulo: Livraria Martins Editora, 1959.
Cardoso, Fernando Henrique. *Charting a New Course: The Politics of Globalization and Social Transformation.* Lanham, MD: Rowman & Littlefield Publishers, Inc., 2001.
——— and Enzo Faletto. *Dependency and Development in Latin America*, trans. Marjory Mattingly Urquidi. Berkeley: University of California Press, 1979.
Carpenter, Humphrey. *A Serious Character: The Life of Ezra Pound.* New York: Delta, 1988.
Casillo, Robert. "Fascists of the Final Hour: Pound's Italian Cantos." *Fascism, Aesthetics, and Culture*, ed. Richard J. Golsan. Hanover, NH: University Press of New England, 1992.
———. *The Genealogy of Demons.* Evanston, IL: Northwestern University Press, 1988.
Castillo, Debra A. *Redreaming America: Toward a Bilingual American Culture.* Albany, NY: State University of New York Press, 2005.
Castro-Klarén, Sarah. "A Genealogy for the 'Manifesto Antropófago.'" *Nepantla*, 1.2 (2000): 295–322.
Cohn, Deborah N. *History and Memory in the Two Souths: Recent Southern and South American Fiction.* Nashville: Vanderbilt University Press, 1999.
Comité International en Faveur d'Ezra Pound. "Letter of Appeal for Signatures on a Petition to the President of the United States for the Release of Ezra Pound from Confinement in St. Elizabeth's Hospital, Washington, DC." 1948.

Cornejo Polar, Antonio. *Escribir en el aire: Ensayo sobre la heterogeneidad socio-cultural en las literaturas andinas*. 1st ed. Lima: Editorial Horizonte, 1994.

Darío, Rubén. *Poesía*, ed. Ernesto Mejía Sánchez. Caracas: Biblioteca Ayacucho, 1977.

Dasenbrock, Reed Way. "Cantos 72 and 73: What Kind of Textbook?" *Paideuma*, 19.3 (Winter 1990): 129–131.

——. "Jefferson and/or Adams: A Shifting Mirror for Mussolini in the Middle Cantos." *ELH*, 55.2 (Summer 1988): 505–526.

De Man, Paul. *Blindness and Insight: Essays in the Rhetoric of Contemporary Criticism*. Minneapolis: University of Minnesota Press, 1983.

——. *The Rhetoric of Romanticism*. New York: Columbia University Press, 1984.

Eastman, Barbara C. "The Gap in *The Cantos*: 72 and 73." *Paideuma*, 8.3 (Winter 1979): 415–427.

Fenollosa, Ernest. "The Chinese Written Character as a Medium for Poetry." *Instigations*, ed. Ezra Pound. Freeport, NY: Books for Libraries Press, Inc., 1967. Orig. pub. 1920.

Fernández Retamar, Roberto. *Calibán: Apuntes sobre la cultura en nuestra América*. México, DF: Editorial Diógenes, 1971.

——. *Para una teoría de la literatura hispanoamericana*. México, DF: Editorial Nuestro Tiempo, 1981.

Fitz, Earl E. *Rediscovering the New World: Inter-American Literature in a Comparative Context*. Iowa City: University of Iowa Press, 1991.

Foster, David William. "Mário de Andrade: On Being São Paulo-Wise in *Paulicéia desvairada*." *Iberoamericana. América Latina—España—Portugal*, 5.19 (2005): 27–40.

Freyre, Gilberto. *Casa-grande e senzala: Formação da família brasileira sob o regime de economia patriarcal*, 2 vols. Rio de Janeiro: Livraria José Olympio, 1943.

García Canclini, Néstor. *Culturas híbridas: Estrategias para entrar y salir de la modernidad*. Buenos Aires: Editorial Sudamericana, 1992.

Greg, W. W. "The Rationale of the Copy-Text." *Studies in Bibliography*, 3 (1950–1951): 19–36.

Guillory, John. *Cultural Capital: The Problem of Literary Canon Formation*. Chicago: University of Chicago Press, 1993.

H. H. (James Laughlin). "Notes on the Cantos." Saddle-stitched pamphlet insert to Ezra Pound, *Cantos LII–LXXI*. New York: New Directions, 1940.

Halperín Donghi, Tulio. *The Contemporary History of Latin America*, trans. John Charles Chasteen. Durham, NC: Duke University Press, 1993.

Hatlen, Burton. "Openness and Closure in Williams' *Spring and All*." *William Carlos Williams Review*, 20.2 (Fall 1994):15–29.

Henríquez Ureña, Pedro. *Seis ensayos en busca de nuestra expresión*. In: *Obra Crítica*, ed. Emma Susana Speratti Piñero. México, DF: Fondo de Cultura Económica, 1960. Orig. pub. 1928.

Huidobro, Vicente. *Altazor de puño y letra*, 2 vols. Santiago de Chile: Banco del Estado de Chile, 1999.

———. *Altazor, Edición facsimilar.* Santiago de Chile: Editorial Universitaria, 1991. Orig. pub. 1931.

———. *Altazor, or a Voyage in Parachute*, trans. Eliot Weinberger. Hanover, NH: Wesleyan University Press, 2004.

———. *Altazor/Temblor del cielo*, ed. René de Costa. Madrid: Cátedra, 1981.

———. "Altazur: Fragmento de 'Un viaje en paracaídas,' traducción de Jean Emar." *Notas de arte*, no. 42, in *La nación* vol. 30 (Wednesday, April 29, 1925), A7.

———. "Fragment d'Altazor." *transition*, nos. 19–20 (June 1930): 194–195.

———. *Obras completas*. Santiago de Chile: Editorial Andrés Bello, 1976.

Instituto Brasileiro de Geografia e Estatísticas. *Sinopse estatística do Brasil, Ano IV.* Rio de Janeiro, 1938.

Jakobson, Roman. *Language and Literature.* Cambridge, MA: Belknap Press, 1987.

Johnson, Randal. "The Institutionalization of Brazilian Modernism." *Brasil/Brazil: Revista de Literatura Brasileira/Journal of Brazilian Literature*, 3.4 (1990): 5–23.

Kadir, Djelal. *Columbus and the Ends of the Earth: Europe's Prophetic Rhetoric as Conquering Ideology.* Berkeley: University of California Press, 1992.

———. "Introduction: America and Its Studies." *PMLA*, 118.1 (January 2003): 9–24.

Kenner, Hugh. *The Pound Era.* Berkeley, CA: University of California Press, 1971.

Kracauer, Siegfried. *The Mass Ornament: Weimar Essays*, trans. Thomas Y. Levin. Cambridge, MA: Harvard University Press, 1995.

Kutzinski, Vera. *Against the American Grain: Myth and History in William Carlos Williams, Jay Wright, and Nicolás Guillén.* Baltimore: The Johns Hopkins University Press, 1987.

Lafetá, João Luiz. *Figuração da intimidade: Imagens na poesia de Mário de Andrade.* São Paulo: Martins Fontes, 1986.

Lajolo, Marisa and Regina Zilberman. *A formação da leitura no Brasil.* São Paulo: Editora Ática, 1996.

Larrea, Juan. *Torres de Dios: Poetas.* Madrid: Editora Nacional/Libros de Poesía, 1982.

Levander, Caroline F. and Robert S. Levine, eds. *Hemispheric American Studies.* Camden, NJ: Rutgers University Press, 2007.

Litz, A. Walton and Christopher MacGowan. "Appendix A: A Note on the Text." *The Collected Poems of William Carlos Williams, Vol. 1*, ed. A. Walton Litz and Christopher MacGowan. New York: New Directions, 1986.

Lopes, Telê Porto Ancona. *Mariodeandradiando.* São Paulo: Editora HUCITEC, 1996.

Lowell, Robert. *Collected Prose*. New York: Farrar, Straus, Giroux, 1987.
Machado de Assis, Joaquim. *The Posthumous Memories of Brás Cubas*, trans. Gregory Rabassa. Oxford: Oxford University Press, 1997. Orig. pub. 1881.
Macy, John. *The Spirit of American Literature*. Garden City, NY: Doubleday, Page, & Co., 1913.
Madureira, Luiz. *Cannibal Modernities: Postcoloniality and the Avant-Garde in Caribbean and Brazilian Literature*. Charlottesville, VA: University of Virginia Press, 2005.
Mallarmé, Stéphane. *Selected Poetry and Prose*, trans. Hubert Creekmore. New York: New Directions, 1982.
Martí, José. "Our America," trans. John D. Blanco. In: Julio Ramos, *Divergent Modernities: Culture and Politics in 19th Century Latin America*. Durham, NC: Duke University Press, 2001.
Marzán, Julio. *The Spanish-American Roots of William Carlos Williams*. Austin, TX: University of Texas Press, 1994.
McCann, Bryan. *Hello, Hello Brazil: Popular Music and the Making of Modern Brazil*. Durham, NC: Duke University Press, 2004.
McGann, Jerome J. *A Critique of Modern Textual Criticism*. Charlottesville, VA: University of Virginia Press, 1983.
Mignolo, Walter. *The Darker Side of the Renaissance: Literacy, Territoriality, and Colonization*. Ann Arbor, MI: University of Michigan Press, 1995.
———. *Local Histories/Global Designs: Coloniality, Subaltern Knowledges, and Border Thinking*. Princeton, NJ: Princeton University Press, 2000.
Mohr, Bill. "The Wheelbarrow in Question: Ideology and the Radical Pellucidity of William Carlos Williams' Images." *William Carlos Williams Review*, 24.2 (Fall 2004): 27–39.
Morales, Andrés. "Un manuscrito que abre mil puertas." In: Vicente Huidobro, *Altazor de puño y letra*. Santiago de Chile: Banco del Estado de Chile, 1999.
Moreiras, Alberto. *The Exhaustion of Difference: The Politics of Latin American Cultural Studies*. Durham, NC: Duke University Press, 2001.
Morse, Richard A. *From Community to Metropolis: A Biography of São Paulo, Brazil*. Gainesville, FL: University of Florida Press, 1958.
———. *New World Soundings*. Baltimore: The Johns Hopkins University Press, 1989.
Murphy, Gretchen. *Hemispheric Imaginings: The Monroe Doctrine and Narratives of U.S. Empire*. Durham, NC: Duke University Press, 2005.
Nancy, Jean-Luc. *The Inoperative Community*. Minneapolis: University of Minnesota Press, 1991.
Norman, Charles, ed. *The Case of Ezra Pound*. New York: The Bodley Press, 1948.
Nunes, Benedito. "Mário de Andrade: As Enfibraturas do Modernismo." *Revista Iberoamericana*, No. 126 (Enero–Marzo 1984): 63–75.
Ortiz, Fernando. *Contrapunteo del tabaco y el azúcar*. Barcelona: Editorial Ariel, 1963. Orig. pub. 1940.

Paz, Octavio. *Alternating Current*, trans. Helen R. Lane. New York: The Viking Press, 1973.
Pease, Donald. "National Identities, Postmodern Artifacts, and Postnational Narratives." *New Americanists: Revisionist Interventions into the Canon 2*, ed. Donald Pease. Spec. issue of *boundary 2*, 19.1 (1992): 1–13.
Perrone, Charles A. "Presentation and Representation of Self and City in *Paulicéia desvairada*." *Chasqui: Revista de literatura latinoamericana*, 31.1 (May 2002): 18–27.
———. *Seven Faces: Brazilian Poetry since Modernism*. Durham, NC: Duke University Press, 1996.
Porter, James I. *Nietzsche and the Philology of the Future*. Stanford, CA: Stanford University Press, 2000.
Pound, Ezra. *The Cantos of Ezra Pound*. New York: New Directions, 1996. Fifth paperbound printing.
———. *Cantos LII–LXXI*. New York: New Directions, 1940.
———. *Instigations*. Freeport, NY: Books for Libraries Press, Inc., 1967. Orig. pub. 1920.
———and James Laughlin. *Selected Letters*, ed. David M. Gordon. New York: W.W. Norton & Co., 1994.
Prefeitura de São Paulo. "Programa de desenvolvimento da Zona Leste." Online http://ww1.prefeitura.sp.gov.br/portal/a_cidade/urbanismo/zona_leste/index.php?p=372&more=1&c=1&tb=1&pb=1, 2004 (accessed March 2006).
Quijano, Aníbal and Immanuel Wallerstein. "Americanity as a Concept, or the Americas in the Modern World-System." *International Journal of Social Sciences* (UNESCO), No. 134 (November 1992): 549–557
Rama, Angel. *La ciudad letrada*. Hanover, NH: Ediciones del Norte, 1984.
———. *The Lettered City*, trans. John Charles Chasteen. Durham, NC: Duke University Press, 1996.
———. *Transculturación narrativa en América Latina*. México, DF: Siglo Veintiuno Editores, 1982.
Ramos, Julio. *Divergent Modernities: Culture and Politics in 19th Century Latin America*. Durham, NC: Duke University Press, 2001.
———. *Paradojas de la letra*. Caracas: Ediciones eXcultura, 1996.
Read, Justin. "Manners of Mistranslation: The *Antropofagismo* of Elizabeth Bishop's Prose and Poetry." *CR: New Centennial Review*, 3.3 (2003): 297–327.
Redman, Tim. *Ezra Pound and Italian Fascism*. New York: Cambridge University Press, 1991.
Rodríguez Monegal, Emir with Thomas Colchie, eds. *The Borzoi Anthology of Latin American Literature*. New York: Alfred A. Knopf, 1992.
Rosenberg, Fernando. *The Avant-Garde and Geopolitics in Latin America*. Pittsburgh: University of Pittsburgh Press, 2006.
Said, Edward W. *Orientalism*. New York: Vintage Books, 1978.
Saldívar, José David. *Border Matters: Remapping American Cultural Studies*. Berkeley: University of California Press, 1997.

Saldívar, José David. *The Dialectics of Our America: Genealogy, Cultural Critique, and Literary History*. Durham, NC: Duke University Press, 1991.
Santiago, Silviano. *The Space In-Between: Essays on Latin American Culture*. Durham, NC: Duke University Press, 2001.
———. *Uma literatura nos trópicos: Ensaios sobre dependência cultural*. São Paulo: Editora Perspectiva, 1978.
Saussure, Ferdinand de. *Course in General Linguistics*, trans. Roy Harris. La Salle, IL: Open Court, 1986.
Schwartz, Jorge. "¡Abajo Tordesillas!" *Casa de las Américas*, 33.191 (April–June 1993): 26–35.
———, ed. *Caixa modernista*. São Paulo: Edusp, 2003.
———, ed. *Las vanguardias latinoamericanas: Textos programáticos y críticos*. Madrid: Cátedra, 1991.
Schwarz, Roberto. *Misplaced Ideas: Essays on Brazilian Culture*. London: Verso, 1992.
S. D. (Delmore Schwartz). "Notes on the Versification of the Cantos." Saddle-stitched pamphlet insert to Ezra Pound, *Cantos LII–LXXI*. New York: New Directions, 1940.
Sevcenko, Nicolau. *Orfeu Extático na Metrópole*. São Paulo: Companhia de Letras, 1992.
Sollors, Werner, ed. *Multilingualism in America: Transnationalism, Ethnicity, and the Languages of American Literature*. New York: New York University Press, 1998.
Spiller, Robert E. "The Cycle and the Roots: National Identity in American Literature." *Toward a New American Literary History*, ed. Louis J. Budd, Edwin H. Cody, and Carl L. Anderson. Durham, NC: Duke University Press, 1980. 3–18.
Spillers, Hortense J., ed. *Comparative American Identities: Race, Sex, and Nationality in the Modern Text*. New York: Routledge, 1991.
Spivak, Gayatri Chakravorty. "Can the Subaltern Speak?" *The Post-Colonial Studies Reader*, ed. Bill Ashcroft, Gareth Griffiths, and Helen Tiffin. London: Routledge, 1995. 66–111.
Tanselle, G. Thomas. *Textual Criticism since Greg: A Chronicle, 1950–1985*. Charlottesville, VA: University of Virginia Press, 1987.
Terrell, Carroll F. *A Companion to* The Cantos of Ezra Pound. Berkeley: University of California Press, 1993.
Unruh, Vicky. *Latin American Vanguards: The Art of Contentious Encounter*. Berkeley: University of California Press, 1994.
Vallejo, César. "Contra el secreto profesional." *Las vanguardias literarias en Hispanoamérica*, ed. Hugo J. Verani. México, DF: Fondo de Cultura Económica, 1986.
Webster's New World Dictionary, Third College Edition. New York: Prentice Hall, 1994.
Wesling, Donald. "Emotion Deriving from Sequence in William Carlos Williams's *Spring and All*." *William Carlos Williams Review*, 24.2 (Fall 2004): 41–47.

Whittemore, Reed. *William Carlos Williams, Poet from New Jersey.* Boston: Houghton Mifflin Company, 1975.

Williams, William Carlos. *The Collected Earlier Poems.* New York: New Directions, 1951.

———. *Collected Poems, 1921–1931.* New York: Objectivist Press, 1934.

———. *The Collected Poems of William Carlos Williams,* 2 vols., ed. A. Walton Litz and Christopher MacGowan. New York: New Directions, 1986.

———. *The Complete Collected Poems, 1906–1938.* New York: New Directions, 1938.

———. *Go Go.* New York: Monroe Wheeler, 1923.

———. *I Wanted to Write a Poem: The Autobiography of the Works of a Poet,* ed. Edith Heal. Boston: Beacon Press, 1958.

———. *Imaginations.* New York: New Directions, 1970.

———. *In the American Grain.* New York: New Directions, 1956.

———. *Selected Essays.* New York: New Directions, 1954.

———. *Spring and All.* 1st ed. Paris: Contact Publishing Co., 1923.

Yúdice, George. *Vicente Huidobro y la motivación del lenguaje.* Buenos Aires: Editorial Galerna, 1978.

Index

Adams, Charles Francis, 169
Adams, John, xxvii, 164, 169, 177–8, 189
Alencar, José de, 207 n33
Altazor, xxvi, 103–55, 193
   Cantos: Prefacio, 118, 120–4; Canto I, 127–8; Canto II, 128–9; Canto III, 129–31; Canto IV, 131–2, 139; Canto V, 132–4; Canto VI, 134–6, 137; Canto VII, 117–18, 136–7
   Manuscript, 140–50, 142 (Fig. 3.2), 146 (Fig. 3.3), 147 (Fig. 3.4), 153 (Fig. 3.7), 154 (Fig. 3.8)
   "Molinos," 132–4, 134 (Fig. 3.1), 141–2, 142 (Fig. 3.2), 152 (Fig. 3.6), 154 (Fig. 3.8)
   Rhetoric, 123–6
   Textual history, 138–50
American New Criticism, xii, 10, 14, 105, 108
American Studies Association (ASA), xiii
Anderson, Benedict, 4, 61, 94
Andrade, Mário de, xxvi, 17, 29, 59–102
   Ethnic identity, 68, 205 n20
   see also Paulicéia desvairada
Andrade, Oswald de, xxiii, 9, 17–22, 25, 26, 61, 67
   "Manifesto Antropófago" ["Cannibalist Manifesto"], 18–20, 201–2 n19
   "Manifesto Pau-Brasil" ["Brazilwood Manifesto"], 18–19
   "pobre alimária" ["poor beast"], 93
   "a roça" ["the farm"], 20–1, 28, 38–9
Anthropophagy, *see* Cannibalism
Anti-Semitism, 56–7, 160–3, 169, 179–86, 188, 190–2
Anzaldúa, Gloria, xv
Arnaut, Daniel, 212 n16
Austin, J. L., 22

Bacigalupo, Massimo, 211 n7
Bakhtin, Mikhail, 22, 70
Baroque, 11–12, 17, 33, 34
Bary, David, 138–9
Baudelaire, Charles, 149
Bello, Andrés, xx
Benjamin, Walter, 56, 116
Bhabha, Homi, 19
Bilac, Olavo, 72
Borges, Jorge Luis, 9–10
Bouguereau, William-Adolfe, 81
Bourdieu, Pierre, 211 n9
Brazil, history, 61–3
Breslin, James, 44–5
Brickhouse, Anna, xiv
Bronson, Walter C., xviii
Bürger, Peter, 107
Bush, Ronald, 213 n25

Campos, Augusto de, 171, 212 n17
Campos, Haroldo de, xxv, xxvii, 19, 171–6, 190
  "Da razão antropofágica" ("Anthropophagic Reason"), 176–7
  "Ideograma, Anagrama, Diagrama," 171–6
  Suggestive pseudo-etymology, 172–6
Candido, Antonio, xx, 206 n27
Cannibalism (*antropofagia*), xxiii, 18–19, 29, 67, 90, 171, 176–7, 189, 191–2, 201–2 n19, 202 n38, 206 n32
Canon debates, *see* Literary canon
Cansinos-Asséns, Rafael, 149
The Cantos of Ezra Pound, xxvi, 157–92, 194
  Cantos: Canto 1, 167; Canto 52, 158–61, 169, 179, 181 (Figs. 4.2 and Fig. 4.3), 180–4; Canto 53, 168; Canto 54, 179; Canto 56, 177; Canto 61, 168; Canto 62, 168, 188; Canto 64, 188–9; Cantos 71 and 72, 159, 162
  Copyright, 186–7
  Orientalism in, 167–71
  Table of contents (*Cantos LII–LXXI*), 184 (Fig. 4.4), 184–5
  Textual history, 179–88, 212 n12
Cardoso, Fernando Enrique, 26–9, 61
Casa de las Américas, 8
Casillo, Robert, 162, 211 n7
Castillo, Debra, xiv
Castro-Klarén, Sarah, 201–2 n19
Censorship, 158–9, 161, 164–5, 166, 178–9, 180–90, 192, 211 n9
CEPAL (United Nations Economic Committee on Latin America"), 26
Cohn, Deborah, xiv

Confucius, xxvii, 167, 169, 177–8, 189
Cornejo Polar, Antonio, xxii
Cummings, E. E., 162

Darío, Rubén, xix
Dasenbrock, Reed Way, 162
Deconstruction, xii, 2, 11, 19, 103, 108–12, 116, 124–6, 173, 176, 193
De Man, Paul, 108–12, 116, 124–5
Dependency theory, xxvi, 20–9, 52, 54–5, 57, 193
Derrida, Jacques, 108, 174
De Torre, Guillermo, 112, 114
Development (Underdevelopment), xvi, 16–7, 20, 25–8, 54, 93
Divus of Justinopolis, Andreas, 167
Djelal Kadir, xiii, xiv, 7
Douglas, Major C. H., 210 n2
Dussel, Enrique, 26

Eastman, Barbara C., 211 n7
Eisenstein, Sergei, 174
Eliot, Thomas Stearns, 14, 15, 17, 182–3
Emar, Jean (Juan), 139
"Empty time," 4, 94
Eurocentrism, 9, 10, 18–9, 24–5, 67, 80, 106
Exceptionalism, xiii

Faletto, Enzo, 26–9
Fenollosa, Ernest, 170–2, 174, 176, 185, 192
Fernández Retamar, Fernando, xiv, 7–10
Fitz, Earl, xiii, xiv, xvii
Foster, David William, 95–6
Foucault, Michel, 39
Franklin, Benjamin, 161, 210 n3
Free Trade and Hemispheric studies, xv–xvii
Freyre, Gilberto, 77
Functionalism, 21, 27–8
Fundación Vicente Huidobro, 140

García Canclini, Nestor, xv
Góngora, Luis de, 11–12, 17
Gourmont, Remy de, 167–8
Gramsci, Antonio, 8
Greg-Bowers school of critical editing, 47–8, 203 n45
Gris, Juan, 115
Guillory, John, 8

Halperín Donghi, Tulio, 63–4
Hatlen, Burton, 203 n46
Hegel, Georg, 19, 66–7, 143
Hegemony, xiii, xix, 7–8, 22, 195
Heidegger, Martin, 54, 108
Henríquez Ureña, Pedro, xx
Historical-Structuralism, 28
Hitler, Adolf, 185–6
Homer, 167
Hugo, Victor, 72
Huidobro, Vicente
    Biography, 103–6, 114–15
    Creationism, 113–14
    El espejo de agua, 114
    Manifestoes: "La creación pura," 112; "La poesía," 112
    Relation to autobiography, 103–6, 115–16
    Vientos contrarios, 104–6
    see also Altazor
Hybridity, xxiii, 2, 78, 170

Ideogram, 168, 170–9, 184, 185, 187–92, *see also* Pound, Ezra

Jakobson, Roman, 36, 119–20, 133, 141, 173
Jefferson, Thomas, 167
Jolas, Eugene, 139

Koine, 22–3, 57
Kracauer, Siegfried, 55
Kutzinkski, Vera, xiii

Lafetá, João Luiz, 75–6
Larrea, Juan, 208 n8

Latin American Studies Association (LASA), xiii
Latinidad, 12, 16
Laughlin, J., 183–6, 212 n12
Lautréamont, Comte de, 127, 148
Lei da Vacina Obrigatória ["Law of Obligatory Vaccine"], 76–8
Letradismo [Lettered City], 62, 67, 68, 69, 103, 106
Levander, Caroline, xiv
Levine, Robert, xiv
Literary canon, 6–10, 42
Litz, A. Walton, 45, 47–8
Lope de Vega, 17
Lopes, Telê Porto Ancona, 99
Lowell, Amy, 13
Lowell, James Russell, 13
Lowell, Robert, 13–15

MacGowan, Christopher, 45, 47–8
Machado de Assis, Joaquim Maria, 60, 77
Macy, John, xviii
Madureira, Luíz, xiv, 18–19
Malatesta, Sigismundo, 167
Malfatti, Anita, 67, 112
Mallarmé, Stéphane, 72, 148–9
Martí, José, 7–8, 9
Marzán, Julio, 11–12, 17, 200–1 n10
Mestizaje, xxii, 165
Mignolo, Walter, xv, xxii, xxv, 23–5
Migration, xxi, xxv, xxvii, 1–6, 8–9, 10–11, 17, 22, 52, 57, 63, 65, 90, 155, 157, 165–6, 171, 176, 178, 193–5
Mistral, Gabriela, 162
Modernism, xxv–xxvii, 6–10, 13, 16, 17–20, 26, 28–9, 42, 55, 57, 199–200 n28
    With respect to Brazilian *modernismo*, 17–20, 28–9, 199–200 n28
    With respect to Spanish-American *vanguardismo*, 26, 199–200 n28

Modernismo [Brazilian], 17–20, 28–9, 63, 66, 67–9, *see also* Modernism
Modernity, xxiv–xxvii, 10, 19, 24–7, 64, 93, 123, 144–5
Montaigne, Michel de, 202 n38
Morales, Andrés, 140–1
Moreiras, Alberto, xxiii, 200 n1
Morse, Richard, xiv, 7, 17–23, 25, 31, 38–9, 42, 65
Moya, Antonio, 99–100
Moyriac de Mailla, J. A. M. de, 169, 177, 189
Murphy, Gretchen, xiv
Mussolini, Benito, 158, 210 n3

Nancy, Jean-Luc, 59–61, 97
Nation (Nationalism), 2–6, 8, 14–5, 18, 22–3, 27–9, 54, 57, 61–4, 75–6, 81–2, 84, 94, 97, 103, 106–7, 126, 142–5, 154–5, 161, 165, 176, 191–3
Nietzsche, Friedrich, 19, 106, 144–5
Noigandres (Brazilian *poesia concreta*), 171, 175–6, 212 n16
Non-conciliation, xxiv, xxvi, 2, 95, 97, 152, 155, 165, 191
Nord-Sud, 112
North American Free Trade Agreement (NAFTA), xv–xvi
Nunes, Benedito, 68, 81

Object, *see* Subject
Objectivity, xxiv, xxvi, 1–2, 6, 12–13, 16–17, 30–2, 38–9, 41, 44, 49–51, 55–7, 61, 97–102, 107–8, 113, 121–5, 136, 138, 164, 192–5, 209 n17
Orientalism, 79–80, 166–7, 170–1
Origins (Originality), xxi–xxii, xxvii, 1–4, 9, 16, 22, 43–4, 46, 51, 53–4, 60, 75, 87–9, 99, 113, 116, 120–6, 132, 137–42, 144–5, 148, 150–5, 157, 167–9, 175, 184, 192, 193–5
Ortiz, Fernando, xxii

Paulicéia desvairada, xxvi, 59–102, 107, 193
"As enfibraturas do Ipiranga," 77–86
Covers, 100 (Fig. 2.1), 101 (Fig. 2.2)
Dedicatory, 98–99
Harmonic verse (polyphony), 69–73, 86–7, 94–5, 98–102
Phonetics, 87–8, 90
Poems: "Anhangabaú," 89; "Colloque sentimental," 91; "Domingo," 91–2; "Inspiração," 87–9; "Noturno," 92–4; "Ode ao burguês," 67–8; "O rebanho," 97; "Os cortejos," 90–1; "Paisagem No. 1," 96–7; "Tu," 90
"Prefácio interessantíssmo," 69–77
Subjectivity, 73–7, 94–5, 97–102
Textual history, 97–102
Pease, Donald, xiv
Peirce, Charles, 174
Perrone, Charles A., 85, 95–6
Pignatari, Décio, 171
Poetic function, 36, 133, 141, 155, 173, *see also* Jakobson, Roman
Porter, James I., 144–5
Post-structuralism, xii
Pound, Ezra, xxvi–xxvii, 17, 42, 112
Anti-Semitism, 160–3, 169, 179–86, 188, 190–2
Biography, 157–64
Cantos LII–LXXI (The China/Adams Cantos), xxvi–xxvii, 161, 164, 168
A Draft of XXX Cantos, 168
Ideogrammic method, 170–9, 192
Pisan Cantos, 168, 210 n3
see also The Cantos of Ezra Pound
Puerto Rico, 10, 12–13

Quijano, Aníbal, xxv, 26

Race (Racism), xvii, 6–7, 24, 40–1, 43–4, 61–2, 68, 92, 103, 106, 205 n20, *see also* Anti-Semitism
Rama, Angel, xxii, 106
Ramos, Julio, 155
Ransom, John Crowe, 13
Raynal, Maurice, 208 n8
Redman, Tim, 162
Rodríguez Monegal, Emir, xx
Romanticism, German, 142–3
Rosa, Liliana, 140
Rosenberg, Fernando, xiv
Rothschild family, 182

Said, Edward, 166–7
Saldívar, José David, xv, 6–8
Santiago, Silviano, xxiii
São Paulo, history, 63–5
Sapir-Whorf semantics, 174
Sarabia, Rosa, 140
Saussure, Ferdinand de, 22, 30, 72, 122, 174, 176
Schwartz, Delmore, 185
Schwartz, Jorge, xiv, 207 n40
Schwarz, Roberto, 93
Semana de Arte Moderna [São Paulo Modern Art Week, 1922], 67–8
Sevcenko, Nicolau, 65
Shapiro, Karl, 14
Soffici, Ardengo, 99
Sollors, Werner, xiv
Spiller, Robert E., xviii
Spillers, Hortense J., xix
Spivak, Gayatri, 8
Spring and All, xxv–xxvi, 1–57, 61, 107, 192
 Grammar, 33–7
 Imagery, 30, 37–8, 40–1
 Poems: "At the Ball Game" ("XXVI"), 55–7; "The Farmer" ("III"), 49–50; "The Hermaphroditic Telephones," 46; "Quietness" ("XXI"), 46; "The Red Wheelbarrow" ("XXII"), 10, 20–2, 28, 30–2, 42–8, 201 n10; "Spring and All" ("I"), 37–9; "To Elsie" ("XVII"), 2–6; "To Have Done Nothing" ("VI"), 32–7; "The Wildflower" ("XXVII"), 39–42
 Prose sections, 48–54
 Textual history, 42–8
 Versification, 31–2, 40
Structural functionalism, *see* Functionalism
Structuralism, xii, 28, 105, 108, 126
Subalterity, xxiv, 6–10, 200 n1
Subject, *see* Object
Subjectivity, xix, xxiii–xxiv, xxvi–xxvii, 1–7, 12–13, 16–17, 18–19, 49, 52, 57, 62, 73–7, 78, 81, 90, 92, 94–5, 97–8, 108–12, 116, 124–5, 128, 157, 164–6, 191, 192–5

Tate, Allen, 13
Transculturation, xxii–xxiii, xxv, 2–6, 19, 89–90, 165–6, 171, 176, 178, 190–2
Translation, xxiii, xxv, xxvii, 1–2, 5, 33, 73, 89–90, 94, 99–102, 116, 117, 121, 132, 139, 145–55, 157, 166, 167, 169–79, 187, 189, 192, 193–5
Tomlins, Jack E., 205 n17

Ultraísmo, 112–13, 150
Underdevelopment, *see* Development
Unruh, Vicky, 78–9, 84

Vallejo, César, xix
Vanguardismo [Spanish-American], 26, 113–14, 138, 150, 199–200 n28, *see also* Modernism

Vargas, Getúlio, 62, 63
Verhaeren, Émile, 207 n39

Wallerstein, Immanuel, xxv, 23
Weinberger, Eliot, 132, 208 n15
Wesling, Donald, 50, 52
West, Rebecca, 16
Williams, William Carlos, xxv–xxvi, 1–57, 61, 107, 192
  Biography, 4, 10–11
  Ethnic identity, xxv, 10–13, 15–17, 43–4
  Go Go, 45–7
  Prose works: *In the American Grain*, 43–4; "A Memory of Tropical Fruit," 12–13; "The Poem as a Field of Action," 15; "A Point for American Criticism," 16
  Versification, 15, 31–2, 41–2
  see also Spring and All
Wittgenstein, Ludwig, 108
Wordsworth, William, 109
World order, xxv, 9, 18–19, 22–6, 28–9, 54–5

Yúdice, George, 125–7, 145

Zukofsky, Louis, 162

GPSR Compliance
The European Union's (EU) General Product Safety Regulation (GPSR) is a set of rules that requires consumer products to be safe and our obligations to ensure this.

If you have any concerns about our products, you can contact us on

ProductSafety@springernature.com

In case Publisher is established outside the EU, the EU authorized representative is:

Springer Nature Customer Service Center GmbH
Europaplatz 3
69115 Heidelberg, Germany

www.ingramcontent.com/pod-product-compliance
Lightning Source LLC
LaVergne TN
LVHW011810060526
838200LV00053B/3730